IMAGES

A Resource Guide for Improving Measurement and Geometry in Elementary Schools

http://images.rbs.org

Edited by
Janie L. Zimmer
Arlene Dowshen
Dennis Ebersole

Second edition

RBS

Mid-Atlantic Eisenhower Consortium for Mathematics and Science Education
at Research for Better Schools

ISBN 1-56602-054-9

This publication is a product of the Mid-Atlantic Eisenhower Regional Consortium for Mathematics and Science Education at Research for Better Schools under funding from the Office of Elementary and Secondary Education, U. S. Department of Education, under grant number R319A000009-03. The content does not necessarily reflect the views of the Department or any other agency of the U.S. Government.

This document may be reproduced for educational purposes without permission.

The contents of this publication are available on the Web site, http://images.rbs.org. Additional copies may be obtained by contacting:

Research for Better Schools
112 North Broad Street, 12th Floor
Philadelphia, PA 19102
Phone: (215) 568-6150
Fax: (215) 568-7260
E-mail: info@rbs.org
Web: http://www.rbs.org

First printing of second edition, 2004
Printed in the United States of America

Acknowledgments

The materials for IMAGES were prepared under the leadership of Janie Zimmer and the Pennsylvania State Team of the Mid-Atlantic Eisenhower Consortium at Research for Better Schools (RBS). The editorial team for the second edition—Janie Zimmer, Arlene Dowshen, and Dennis Ebersole—has contributed much expertise, time, energy, and creativity to this project. Thanks to the many dedicated individuals who were so generous in bringing their considerable knowledge to bear in developing content and guiding the materials through the final stages of editing. Finally, thanks to the teachers and students at St. Patrick's School in Woodbury, N.J. for allowing us to take the photos included in this publication.

Contributors

Linda Benedetto
Higher Education Associate
Pennsylvania Department of Education

Penny Barchfeld-Venet
Assessment Specialist
TERC

Midge Barilla
Director of Curriculum and Instruction
Owen J. Roberts School District

Judy Basara
Mathematics Teacher
Archdiocese of Philadelphia

Thaddeus Basara
Science Teacher, retired

Arlene Dowshen*
Assoc. Professor of Mathematics Education
Widener University

Dennis Ebersole*
Professor of Mathematics and Computer Science
Northampton Community College

Jane Konrad
Research Associate
University of Pittsburgh

Robert Jesberg*
Education Consultant
K'NEX Education

Connie Logan
Teacher/Specialist
Kennett Consolidated School District

John Martin
Professor Emeritus of Mathematics
Shippensburg University

Ann Massey
Professor Emeritus
Indiana University of Pennsylvania

David Reese
Director of Human Resources
Northeastern Educational I.U. #19

Kenneth Schroder
Director
Commonwealth Excellence in Science Teaching Alliance (CESTA)

Patty L. Schumacher
Teacher/Educational Consultant
Telford, PA

Josephine Shirey
Assistant Director
North Central Math/Science Collaborative
Clarion University

Michael Speziale*
Assistant Superintendent
Dallas School District

Harry Stratigos
Mathematics Specialist, retired
Pennsylvania Department of Education

Florence Waring*
Teacher
CORA Services

Janie L. Zimmer*
Mathematics Associate and Liaison to the Pennsylvania State Team for Mathematics and Science Education
Research for Better Schools

Editorial Support

Wendy Coffman*
Communications Consultant

Debra Gingerich*
Communications Manager
Research for Better Schools

Jim Harper
former Communications Manager
Research for Better Schools

Alison Rooney*
Communications Consultant

Expert Reviewers

Francis (Skip) Fennell
Professor of Education
Western Maryland College

Mary Montgomery Lindquist
Professor Emeritus
Columbus State University

Graphics and Technology

Bill Halverson*
Systems Administrator
Research for Better Schools

Todd Laffler*
Freelance Graphic Designer

Tom Lorenz*
Manager of Information Services
Research for Better Schools

David Reese
Director of Human Resources
Northeastern Educational I.U. #19

Michael Speziale*
Assistant Superintendent
Dallas School District

Michael Streubert
Graphic Design Specialist

* Made additional contributions to the second edition

Research for Better Schools (RBS) is a nonprofit educational research and development firm that has been serving educators in the mid-Atlantic region of Delaware, the District of Columbia, Maryland, New Jersey, and Pennsylvania since 1966. Its mission is to help students achieve by supporting improvement efforts in schools and other educational programs, focusing on mathematics, science, and technology.

The Mid-Atlantic Eisenhower Consortium for Mathematics and Science Education at RBS aims to improve school mathematics and science through its educators in the District of Columbia, Delaware, Maryland, New Jersey, and Pennsylvania. It offers technical assistance, workshops, and conferences aimed at helping school and district staff improve student learning and achievement.

Preface

This second edition of IMAGES makes use of the experience gained during the 2002 and 2003 IMAGES Institutes, held in Pennsylvania and Maryland for 343 educators. Observing how they made use of the materials presented was extremely valuable as we continually revisit how to best support the teaching of geometry and measurement. As a result of these Institutes, secondary workshops were conducted by these participants, and to date more than 2,000 teachers have had some training with the IMAGES program.

We also sought to show evidence of effectiveness since the first printing of the book in 2002. Part of this effort was to measure change in content knowledge by administering pre- and post-tests at each of the five IMAGES Institutes conducted since the summer of 2002. The pre-tests from each of these five institutes indicated that teachers had misunderstandings of basic geometry and measurement concepts, and in the post-tests teachers showed statistically significant growth in their knowledge of these concepts. Furthermore, after engaging in the IMAGES professional development training:

- 88 percent of participants stated that they had an increased knowledge of geometry and measurement
- 82 percent of participants reported feeling more competent in their ability to teach geometry and measurement
- 90 percent of participants agreed they were comfortable using manipulatives to teach geometry and measurement concepts
- 93 percent of participants reported being more aware of places to find appropriate technologies (e.g., the Web and appropriate software) to help them plan and teach geometry and measurement.[1]

We are proud to know that our efforts are having a positive impact. One elementary principal who attended the IMAGES 2002 Institute wrote, "All 3 of my fifth grade teachers attended IMAGES last summer. . . . I was thrilled that my 5th grade PSSA math scores continued to rise this year. . . . I couldn't help but note that my building was the only elementary building in our district with scores well above the state average in measurement and geometry. Proof to me that the IMAGES workshop we attended was well worth the time."[2]

With the publication of this second edition, we are continuing to gather evidence of effectiveness of the IMAGES program.

---

[1] Analysis of IMAGES Institutes, conducted August 2002–February 2004.
[2] E-mail from Linda Lemmon, then Principal of Dillsburg Elementary School in Dillsburg, Pa., to Janie Zimmer, July 23, 2003.

Table of Contents

Chapter 4

Chapter 5

Chapter 6

Appendices

RATIONALE

The Pennsylvania State Team of the Mid-Atlantic Eisenhower Consortium at Research for Better Schools (RBS) has developed IMAGES (Improving Measurement and Geometry in Elementary Schools) to assist teachers and students in grades K–5 in improving their concepts and skills in these areas. Through this publication we hope to play a part in inspiring teachers to provide a firm foundation in mathematics that integrates geometry and measurement with sound teaching strategies that make use of the best educational research and teaching experience.

The Third International Mathematics and Science Study (TIMSS), conducted in 1995, clearly indicated that American students need to improve their understanding of geometric concepts and improve their basic knowledge in measurement and proportionality.[3] This problem has been recognized by state educational agencies, the U.S. Department of Education, the National Council of Teachers of Mathematics (NCTM), institutions of higher education, school districts, and many educational publishers.[4] Since the release of the TIMSS 1995 data, some mathematics projects have been highlighted as being exemplary or promising and have begun to be used in schools throughout the country.[5] In addition, other publishers have examined these programs and have begun to develop standards-based mathematics textbooks and resource materials with strong content and an emphasis on big ideas. A review of states' test scores, the Third International Mathematics and Science Study-Repeat (TIMSS-R, conducted in 1999), and the *Nation's Report Card*[6] shows that the need for improvement in geometry and measurement continues. Additional time and more intensive professional development for teachers is needed to have the desired impact on student learning and achievement in these areas.

The Pennsylvania Governor's Institutes and Urban Academy programs during the summer of 2001 revealed many elementary teachers' limited knowledge of geometry. When it was announced by the Pennsylvania Department of Education that the

---

[3] U.S. Department of Education, National Center for Education Statistics, *Pursuing Excellence: A Study of U.S. Fourth-Grade Mathematics and Science Achievement in International Context* (Washington, D.C.: U.S. Government Printing Office, 1997), pp. 28–29; U.S. Department of Education, National Center for Education Statistics, *Pursuing Excellence: A Study of U.S. Eighth-Grade Mathematics and Science Teaching, Learning, Curriculum, and Achievement in International Context* (Washington, D.C.: U.S. Government Printing Office, 1996), pp. 28–29. Both are available online at http://nces.ed.gov/timss.

[4] U.S. Department of Education, National Commission on Mathematics and Science Teaching for the 21st Century, *Before It's Too Late: A Report on the Nation* (Washington, D.C.: U.S. Government Printing Office, September 2000), available online at http://www.ed.gov/inits/Math/glenn/index.html; Tom Loveless and Paul Diperna, *The Brown Center Report on American Education: How Well Are American Students Learning? Focus on Math Achievement* (Washington, D.C.: Brookings Institution, 2000); National Council of Teachers of Mathematics, *Principles and Standards for School Mathematics* (Reston, Va.: National Council of Teachers of Mathematics, 2000).

[5] U.S. Department of Education's Math and Science Education Expert Panel, *Exemplary and Promising Mathematics Programs* (Washington, D.C.: U.S. Department of Education, 1999), available online at http://www.enc.org/professional/federalresources/exemplary/promising.

[6] National Center for Education Statistics, *Nation's Report Card* (Washington, D.C.: National Center for Education Statistics, 2003), available online at http://nces.ed.gov/nationsreportcard/.

Governor's summer professional development programs for teachers would focus on geometry, the number of applications for admission to those institutes doubled and tripled.[7] Additionally, instructors' records indicate that participants who took the pre-test performed very poorly. In the Urban Academy for kindergarten through eighth grade teachers, only a few achieved a passing grade in the pre-test. In one group of 28 elementary teachers, only one passed the pre-test.[8]

While many educational agencies are striving to determine the causes for the lack of improvement in these areas, it is becoming clearer that many elementary teachers (through no fault of their own) have limited and faulty knowledge of geometric concepts and skills. Furthermore, research needs to inform instructional strategies and curriculum content for geometry and measurement in the classroom.

The benefits of geometry and measurement skills for students go beyond these specific content areas, and also help students with broader cognitive tasks, such as organization, problem solving, enhancing visualization, and even following directions.

To fulfill its goal of improving the quality of the teaching of geometry and measurement, IMAGES addresses elements that are integral to developing local school capacity:
- rich, rigorous academic content in geometry and measurement for K–5 teachers
- strategies to develop the skills and concepts students must have to meet or exceed state measurement and geometry standards
- a trained cohort of educators to share the program content with teachers in their district and surrounding districts
- support for the trained cohort after the initial summer institutes
- continuing professional education hours or graduate credit needed for recertification requirements
- a dynamic presence on the Web, with a site that will continue to grow and change, based on feedback and use of the materials.

IMAGES differs from other resources in that it comprehensively covers the geometry and measurement content expectations for teachers and for students in kindergarten through grade five. It also provides a broad collection of varying print and non-print resources addressing issues such as cognition and development, brain research, children's literature, assessment, and software.

IMAGES will continue to improve teachers' content knowledge, increase their use of best practices, change attitudes toward geometry and measurement, and provide a better understanding of how students learn. Our hope is that this will make a difference in classroom instruction as well as on students' performance in measurement and geometry.

---

[7] Telephone interview with Linda Benedetto, Higher Education Associate at the Pennsylvania Department of Education, conducted by Janie Zimmer, October 2001.
[8] Telephone interview with Linda Benedetto, October 2001.

HOW TO USE IMAGES

This print version of IMAGES has been created in conjunction with a Web site, http://images.rbs.org, which will continue to grow as the program evolves. The resources are intended for: classroom teachers to use in furthering their own knowledge and in planning lessons; school administrators conducting professional development; other leaders within a school; and mathematics specialists and coordinators in a school or school district. IMAGES resources are keyed to both national and state standards. The relevant mathematics standards of several states appear in the appendices to this book; others are available on the IMAGES Web site.

The IMAGES team encourages educators to use these materials:
- as a resource to help implement state and national standards
- as a guide to determine what big ideas in geometry and measurement content are most important for students
- as a reminder that their own understanding of geometry and measurement is critical to their students' learning
- as sample lessons and activities, both to use as is and as the basis for creating new classroom experiences
- as a source for finding useful manipulatives, videos, technology, children's literature, and links to research and curricula that can improve the teaching and learning of geometry and measurement
- as a source of resources for teachers to improve their own content knowledge in geometry and measurement
- as a means to foster collaboration with other teachers in their schools and school districts, as well as with those in other districts.

One of the most important aspects of these materials is that they make it easier for teachers to see how to implement standards, as well as reinforce the big ideas related to geometry and measurement. This publication begins with an investigation of **how children learn** (cognitive and developmental issues), then presents **what children should learn** (geometry and measurement content) and **how to teach and assess what children learn** (teaching strategies, lesson plans, and assessment). The book finishes with multiple print and non-print resources.

Chapter 1

Cognitive and Developmental Issues

Children have real understanding only of that which they invent themselves, and each time we try to teach them something too quickly, we keep them from reinventing it themselves.

—Jean Piaget[1]

This section provides guidance on issues elementary teachers should consider when designing and teaching an instructional unit to elementary students. It incorporates findings from educational research and other resource documents, including NCTM's *Principles and Standards for School Mathematics*.[2]

Moreover, this chapter provides ideas and information to support teachers in beginning to translate some of the latest educational research into daily classroom practice. Teachers' effectiveness in the classroom has been shown to benefit greatly from looking at various developmental stages of students and considering cognitive science and other contributions from educational research. Too often, teachers do not focus on *how* students learn and the critical importance of these cognitive issues for their teaching.

---

[1] Seymour Papert, "Papert on Piaget." *Time* (March 29, 1999): p. 105, available online at http://www.papert.org/articles/Papertonpiaget.html.

[2] National Council of Teachers of Mathematics, *Principles and Standards for School Mathematics* (Reston, Va.: National Council of Teachers of Mathematics, 2000).

This chapter explores:
- **Van Hiele Levels of Geometric Reasoning**
- **Current Brain Research**
- **Facilitating Developmental Learning**
  - Use Concrete Representations
  - Provide Time to Play
  - Use Examples and Non-Examples
  - Introduce and Implement Technology
  - Use Context and Prior Knowledge
  - Actively Engage Students
  - Implement the Equity Principle
    - Gender equity
    - Multicultural learning environments
- **Learning Styles and Multiple Intelligences**

Van Hiele Levels of Geometric Reasoning

The work of two Dutch educators, Pierre van Hiele and Dina van Hiele-Geldof, has given us a vision around which to design geometry curriculum.[3] Through their research they have identified five levels of understanding spatial concepts through which children move sequentially on their way to geometric thinking.[4] There are four characteristics of these levels of thought:

- The Van Hiele levels of geometric reasoning are sequential. Students must pass through all prior levels to arrive at any specific level.
- These levels are not age-dependent in the way Piaget described development.
- Geometric experiences have the greatest influence on advancement through the levels.
- Instruction and language at a level higher than the level of the student may inhibit learning.[5]

Below are listed the van Hiele levels and activities that would be appropriate for students at each level. Most students in grades K–3 will be at Level 1 (visualization) while students in grades 4–5 may be at Level 2 (analysis) and some possibly at Level 3 (informal deduction). *It is important for elementary school teachers to provide their students with experiences that will help them move from Level 1 to Level 3 by the end of the eighth grade.*

(Note that the five van Hiele levels are sometimes numbered 0–4, as opposed to 1–5, which is used in this document.)

[3] Mary L. Crowley, "The Van Hiele Model of the Development of Geometric Thought," in *Learning and Teaching Geometry, K–12*, ed. Mary M. Lindquist (Reston, Va.: National Council of Teachers of Mathematics, 1987), pp. 1–16.
[4] Pierre M. Van Hiele, "Developing Geometric Thinking Through Activities That Begin with Play," *Teaching Children Mathematics* 5, no. 6 (February 1999): pp. 310–16.
[5] John A. Van de Walle, *Elementary and Middle School Mathematics: Teaching Developmentally*, 4th ed. (New York: Addison Wesley Longman, 2001), pp. 310–11.

1. Visualization

Students can name and recognize shapes by their appearance, but cannot specifically identify properties of shapes. Although they may be able to recognize characteristics, they do not use them for recognition and sorting.

> ### *Suggestions for instruction using visualization[6]*
>
> - sorting, identifying, and describing shapes
> - manipulating physical models
> - seeing different sizes and orientations of the same shape as to distinguish characteristics of a shape and the features that are not relevant
> - building, drawing, making, putting together, and taking apart shapes.

2. Analysis

Students begin to identify properties of shapes and learn to use appropriate vocabulary related to properties, but do not make connections between different shapes and their properties. Irrelevant features, such as size or orientation, become less important, as students are able to focus on all shapes within a class. They are able to think about what properties make a rectangle. Students at this level are able to begin to talk about the relationship between shapes and their properties.

> ### *Suggestions for instruction using analysis*
>
> - shifting from simple identification to properties, by using concrete or virtual models to define, measure, observe, and change properties
> - using models and/or technology to focus on defining properties, making property lists, and discussing sufficient conditions to define a shape
> - doing problem solving, including tasks in which properties of shapes are important components
> - classifying using properties of shapes.

---

[6] Van de Walle, *Elementary and Middle School Mathematics,* pp. 311–12.

3. Informal Deduction

Students are able to recognize relationships between and among properties of shapes or classes of shapes and are able to follow logical arguments using such properties.

> **Suggestions for instruction using informal deduction**
> - doing problem solving, including tasks in which properties of shapes are important components
> - using models and property lists, and discussing which group of properties constitute a necessary and sufficient condition for a specific shape
> - using informal, deductive language ("all," "some," "none," "if-then," "what if," etc.)
> - investigating certain relationships among polygons to establish if the converse is also valid (e.g., "If a quadrilateral is a rectangle, it must have four right angles; if a quadrilateral has four right angles, must it also be a rectangle?")
> - using models and drawings (including dynamic geometry software) as tools to look for generalizations and counter-examples
> - making and testing hypotheses
> - using properties to define a shape or determine if a particular shape is included in a given set.

Note: Students usually do not reach Levels 4 and 5 until high school or college, but teachers should be aware of these levels nonetheless.

4. Deduction

Students can go beyond just identifying characteristics of shapes and are able to construct proofs using postulates or axioms and definitions. A typical high school geometry course should be taught at this level.

5. Rigor

This is the highest level of thought in the van Hiele hierarchy. Students at this level can work in different geometric or axiomatic systems and would most likely be enrolled in a college level course in geometry.

Implications of van Hiele for instruction

Geometry taught in the elementary school should be informal. Such informal geometry activities should be exploratory and hands-on, in order to provide children with the opportunity to investigate, to build and take apart, to create and make drawings, and to make observations about shapes in the world around them.[7] This provides the basis for more formal activities at higher levels.

Teaching a geometry lesson at one van Hiele level when students are functioning at a lower level may hinder student learning. For example, a teacher asks his or her students to play the "What am I?" game with properties of geometric figures, saying, "I have four sides and all of my interior angles are right angles. What am I?" To answer this question, a student must be functioning at Level 2 (analysis) in van Hiele's model of geometric reasoning. If the students in this class are functioning at Level 1 (visualization), where they recognize a figure by its appearance, they will not be able to play the game. If students are at different levels in one class, the teacher must use differentiated instruction to meet the needs of all of his or her students. Diagnostic assessment will help to determine the developmental level in geometry for each student.

Current Brain Research

In recent years researchers have used an interdisciplinary approach to seek to better understand how the brain works. Much of this research has direct implications for the classroom. For example, we know that students remember what they were thinking about at the time when they first learn a new concept. If this thinking is shallow, then their learning will also be shallow.[8] For instance, are students thinking about the straws and gumdrops used to create different shapes, or are they focusing on the goal of the activity: the idea that triangles are necessarily rigid?

To make use of these findings, a teacher should anticipate what students may be thinking about during a lesson, be careful to link the activity to the

---

[7] Van de Walle, *Elementary and Middle School Mathematics*, pp. 311–49.
[8] Daniel T. Willingham, *Cognition: The Thinking Animal* (New York: Prentice Hall, 2001). Also see his column in the American Federation of Teachers' journal, *American Educator*, entitled "How We Learn: Ask the Cognitive Scientist."

mathematical concepts that it is designed to illustrate, and direct student thinking to the mathematical concepts at hand. The teacher should change the activity if students spend too much time thinking about material that is unrelated to the instructional goal of the lesson.

Cognitive science has also shown that the mind tends to remember in very concrete forms. If we want students to have a deeper knowledge of a mathematical concept so that they can apply the knowledge in new situations, we must offer students numerous opportunities to engage with related knowledge, facts, and examples of the concept. Teachers can guide students as they move through several stages in the process of developing deep, flexible knowledge. Teachers should revisit the same concept repeatedly over an extended period, in order to encourage thinking about the similarities and differences in the examples.

Facilitating Developmental Learning

There are a number of ways to support developmental learning in the classroom; in the context of IMAGES we suggest creating a combined approach based on the menu of ideas listed in this section. Only if teachers are constantly reevaluating and readjusting their own strategies to teaching will students continue to learn in new and developmental ways.

Use Concrete Representations

Concepts such as symmetry, translations, reflections, area, and volume can be very abstract and are often not connected to the student's world. When a new concept is introduced, students need tactile and visual experiences to assist them in understanding the concept.[9] For example, area and volume become more real when students cover a rectangle with squares or fill a rectangular solid with cubes. Using manipulatives allows the students to relate new ideas to things they already know and understand. After students feel comfortable with the concepts using manipulatives, students are ready to move from the concrete to the visual. For example, a figure drawn on paper could be folded along its line of symmetry to verify that it is in fact symmetric. The best use of instructional time is to wait to introduce some abstraction until students have moved into van Hiele's Level 2 (analysis).

---

[9] For research in this area, see James Hiebert and Thomas P. Carpenter, "Learning and Teaching with Understanding," in *Handbook of Research on Mathematics Teaching and Learning*, ed. Douglas A. Grouws (New York: Macmillan, 1992), pp. 65–97.

A suggestion for instruction using concrete representations

Use a mirror or Mira™ to illustrate that a pattern block is symmetric about a line. The equilateral triangle has three lines of symmetry and the square has four lines of symmetry. Ask the students to find them.

Have students trace a flat plastic bear (or other animal) in one position, and then move or translate the bear to a new position and trace it again. Explain that this is an example of a geometric transformation, in particular a translation. Ask them: "Are the new figure and the original figure congruent?"

Have students place the bear on one side of a line drawn on a new sheet of paper. Then place a Mira™ on the line. Have them draw the bear they see reflected in the Mira™ on the other side of the line. Students now have a reflection of the bear across the line of reflection.

Ask them to look at properties of the reflection and compare these properties to what happens when they look at their own reflection, or wave, or wink in a mirror. For example, they should note that a particular point on the bear and the reflection of this point (its image) can be connected with a line segment, and that the line of reflection is perpendicular to this line segment and bisects the line segment.

Provide Time to Play

Students can learn significant mathematics—particularly geometry—during play.[10] For example, when playing with tangrams students discover that they must sometimes "flip" a piece over to make it fit into a picture they are creating, while other times they must rotate the piece. Translating a piece from one location to another can change the picture they are creating from one form to another. Students discover that several pieces can be combined to make a larger piece and that the square can be broken up into the seven tangram pieces.

---

[10] Van Hiele, "Developing Geometric Thinking," pp. 310–16.

Also, if students are to use a manipulative to discover a mathematical concept, they first need time to play with the manipulative to become familiar with it. The same is true with computer programs, computer games, and calculators. Once familiar with the new tool, they will stay on task longer as teachers introduce guided activities.

*For an example of how to incorporate time to play, see the **Pattern Block Shapes** activity on page 68.*

Use Examples and Non-Examples

Students are likely to understand concepts, such as mathematical definitions, if a teacher provides them examples of a concept and non-examples.[11] For example, students who are still at van Hiele's Level 1 (visualization) will not develop a solid understanding of what it means to be a triangle if they only see equilateral triangles oriented in the same way. To move students to the next level, a teacher needs to show them examples of similar objects that are not triangles, as well as obtuse and scalene triangles and triangles where the base is not horizontal. Using this approach when introducing each new figure will help students later in their schooling to place figures appropriately in the hierarchy of figures.[12]

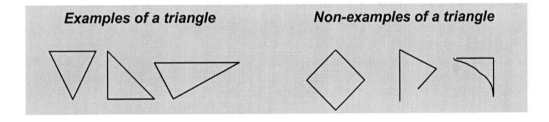

Examples of a triangle   **Non-examples of a triangle**

Introduce and Implement Technology

Technology in the classroom is an effective way to engage students, while also supporting the development of skills that will be critical to them in future years. Appropriate uses of technology can also foster students' understanding of concepts in geometry and measurement. Technology can also assist the teacher in supporting students with special needs. On the other hand, use of inappropriate technology or ill-planned use of the technology can be worse for students than using no technology. A computer program that is too sophisticated for the students will only frustrate them. Using the computer for nothing more than drill and practice does not take advantage of technology's strengths.

---

[11] Annie Selden and John Selden, "The Role of Examples in Learning Mathematics," *The Mathematics Association of America Research Sampler 5* (February 20, 1998).
[12] National Council of Teachers of Mathematics, *Principles and Standards for School Mathematics*, p. 122.

Software such as Logo (turtle graphics) and MicroWorlds™ allows teachers to create activities and pose problems that encourage students to learn mathematics in the context of a problem and help children visualize geometric concepts and properties.[13] For example, students can use geometric concepts to create a house or other shape. Simulations allow students to explore topics they may not be able or willing to do on their own. Students may be able to explore with virtual manipulatives in a way that would not otherwise be possible. Software such as the Geometer's Sketchpad® allows students to explore shapes like triangles and quadrilaterals in a dynamic environment.[14] Students can also use the software to transform a figure, helping students to understand geometric transformations. Using the software to measure lengths and areas allows students to explore the concepts of area and perimeter. In addition, using calculators can allow students to focus on conceptual understanding and mathematical reasoning rather than solely on computation.

Using the Geometer's Sketchpad® to Explore Area and Perimeter

A. Create a triangle using Sketchpad:
   1. Plot three points.
   2. Select the three points.
   3. Have Sketchpad create the polygon interior— a triangle.

B. Find the perimeter and area of the triangle:
   1. While still selecting the interior, have Sketchpad measure the perimeter and area of the triangle.
   2. Grab one of the vertices and move it around the screen until you have a triangle that is close to an equilateral triangle. Record the area and the perimeter.

C. Dynamically alter the triangle and observe what happens to the area and perimeter:
   1. Move the vertex to create a skinny obtuse triangle (a triangle with one angle with measure more than 90 degrees) that has approximately the same perimeter. What has happened to the area?

(continued on next page)

---

[13] Michael T. Battista and Douglas H. Clements, "Using Spatial Imagery in Geometric Reasoning," *Arithmetic Teacher* 39, no. 3 (November 1991): pp. 18–21.

[14] Azita Manouchehri, Mary C. Enderson, and Lyle A. Pagnucco, "Exploring Geometry with Technology," *Mathematics Teaching in the Middle School* 3, no. 6 (January 1998): pp. 436–42.

Using the Geometer's Sketchpad® (continued)

2. Can you make the perimeter larger than the perimeter of the equilateral triangle while keeping the area smaller than that of the equilateral triangle?
3. Which triangles have the smallest area if you keep the perimeter (approximately) the same?
4. If you keep the triangle an equilateral triangle, what happens to the area when you increase the perimeter?
5. If you try different triangles with (approximately) the same perimeter, which triangle has the largest area?
6. Create different triangles with approximately the same area as the recorded area of the equilateral triangle. Can you find any with a much larger perimeter?

D. Repeat this investigation with quadrilaterals, starting with a square.

E. Repeat this investigation with pentagons, starting with a regular pentagon (all five sides are equal in length and all five interior angles have the same measure).

Students should discover that, if the new polygon is similar to the original polygon, increasing the perimeter increases the area.

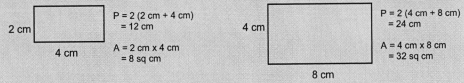

If the figures are not similar, increasing the perimeter will often, but not necessarily, increase the area.

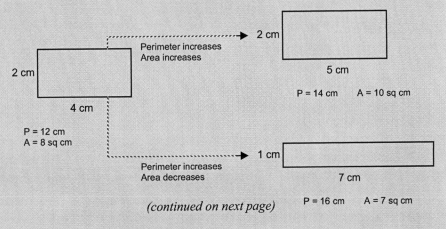

(continued on next page)

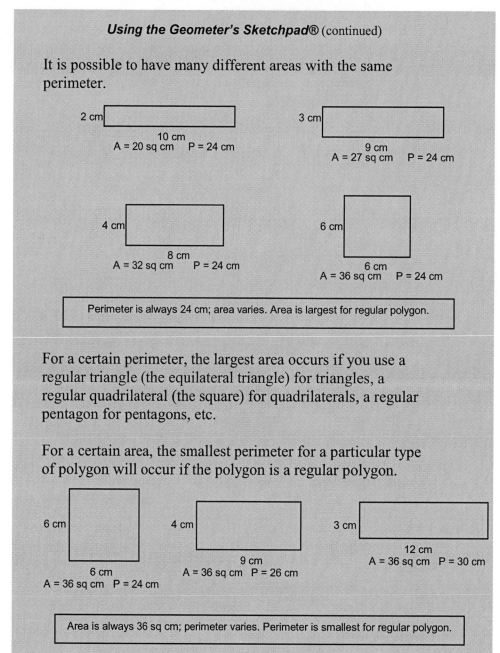

Using the Geometer's Sketchpad® (continued)

It is possible to have many different areas with the same perimeter.

2 cm
10 cm
A = 20 sq cm   P = 24 cm

3 cm
9 cm
A = 27 sq cm   P = 24 cm

4 cm
8 cm
A = 32 sq cm   P = 24 cm

6 cm
6 cm
A = 36 sq cm   P = 24 cm

Perimeter is always 24 cm; area varies. Area is largest for regular polygon.

For a certain perimeter, the largest area occurs if you use a regular triangle (the equilateral triangle) for triangles, a regular quadrilateral (the square) for quadrilaterals, a regular pentagon for pentagons, etc.

For a certain area, the smallest perimeter for a particular type of polygon will occur if the polygon is a regular polygon.

6 cm
6 cm
A = 36 sq cm   P = 24 cm

4 cm
9 cm
A = 36 sq cm   P = 26 cm

3 cm
12 cm
A = 36 sq cm   P = 30 cm

Area is always 36 sq cm; perimeter varies. Perimeter is smallest for regular polygon.

Use Context and Prior Knowledge

Students try to use what they already know to make sense of new mathematical concepts.[15] Good teachers make these connections explicit, determining what their students already know and helping students see how the new concept is related to that knowledge.

For example, students may understand area as the number of squares required to cover a region or figure and understand perimeter as the length of string

---

[15] Hiebert and Carpenter, "Learning and Teaching with Understanding," p. 80.

required to surround the region. A teacher can approach the concept of volume as a natural extension of the concept of area; it is the number of cubes required to fill an object or open figure such as an open box. Similarly, surface area is the three-dimensional equivalent of the two-dimensional concept of perimeter; it is the amount of material needed to surround the object. Students will remember and have a stronger conceptual understanding because the teacher built on prior knowledge.

A teacher can make this connection even stronger by using objects that students are familiar with (such as a cereal box) and by introducing the concepts as part of a problem ("How much cereal will fit in the box and how much paper is needed to cover the cardboard?"). Because it is difficult to transfer knowledge from one discipline to another, students should have experience applying mathematical knowledge to other disciplines. This will also motivate the need for learning mathematics.

Integrating mathematics and science or mathematics and art instruction is an excellent way to facilitate teaching in context. Small group work that asks students to investigate a concept or explore possible solutions to a problem encourages them to discuss what they already know and communicate mathematically how this knowledge could be applied in a new situation. Clustering ideas, as discussed in the "Teaching Strategies" section (see page 56), is another way of helping students see connections within mathematics.

Actively Engage Students

"Students' understanding will increase if they are actively engaged in tasks and experiences designed to deepen and connect their knowledge of mathematical concepts."[16]

An ideal atmosphere for actively engaging students is one in which:
- student discussion and collaboration are encouraged
- students are expected to justify their thinking
- students feel comfortable questioning the reasoning of the teacher and other students
- students respect each other and the teacher
- students feel comfortable making conjectures and suggesting alternative problem-solving strategies
- students feel comfortable presenting results.

---

[16] John Sutton and Alice Krueger, eds., *EDThoughts: What We Know about Mathematics Teaching and Learning* (Aurora, Co.: Mid-Continent Research for Education and Learning [MCREL], 2002), p. 91.

This atmosphere requires the teacher to be a facilitator of learning rather than a dispenser of knowledge.

> ### Teaching by Engaging vs. Teaching by Telling
>
> Teaching by *Telling*: The teacher states the definition of a convex polygon and draws a picture of one (or several) on the board.
>
> Teaching by *Engaging*: The teacher gives examples (verbal and visual) of convex and non-convex polygons and asks the students to create a definition (in writing, either individually or in teams) and to justify their choices. Students then share their definitions and try to derive *one* definition.

Implement the Equity Principle[17]

A critical aspect of supporting students in learning developmentally is providing each student an equal opportunity to learn—a goal that has been made explicit in the NCTM's *Principles and Standards for School Mathematics*. A teacher should provide equal opportunity for all students, regardless of gender or other personal characteristics, to learn mathematics; educational equity requires that teachers have high expectations for all students.[18] Teachers are responsible for challenging their own biases, which may be unintentional. The information in this section is intended as a reminder of the goals that we as educators must constantly keep in mind.

Gender equity

The under-representation of women in mathematics-related fields has been well documented, and educational research has examined factors related to this and to the lower achievement of females than males in mathematics.[19] Although gender differences in mathematics achievement have continued to decrease, teachers need to create learning environments where both girls and

---

[17] For an extensive listing of equity and gender and multicultural education resources, see Andria P Troutman and Betty K. Lichtenberg, *Mathematics a Good Beginning* (Belmont, Ca.: Wadsworth/ Thomson Learning, 2003), pp. 570–72.

[18] National Council of Teachers of Mathematics, *Principles and Standards for School Mathematics*, p. 12–14.

[19] Gila Hanna, "Reaching Gender Equity in Mathematics Education," *The Educational Forum* 67, no. 3 (spring 2003): pp. 204–14.

boys are equally encouraged to learn and achieve in mathematics. Approaches that bridge the gap between the sexes in learning mathematics include:

- using cooperative learning
- using cooperative rather than competitive mathematical games
- calling on girls as often as boys
- allowing sufficient wait time for a response to a question
- praising both sexes for their responses
- creating an atmosphere that encourages all students to take risks
- having high expectations for all students
- encouraging communication about mathematics
- emphasizing the social nature of learning mathematics

Multicultural learning environments[20]

There is a pervasive belief in the United States that some students do not have the "math gene" and therefore cannot learn significant mathematics. Traditionally, these students have included students living in poverty, students for whom English is a second language, and non-whites. Research suggests that all students can learn significant mathematics if they receive a quality educational experience with the extra support that they need,[21] but teachers must have high expectations for all students.

One way for teachers to combat the belief that some students cannot learn mathematics is to highlight the contributions to mathematics of different countries, including Africa, India, China, and South America. This awareness and the ability to identify with the mathematics accomplishments of others from similar cultural backgrounds can motivate some students to learn the mathematics teachers are presenting. For example, tessellations, symmetry, and geometric transformations are found in Native American and African designs.[22]

---

[20] For discussion of this topic and listing of resources, see Geneva Gay, "The Importance of Multicultural Education," *Educational Leadership* 61, no. 4 (December 2003/January 2004): pp. 30–35; Lynda R. Wiest, "Multicultural Mathematics Instruction: Approaches and Resources," *Teaching Children Mathematics* 9, no. 1 (September 2002): pp. 49–55; and Claudia Zaslavsky, "Exploring World Cultures in Math Class," *Educational Leadership* 60, no. 2 (October 2002): pp. 66–69.

[21] Janet Trentacosta, ed., *Multicultural and Gender Equity in the Mathematics Classroom: The Gift of Diversity* (Reston, Va.: NCTM, 1997).

[22] Lyn Taylor et al., "American Indians, Mathematical Attitudes, and the *Standards*," *Arithmetic Teacher* 38, no. 6 (February 1991): pp. 14–21; Claudia Zaslavsky, "Multicultural Mathematics Education for the Middle Grades," *Arithmetic Teacher* 38, no. 6 (February 1991): pp. 8–13. Other sources of multicultural mathematics activities include: Clare V. Bell, "Learning Geometric Concepts through Ceramic Tile Design," *Mathematics Teaching in the Middle School* 9, no. 3 (November 2003): pp. 134–40; Marina C. Krause, *Multicultural Mathematics Materials*, 2nd ed. (Reston, Va.: NCTM, 2000); Maureen D. Neumann, "The Mathematics of Native American Star Quilts," *Mathematics Teaching in the Middle School* 9, no. 4 (December 2003): pp. 230–36; and Lynda S. Paznokas, "Teaching Mathematics through Cultural Quilting," *Teaching Children Mathematics* 9, no. 4 (December 2003): pp. 250–56.

Learning Styles and Multiple Intelligences

Just as many students have a preferred learning style, many teachers have a preferred teaching style. If a teacher uses one preferred teaching style almost exclusively and does not adjust to the learning styles of some students, the students suffer.[23] A teacher needs to be aware of his or her preferred teaching style and the preferred learning styles of each of his or her students. Only then can a teacher design learning experiences that accommodate the needs of all students. In the United States, we tend to stress verbal and mathematical reasoning skills more than many of the other multiple intelligences identified by Howard Gardner.[24] Many believe that, by recognizing the other intelligences in students, a teacher can take advantage of these abilities.

If several students have a strong musical intelligence, for example, a teacher can create activities that use music as a bridge to a mathematical concept, such as time signatures and note values to discuss the measurement of time.[25]

Gardner's eight intelligences

- visual/spatial intelligence
- musical intelligence
- verbal/linguistic intelligence
- logical/mathematical intelligence
- interpersonal intelligence
- intrapersonal intelligence
- bodily/kinesthetic intelligence
- naturalist intelligence.

---

[23] Sutton and Krueger, *EDThoughts*, p. 9.

[24] Howard Gardner, *Frames of Mind: The Theory of Multiple Intelligences* (New York: Basic Books), 1983. Also see Linda Campbell, Bruce Campbell, and Dee Dickinson, *Teaching and Learning Through Multiple Intelligences*, 2nd ed. (Boston: Allyn & Bacon, 1999); Stefanie Weiss, "Howard Gardner: All Kinds of Smarts," *NEA Today* 17, no. 6 (March 1999): p. 42 (available online at http://www.nea.org/neatoday/9903/gardner.html); and visit http://www.america-tomorrow.com/ati/nhl80402.htm.

[25] Gayle Cloke, Nola Ewing, and Dory Stevens, eds., "The Fine Art of Mathematics," *Teaching Children Mathematics* 8, no. 2 (2001): pp. 108–10; Tim Granger, "Math Is Art," *Teaching Children Mathematics* 7, no. 1 (2000): pp. 10–13; Gretchen L. Johnson and R. Jill Edelson, "Integrating Music and Mathematics in the Elementary Classroom," *Teaching Children Mathematics* 9, no. 8 (2003): pp. 474–79; and Patricia S. Moyer, "Patterns and Symmetry: Reflections of Culture," *Teaching Children Mathematics* 8, no. 3 (2001): pp. 140–44. Also see the lesson plan: "A Gigabyte of Music, How Much Is That?" (available at http://www.pbs.org/newshour/extra/teachers/lessonplans/math/download_10-2.html) from the PBS (Public Broadcasting Service) "News Hour Extra" Teacher Resources.

Summary of Cognitive and Developmental Issues

A teacher should be aware of the **van Hiele levels** of his or her students and use appropriate language and symbols. A teacher should design activities to move students from van Hiele Level 1 (visualization) in kindergarten, through Level 2 (analysis), to Level 3 (informal deduction) by grade eight.

Brain research, in areas such as memory retention and the learning of new concepts, has significant implications for instruction. Teachers need to stay informed about the latest research concerning education and work to implement that research in the classroom.

Geometry and measurement at the elementary school level should be informal, exploratory, and hands-on. When introducing new concepts, a teacher should start with **concrete representations** (e.g., manipulatives) and introduce visual representations and abstract symbolism as students increase their level of understanding.

When introducing a new manipulative or technology, a teacher should give students **time to play** and become familiar with the new educational tool.

When introducing a new geometric shape, a teacher should show both **examples and non-examples** of the shape as well as different sizes and orientations.

The amount and type of **technology** will vary by grade level. A teacher should be sure that his or her students are developmentally ready for the technology used.

A teacher should teach geometry and measurement in **context**, making connections between the concepts and the students' world as well as to other areas of mathematics and other disciplines.

A teacher should carefully plan experiences with geometry and measurement to take advantage of **prior knowledge** and to challenge students' misconceptions.

A teacher must **actively engage students** in the learning process, so students construct their own knowledge.

A teacher should provide **equal opportunity for all students** to learn mathematics, regardless of gender or other personal characteristics; educational equity requires that teachers have high expectations for all students.

Whenever feasible, a teacher should make students aware of the **contributions of all cultures** to geometry and measurement.

A teacher should take into account the different **learning styles** of his or her students and take advantage of their **multiple intelligences**.

Chapter 2

Content Strands

Improving teachers' mathematical knowledge and their capacity to use it to do the work of teaching is crucial in developing students' mathematical proficiency.

—*Adding It Up*[1]

Content for the IMAGES program covers five different strands:
- Visualization and Spatial Reasoning
- Two- and Three-Dimensional Geometry
- Coordinate Geometry
- Transformational Geometry
- Measurement

These strands were chosen to be consistent with international (TIMSS: the Third International Mathematics and Science Study), national (NAEP: the National Assessment of Educational Progress), and state standards and expectations.

Because teachers need to know material that reaches beyond the level of the geometry and measurement that they themselves are teaching, IMAGES includes content beyond grades K–5, in support of what students will need to know in subsequent years. In designing this publication, determining how to present the K–5 student expectations posed a dilemma, as the NCTM standards are divided pre-K–2 and 3–5, while many states have traditionally required assessments at grades 3, 5, and 8. In order to be teacher-friendly, IMAGES clusters content for grades K–3 and 4–5 to help guide teachers for state benchmark assessments.[2]

---

[1] Jeremy Kilpatrick, Jane Swanford, and Bradford Findell, eds., *Adding It Up: Helping Children Learn Mathematics* (Washington, D.C.: National Academy Press, 2001), p. 372.

[2] While President Bush's 2001 "No Child Left Behind" initiative requires testing at every grade level, we anticipate that the larger, statewide mathematics benchmarks will remain at grades 3, 5, and 8, as they were when this resource book went to press. See pamphlet published by the U.S. Department of Education, Office of the Secretary, *Back to School, Moving Forward: What 'No Child Left Behind' Means for America's Communities* (Washington, D.C., 2001).

It is crucial that a teacher creates and follows a coherent curriculum; simply adding a few geometry and measurement activities is not sufficient. Students best understand this geometry and measurement content when their teacher integrates it within mathematics and relates it to other disciplines and information that students already know. A teacher can do this through overlapping and clustering geometry and measurement content areas, both across strands and within a single strand. (For more information on clustering, see page 56.)

Each content strand refers to grade-appropriate activities and lesson plans, which are provided in detail in Chapter 4. To explore how the IMAGES content strands correlate to state standards for assessment, refer to Appendix A, which lists, by content strand, those standards that apply to various sample state standards.

This content chapter is meant to provide models for teachers to use in creating and adapting their own original lessons, incorporate the content of geometry and measurement, and also expand the framework of the state standards and the NCTM *Principles and Standards for School Mathematics*.

This chapter presents the following components for each of the five content strands:
- essential content for elementary teachers in kindergarten through grade eight
- essential content for students in kindergarten through grade three
- essential content for students in grades four and five
- sample instructional activities
- sample lesson plans.

A note on language: While some state standards seem to use the terms "figure" and "shape" interchangeably, IMAGES consistently uses the term "geometric shape."

Visualization and Spatial Reasoning

Essential content for elementary teachers

I.   Become familiar with projections, cross-sections, and decompositions of common two- and three-dimensional geometric shapes.[3]

II. Construct three-dimensional geometric shapes from two-dimensional shapes and use a two-dimensional representation for three-dimensional shapes.

III. Create and recognize a geometric shape from different perspectives (top, bottom, side).

IV. Use appropriate software (such as the Geometer's Sketchpad®) for showing representations of geometric shapes.

Essential content for students grades K–3

I.   Specify locations and describe spatial relationships using representational systems.[4]
     A. Describe relative positions in space; interpret and apply ideas about relative position.

II. Use visualization and spatial reasoning to solve problems.[5]
     A. Use spatial visualization to create mental images of geometric shapes.
     B. Identify and draw geometric shapes from different perspectives.
     C. Recognize geometric shapes and structures in their environment.
     D. Build and draw geometric objects from mental images.

Essential content for students grades 4–5

I.   Maintain and expand on concepts introduced in primary grades.

II. Specify locations and describe spatial relationships using representational systems.[6]
     A. Use appropriate geometric vocabulary to describe location, movement, and relative position.

(continued on next page)

---

[3] Conference Board of the Mathematical Sciences, *The Mathematical Education of Teachers*, part 1. (Washington, D.C.: Mathematical Association of America, 2000), p. 80.
[4] National Council of Teachers of Mathematics, *Principles and Standards for School Mathematics*, (Reston, Va.: National Council of Teachers of Mathematics), p. 396
[5] Ibid.
[6] Ibid.

> **Essential content for students grades 4–5** (continued)
>
> III. Use visualization and spatial reasoning to solve problems.[7]
> A. Identify and build a three-dimensional object from two-dimensional representations.
> B. Draw a two-dimensional representation of a three-dimensional object.
> C. Recognize that geometric ideas and relationships can be applied to other disciplines and can be related to problems in everyday life.

See *Appendix A* for a list of sample state standards for mathematics.

Instructional activities and lesson plans for visualization and spatial reasoning

The activities and lesson plans listed here (by grade level) are described more extensively in Chapter 4, where they are listed alphabetically.

Note: The ⌨ symbol indicates that the full description of this activity includes a link to an online resource.

ACTIVITY	DESCRIPTION
Creating Tilings grades K–5 (p. 63)	Have students create tilings with pattern block pieces and draw their tilings on triangle dot paper. Have upper-level students discuss why certain shapes tile and others do not.
Draw a Shape from Memory grades K–5 (p. 64)	Show students a shape for a few seconds and then have them try to draw the shape from memory. Start with simpler shapes and then draw more complex ones.
Geoboard Polygons grades 1–4 (p. 65)	Have students duplicate shapes on a geoboard and then break them into smaller shapes. For an irregular shape, have students find as many triangles, squares, or rectangles within the shape as possible.
Creating Tessellations grades 1–5 (p. 62)	Have students use index cards to create a shape that will tessellate the plane. Display their tessellations on a bulletin board. This activity can be connected to the art of M. C. Esher.
Origami grades 2–5 (p. 68)	Use origami to explore spatial relations and to investigate shapes and their properties. Some of the concepts to explore are similarity, congruence, and classification of triangles. As students do the folding, introduce mathematical terms such as *diagonal* and *midpoint*.⌨
Build a Shape grades 3–5 (p. 60)	Have students use cubes to build a shape and then draw the shapes on graph paper, showing how they would look from the front, back, side, top, and bottom. *(continued on next page)*

---

[7] Ibid.

Creating Nets grades 4–5 (p. 62)	Have students build shapes with wooden cubes then create nets to wrap the shapes. Use the nets to discuss surface area.
Creating Pentominoes grades 4–5 (p. 62)	Have students work together, using square tiles, to find the 12 different pentomino shapes. Have them record results on graph paper or square dot paper. Have students use transformations to verify uniqueness of shapes.
Pentomino Boxes grades 4–5 (p. 69)	Have students try to visualize which of the 12 pentomino pieces can be folded to make a box without a top. Have students make the pentomino pieces on one-inch square grid paper and fold to confirm their conjectures.
LESSON PLAN	**DESCRIPTION**
Tiling the Plane grades 2–3 (p. 145)	Students use pattern blocks and triangle paper to develop an understanding of tessellations while reviewing names of geometric shapes.
Rep Tiles grade 3 (p. 121)	Students develop a deeper understanding of similarity and how perimeter changes as a result of increase in size. They create "rep tiles" using four pattern blocks ("rep-4 tiles").
Visualizing Multiplication grades 3–5 (p. 159)	Students use an area model to do multiplication.
Rep Tiles grades 4–5 (p. 127)	Similar to the grade 3 lesson above, with added element of how area changes as a result of an increase in size.
Investigating Nets and Polyhedra grade 5 (p. 101)	Students explore nets for three-dimensional shapes.
Tiling the Plane grade 5 (p. 149)	Similar to the grades 2–3 lesson above, and addressing more complex tessellations.

Two- and Three-Dimensional Geometry

Essential content for elementary teachers

I. Develop an understanding of basic geometric concepts including: point, line, plane, space, line segment, betweenness, ray, angle, vertex, parallelism, perpendicularity, congruency, similarity, simple closed curve, Pythagorean relationship.

II. Identify types of angles including acute, right, obtuse, straight, reflex, vertical, supplementary, complementary, corresponding, alternate interior, and alternate exterior.

III. Recognize and define common geometric shapes.
   A. Two-dimensional geometric shapes
       1. Triangles: be able to classify by sides (equilateral, scalene, isosceles) and classify by angle (right, acute, obtuse)
       2. Quadrilaterals (trapezoid, parallelogram, rectangle, square, rhombus, kite): identify characteristics and relationships among these shapes
       3. Polygons, regular polygons
       4. Circle
   B. Three-dimensional geometric shapes
       1. Polyhedra (prisms, pyramids), regular polyhedra (Platonic solids): connecting polyhedra to polygons, nets
       2. Cylinder, cone, sphere

Essential content for students K–3

I. Analyze characteristics and properties of two- and three-dimensional geometric shapes and develop mathematical arguments about geometric relationships.[8]
   A. Two-dimensional geometric shapes
       1. Recognize, name, build, draw, compare, and sort shapes.
       2. Describe attributes and parts of shapes: circle, rectangle, square, triangle, parallelogram (sides and vertices); locate interior (inside) and exterior (outside) angles.
       3. Compare shapes made with line segments (polygons) and identify congruent and similar geometric shapes.
       4. Identify right angles in polygons.
       5. Investigate and predict the results of putting together and taking apart shapes.
   B. Three-dimensional geometric shapes
       1. Recognize, name, build, draw, compare, and sort shapes: sphere (ball), cone, cylinder (can), pyramid, prism (box), cube.
       2. Describe attributes and parts of shapes: identify faces, edges, vertices (corners).

(continued on next page)

---

[8] Ibid.

> ### *Essential content for students K–3* (continued)
>
> 3. Sort using similar attributes (curved surfaces, flat surfaces).
> 4. Investigate and predict the results of putting together and taking apart shapes.
>
> II. Develop vocabulary and concepts related to two- and three-dimensional geometric shapes.
>   A. Two-dimensional shapes: angle, circle, congruency, line segment, parallelogram, polygon, rectangle, similarity, square, triangle
>   B. Three-dimensional shapes: cone, cube, cylinder, edge, face, prism, pyramid, sphere, vertices

> ### *Essential content for students grades 4–5*
>
> I. Maintain and expand on concepts introduced in primary grades.
>
> II. Analyze characteristics and properties of two- and three-dimensional geometric shapes and develop mathematical arguments about geometric relationships.[9]
>   A. Two-dimensional geometric shapes
>   1. Identify, compare, and analyze attributes of shapes, and develop vocabulary to describe the attributes.
>   a. Angles (right, acute, obtuse, straight)
>   b. Circles (diameter, radius, center, arc, circumference)
>   c. Lines (parallel, intersecting, perpendicular)
>   d. Line segments
>   e. Polygons (vertex, side, diagonal, perimeter); classification by number of sides (quadrilaterals, pentagon, hexagon)
>   2. Classify shapes according to their properties.
>   a. Triangles (classify by angles and sides)
>   b. Quadrilaterals (square, rectangle, parallelogram, rhombus, trapezoid, kite)
>   3. Investigate, describe, and reason about the results of subdividing, combining, and transforming shapes.
>   4. Explore and identify congruence and similarity.
>   5. Make and test conjectures about geometric properties and relationships and develop logical arguments to justify conclusions.
>   B. Three-dimensional geometric shapes
>   1. Identify shapes (cylinder, cone, sphere, pyramid, prism).
>   2. Apply terms (face, edge, vertex).
>   3. Classify shapes according to their properties and develop definitions of classes of shapes such as triangles and pyramids.
>   4. Investigate, describe, and reason about the results of subdividing, combining, and transforming shapes.

*See **Appendix A** for a list of sample state standards for mathematics.*

---

[9] Ibid.

Instructional activities and lesson plans for two- and three-dimensional geometry

The activities and lesson plans listed here (by grade level) are described more extensively in Chapter 4, where they are listed alphabetically.

Note: The 🖥 symbol indicates that the full description of this activity includes a link to an online resource. The 📖 symbol indicates that the full description includes a reference to children's literature.

ACTIVITY	DESCRIPTION
Describe the Shape grades K–2 (p. 63)	Help students learn to identify geometric shapes using pattern blocks, a pattern block applet, or triangle grid paper. 🖥📖
Footprints in the Sand grades K–2 (p. 65)	Use blocks of various shapes to make impressions in sand. Students identify the shapes and match the blocks to the impressions. 📖
The Button Box grades K–3 (p. 60)	Have students sort a box of buttons according to different attributes and describe what attributes they used. 📖
Describing Attributes of Shapes grades K–3 (p. 63)	Have students examine and describe the attributes of attribute blocks. Place a block where students cannot see it and have them ask "yes" or "no" questions until they can fully describe the shape.
Nature Walk grades K–3 (p. 67)	Take students on a nature walk and have them identify various shapes in nature. Take photographs to use on a bulletin board display or have students draw what they find. 📖
Shape People grades K–3 (p. 71)	Have students use different polygons and circles to create a person out of shapes. Connect this activity with language arts by having each student write a story about his or her person.
Winter Shapes grades K–3 (p. 73)	Cut various two-dimensional shapes from construction paper and have students use them to make all the winter objects that they can imagine.
Draw a Shape from Memory grades K–5 (p. 64)	Show students a shape for a few seconds and then have them try to draw the shape from memory. Start with simpler shapes and then draw more complex ones.
Pattern Block Shapes grades 2–3 (p. 68)	Develop the relationships between the different pattern block shapes by having students create one shape by using other shapes. Have students draw and color their shapes on triangle grid paper and include a verbal explanation of the picture and the shapes they used.
Shape Journals grades 2–4 (p. 71)	On each page of a journal, have students name a polygon and draw it. Have them look in magazines for a picture of an object that closely resembles the polygon, cut it out, and paste it into the journal. *(continued on next page)*

Writing Stories grades 1–5 (p. 73)	Have students write creative stories using as many geometric terms as possible. Suggest a general topic or theme for their story or relate it to what you are teaching in language arts, science, or social studies.
"Who Am I?" Riddles grades 2–4 (p. 73)	Prepare "Who Am I" riddles for students to solve, such as: "I am a polygon; I have four sides of equal length, but the four angles are not of equal measure. Who am I?" Have students make up the riddles and share them with each other.
Geoboard Polygons grades 1–4 (p. 65)	Have students duplicate shapes on a geoboard and then break them into smaller shapes. Give students an irregular shape and have them find as many triangles, squares, or rectangles as possible.
Go-Together Rules grades 3–4 (p. 65)	Prepare sets of rules for attributes of shapes, with blanks for students to complete, such as "All ____ have ____" or "No ____ have ____." Have students make up rules for each other to complete.
Rope Polygons grades 3–5 (p. 71)	Have a group of three students make different triangles using rope or string. Have students determine how many students are needed for other kinds of polygons.
Shape Puzzles grades 3–5 (p. 71)	Cut out puzzle pieces for a shape and put the pieces into an envelope with the final shape on the outside. Have students arrange the pieces into the shape shown, then make shape puzzles for others to solve.
Connect the Dots grades 3–4 (p. 61)	Have students draw polygons on square dot paper, taking turns drawing one line segment at a time. When students complete a shape, have them put their initials in the shape.
Origami grades 2–5 (p. 68)	Use origami to explore spatial relations, shapes, and their properties. Explore concepts such as congruence and classification of triangles. Introduce mathematical terms such as *diagonal* and *midpoint*. 💻
Build a Shape grades 3–5 (p. 60)	Use cubes to build a shape. Have students draw the shapes on graph paper and show how they look from the front, back, side, top, and bottom.
Building Vocabulary grades 4–5 (p. 60)	Have students make a word bank, looking for common roots in words. Have students use word roots to write definitions of words.
Creating Nets grades 4–5 (p. 62)	Have students build shapes with wooden cubes and create nets to wrap the shapes. Use the nets to discuss surface area.
Creative Writing Activity grades 4–5 (p. 63)	Have students read books such as *Sir Cumference and the First Round Table* and then write their own stories using geometry vocabulary words. 📖
Regular Polygons grades 4–5 (p. 70)	Have students use flexible straws or K'NEX™ materials to make regular polygons and then discuss the attributes of the shapes.
Platonic Solids grades 4–5 (p. 69)	Discuss the Platonic solids and use nets to develop the concepts of edges, faces, and vertices. Make a chart to determine the relationship between the number of edges, vertices, and faces (Euler's Formula).

(continued on next page)

Scale Drawings grades 4–5 (p. 71)	Use scale drawings to help students develop the concept of similarity. Have students make a scale drawing of their classroom, where one square on the graph paper represents one square floor tile.
Using Geometric Software to Explore Triangles grade 5 (p. 72)	Use dynamic geometric software to measure the interior angles and the lengths of the sides of a triangle. Have students create different types of triangles, discover the triangle inequality property, and determine that the sum of interior angles is always 180 degrees.
LESSON PLANS	**DESCRIPTION**
Geoboard Squares grades 2–3 (p. 89)	Students create squares of different sizes on a geoboard and use a system or numeric pattern to determine the number of squares possible on a 10-by-10 geoboard.
Tiling the Plane grades 2–3 (p. 145)	Students use pattern blocks and triangle paper to develop an understanding of tessellations while reviewing names of geometric shapes.
Rep Tiles grade 3 (p. 121)	Students develop a deeper understanding of similarity and how perimeter changes as a result of increase in size. They create "rep tiles" using four pattern blocks ("rep-4 tiles").
Can You Name That Shape? grades 2–4 (p. 81)	Students build and draw geometric objects using manipulatives and develop vocabulary and concepts related to two-dimensional shapes.
It's a 3-D World Out There! grades 2–4 (p. 109)	Students use manipulatives to build, invent, and draw three-dimensional shapes.
Rep Tiles grades 4–5 (p. 127)	Similar to the grade 3 lesson above, with added element of how area changes as a result of an increase in size.
Investigating Nets and Polyhedra grade 5 (p. 101)	Students explore nets for three-dimensional shapes
The Sum of the Interior Angles of a Polygon grades 4-5 (p. 135)	Students use the Geometer's Sketchpad® to find a formula for the sum of the interior angles of a polygon.
Tiling the Plane grade 5 (p. 149)	Similar to the grades 2–3 lesson above, and addressing more complex tessellations.

Coordinate Geometry

Essential content for elementary teachers

I.   Understand distance on a line.

II. Understand the coordinate plane.
  A. Coordinates
  B. Origin
  C. Quadrants
  D. Identify and plot points

III. Use coordinate geometry to investigate properties of shapes and relationships such as congruence, similarity, and the Pythagorean relationship.

Essential content for students grades K–3

I.   Specify locations and describe spatial relationships using coordinate geometry.[10]
  A. Describe, name, and interpret relative positions on a line and on a plane.
  B. Describe, name, and interpret direction and distance in navigating on a line or on a plane and apply ideas about direction and distance.
  C. Find and name locations with simple relationships such as "near to" and in coordinate systems such as maps.

Essential content for students grades 4–5

I.   Maintain and expand on concepts introduced in primary grades.

II. Specify locations and describe spatial relationships using coordinate geometry.[11]
  A. Describe location and movement using common language and geometric vocabulary.
  B. Make and use coordinate systems to specify locations and to describe paths.
  C. Find the distance between points along horizontal and vertical lines of a coordinate system.

---

*See **Appendix A** for a list of sample state standards for mathematics.*

---

[10] National Council of Teachers of Mathematics, *Principles and Standards for School Mathematics*, p. 396.
[11] Ibid.

Instructional activities and lesson plans for coordinate geometry

The brief activities and lesson plans listed here (by grade level) are described more extensively in Chapter 4, where they are listed alphabetically.

Note: The 🖳 symbol indicates that the full description of this activity includes a link to an online resource.

ACTIVITY	DESCRIPTION
Mixed-up Pictures grades K–2 (p. 67)	Showing pictures where some of the items are upside-down and some are right-side-up, have students identify the proper orientation of each item.
Calendar Locations grades 1–3 (p. 61)	Have students use a calendar to locate relative positions in a plane.
Number Line Message grades 1–3 (p. 67)	Have students place specially chosen letters above a series of numbers on the number line, and have them read the message that emerges.
Traveling on a Grid grades 2–3 (p. 72)	Have students use large block graph paper to draw city streets and buildings. Have them describe how to get from one location to another.
Graphing Points on a Line grades 2–4 (p. 65)	Have students identify points on a number line. This activity also includes negatives, scale, a glossary, and links. 🖳
Using Maps grades 3–5 (p. 73)	Have students use road maps to find the distances between cities. Have them describe how to get from one city to another.
Coordinate Games grades 4–5 (p. 61)	Have students play games such as *Battleship*, *Coordinate Tic-Tac-Toe*, *Hurkle*, or *Grid Football*.
The Plane grades 4–5 (p. 69)	Help students learn to plot points on the coordinate plane. Concepts included in this activity are: the plane, finding points, graphing points, and scale. 🖳
Plotting Pictures grades 4–5 (p. 70)	Have students plot and connect sets of coordinates that create shapes and images.
Playground Grids grades 4–5 (p. 69)	Mark off a grid on the playground with X- and Y-axes. Have students walk to points on the grid by traveling along the grid lines. (This can also be done in a classroom that has square floor tiles.)
LESSON PLANS	**DESCRIPTION**
Traveling around Our Town grades 1–2 (p. 155)	Students learn to specify locations on a grid by using the words *right*, *left*, *up*, and *down* and find different paths from one location to another.
Find the Shape grades 4–5 (p. 85)	Students play a game similar to the game *Battleship*. They practice identifying ordered pairs and plotting ordered pairs in the first quadrant. (This lesson can be extended to include the entire coordinate plane.)

Transformational Geometry

Essential content for elementary teachers

I. Understand symmetry and identify line symmetry and rotational symmetry in geometric shapes and objects.

II. Understand transformations of geometric shapes.
  A. Congruence
    1. Translation (slide)
    2. Reflection (flip)
    3. Rotation (turn)
    4. Glide reflection (glide)
  B. Similarity: dilation (enlarge and shrink)
  C. Topological: distortion

III. Define, understand, and develop tessellations by hand and on the computer; understand which shapes will tessellate and why.

Essential content for students grades K–3

I. Apply transformations and use symmetry to analyze mathematical situations.[12]
  A. Identify lines of symmetry in nature, in regular polygons and other two-dimensional geometric shapes; make shapes that have lines of symmetry and fold shapes to find lines of symmetry.
  B. Identify slides, flips, and turns.
  C. Investigate tessellations with regular polygons (square, equilateral triangle, hexagon) and other polygons (quadrilaterals—rectangle, parallelogram, rhombus, kite, and trapezoid).

Essential content for students grades 4–5

I. Maintain and expand on concepts introduced in primary grades.

II. Apply transformations and use symmetry to analyze mathematical situations.[13]
  A. Recognize line and rotational symmetry in two- and three-dimensional geometric shapes and objects.
  B. Use slides, flips, and turns to understand position and congruence of geometric shapes.
  C. Define and create tessellations of simple polygonal shapes; determine regular polygons that can be tessellated; and develop a tessellation by hand and on the computer.

*See **Appendix A** for a list of sample state standards for mathematics.*

---

[12] Ibid.
[13] Ibid.

Instructional activities and lesson plans for transformational geometry

The brief activities and lesson plans listed here (by grade level) are described more extensively in Chapter 4, where they are listed alphabetically.

Note: The ▣ symbol indicates that the full description of this activity includes a link to an online resource. The ▢ symbol indicates that the full description includes a reference to children's literature.

ACTIVITY	DESCRIPTION
Creating Tessellations grades 1-5 (p. 62)	Have students use index cards to create a shape that will tessellate the plane.
Line Symmetry grades K–3 (p. 67)	Have students show lines of symmetry using pattern blocks, a pattern block applet, or paper folding. ▣▢
Simply Symmetrical grades 1–5 (p. 72)	Have students explore the classroom for symmetrical designs with both reflection and rotation symmetry. Have students draw the missing half of an object using reflection symmetry. Have students explore symmetry in block letters. ▣
Geo-Dot Paper grades 3–5 (p. 65)	Have students draw different quadrilaterals on dot paper and then compare their shapes with a partner. Explore properties of shapes, congruent and similar shapes, and translations and reflections.
Regular Polygons grades 4–5 (p. 70)	Have students create regular polygons with flexible straws or K'NEX™ materials and explore which of the regular polygons will tessellate.
Pentomino Pieces grades 3–5 (p. 69)	Have students use pentomino pieces to explore reflection and rotation symmetry. Use paper folding, mirrors, or Miras™.
Creating Pentominoes grades 4–5 (p. 62)	Have students work together, using square tiles, to find the 12 different pentomino shapes and record their results on graph or square dot paper. Have students use transformations to verify the uniqueness of shapes.
LESSON PLAN	**DESCRIPTION**
Tiling the Plane grades 2–3 (p. 145)	Students use pattern blocks and triangle paper to develop an understanding of tessellations while reviewing names of geometric shapes.
Rep Tiles grade 3 (p. 121)	Students develop a deeper understanding of similarity and how perimeter changes as a result of increase in size. They create "rep tiles" using four pattern blocks ("rep-4 tiles").
Rep Tiles grades 4–5 (p. 127)	Similar to the grade 3 lesson above, with added element of how area changes as a result of an increase in size.
Reflections grade 5 (p. 113)	Students discover properties of reflections and glide reflections and review names of shapes and the concepts of congruence and perpendicular lines. Use pattern blocks, Miras™, and protractors.
Tiling the Plane grade 5 (p. 149)	Similar to the grades 2–3 lesson above, and addressing more complex tessellations.

Measurement

Essential content for elementary teachers

I. Know and understand the measurable attributes of objects (time, temperature, length, perimeter, area, volume, capacity, weight, and angle measure).

II. Know and understand the units of measurement, customary and metric systems of measurement, and the measuring process; understand aspects of size, be able to compare units and select the appropriate unit for the attribute being measured, and understand that measurements are approximations.[14]

III. Know how to use non-standard, customary, and metric units of measurement and be able to convert and operate within each system.

IV. Develop formulas for measuring area, surface area, and volume for two- and three-dimensional geometric shapes and explore the independence of perimeter and area, and surface area and volume.

V. Use strategies for estimating (using referents, chunking, unitizing) linear measurement, area, and volume, and verify those estimates by use of non-standard and standard units.

VI. Understand and use appropriate measurement instruments (rulers, scales, thermometers, clocks, calendars, beakers, cups, etc.).

VII. Know and understand the development of measurement in an historical context.

Essential content for students grades K–3

I. Understand measurable attributes of objects and the units, systems, and processes of measurement.[15]
   A. Recognize attributes of objects and use a variety of ways for measuring those attributes (time, temperature, length, area, volume, capacity, weight, perimeter, and angle measure).
   B. Measure objects using non-standard and standard units (customary and metric).
   C. Use the appropriate unit for the attribute being measured.
   D. Compare attributes of different objects and different attributes of a given object.
   (continued on next page)

---

[14] National Council of Teachers of Mathematics, *Principles and Standards for School Mathematics*, p. 81.
[15] National Council of Teachers of Mathematics, *Principles and Standards for School Mathematics*, p. 398.

Essential content for students grades K–3 (continued)

II. Apply appropriate techniques, tools, and formulas to determine measurements.[16]
   A. Recognize, name, and use appropriate tools for measuring objects.
   B. Find the perimeter, area, or volume of objects using concrete objects (string, square tiles, or cubes); then use non-standard and standard measures.
   C. Estimate measures by using common referents to make comparisons, and then verify values.

Essential content for students grades 4–5

I. Maintain and expand on concepts introduced in primary grades.

II. Understand measurable attributes of objects and the units, systems, and processes of measurement.[17]
   A. Understand attributes introduced in primary grades and select the appropriate unit for measuring each.
   B. Identify, compare, and use customary and metric units of measure appropriately.
   C. Convert measurements within the same system (inches to feet or centimeters to meters) and convert different measures to the same unit.
   D. Investigate what happens to the attributes of a geometric shape when the shape is changed, such as what happens to perimeter or area when a two-dimensional shape is changed in some way.

III. Apply appropriate techniques, tools, and formulas to determine measurements.[18]
   A. Develop strategies for measuring irregular geometric shapes.
   B. Use appropriate tools for measuring attributes.
   C. Select and use referents for estimating measurements.
   D. Develop, understand, and use formulas for area of two-dimensional geometric shapes such as rectangles, squares, triangles, and parallelograms and for surface area and volume of rectangular solids.

---

*See **Appendix A** for a list of sample state standards for mathematics.*

---

[16] Ibid.
[17] Ibid.
[18] Ibid.

Instructional activities and lesson plans for measurement

The brief activities and lesson plans listed here (by grade level) are described more extensively in Chapter 4, where they are listed alphabetically.

Note: The 🖥 symbol indicates that the full description of this activity includes a link to an online resource. The 📖 symbol indicates that the full description includes a reference to children's literature.

ACTIVITY	DESCRIPTION
Inching Along grades K–2 (p. 66)	Have students measure objects using non-standard units, such as "inchworm" packing peanuts. 🖥📖
Comparing Lengths of Arms with Links grades K–3 (p. 61)	Have students use commercially available links or large paper clips to make chains as long as their arms. Have students compare their arm-chains and use them to measure objects. 📖
Is My Hand Bigger or Smaller Than Yours? grades K–3 (p. 66)	Have students trace their hands and use their tracings to compare the area of their hands.
Measuring Desktops with Hands grades 1–3 (p. 67)	Have students trace their hands and use the tracings to measure the desktop. Emphasize area as the covering of a region with the same shape.
Determining the Appropriate Unit of Measure grades 1–3 (p. 63)	Have students use different measuring tools to measure various objects around the classroom. Discuss with students which tools and units were easier to use for measuring the different objects.
Finding Perimeter with a Non-Standard Unit grades 3–4 (p. 64)	Have students use pattern blocks to explore perimeter and record their work on triangle grid paper or isometric dot paper. To extend this activity, have students make different shapes with the pattern blocks, draw them on the dot or grid paper, and then identify the perimeter of the shape.
Centimeter by Centimeter or Inch by Inch grades 3–5 (p. 61)	Have students make a meter stick (or one-foot ruler) and use it to measure objects in the classroom. For fourth and fifth grade students, specify appropriate degrees of accuracy. 🖥📖
Fixed Perimeter grades 3–5 (p. 64)	Have students use a piece of ribbon that measures about 10 yards to make different shapes and explore what happens to the area of shapes if the perimeter is held constant. The activity includes possible extensions.
Finding Area with a Non-Standard Unit grades 3–5 (p. 64)	Have students use pattern blocks to explore area and record their work on triangle grid paper or isometric dot paper. Assuming that the green triangle has an area of one square unit, have students find the area of the other shapes and then build other shapes with the pattern blocks and find the area. *(continued on next page)*

Bubble Mania grades 3–5 (p. 60)	Have students create soap bubble prints to explore the concepts of diameter, circumference, and area of a circle. 🖥
Paper-Penny Boxes grades 3–5 (p. 68)	Have students explore the concept of volume by building a paper box that will hold 100 pennies. 📖
Area and Perimeter grades 4–5 (p. 60)	Have students construct various two-dimensional shapes with straws and gumdrops or K'NEX™ rods and connectors, and then calculate perimeter and area.
Lighting the Perimeter grades 4–5 (p. 66)	Have students use their knowledge of perimeter to determine how long a string of lights is needed to decorate the outside of a building or other structure. 🖥
How Many Square Feet in a Square Yard? grades 4–5 (p. 66)	Have students use one-foot linoleum squares to demonstrate that nine square feet are equal to one square yard.
Tree Measurement grades 4-5 (p. 72)	Teach students a method for measuring the height of a tree that is too tall to measure directly. 🖥
Creative Writing Activity grades 4–5 (p. 63)	Have students read books such as *Sir Cumference and the First Round Table* and then write their own stories using geometry vocabulary words. 📖
Creating Nets grades 4–5 (p. 62)	Have students build shapes with wooden cubes and then create nets to wrap the shapes. Use the nets to discuss surface area.
Pumpkin Pi grade 5 (p. 70)	Have students use small pumpkins to explore circumference and diameter and the relationship between these two ideas and pi.
Pi Day grade 5 (p. 69)	Celebrate Pi Day, March 14 (also the birthday of Albert Einstein and Waclaw Sierpinski). Suggestions for celebrating include connection to children's literature, a Pi day contest, a trivia game, a visit to an online museum, and Web resources. 🖥📖
Mini-Metric Olympics grade 5 (p. 67)	Help students to become familiar with metric units by having them estimate and measure in a "Metric Olympic" setting that includes six activities. 🖥 *(continued on next page)*

LESSON PLANS	DESCRIPTION
Can You Build It? grade 3 (p. 77)	Students explore shapes and area using pattern blocks.
Rep Tiles grade 3 (p. 121)	Students develop a deeper understanding of similarity and how perimeter changes as a result of an increase in size. They create "rep tiles" using four pattern blocks ("rep-4 tiles").
Visualizing Multiplication grades 3–5 (p. 159)	Students use an area model to do multiplication.
Rep Tiles grades 4–5 (p. 127)	Similar to the grade 3 lesson above, with added element of how area changes as a result of an increase in size.
How Close Is Our Estimate? grade 5 (p. 95)	Students explore area as the covering of a region and develop an understanding of measuring area in square units.
The Sum of the Interior Angles of a Polygon grades 4-5 (p. 135)	Students use the Geometer's Sketchpad® to find a formula for the sum of the interior angles of a polygon.

Chapter 3

Teaching Strategies

As teachers' pedagogical content knowledge increases within the context of a strong knowledge of mathematical content, their ability to impact student learning also increases.

—*EDThoughts*[1]

Teachers will find that, as they strive to support students' learning, some of the teaching strategies included in this section will be helpful. All of these practices underscore the importance of establishing and working with a standards-based curriculum in a systematic way. Research has shown that use of these strategies is effective in helping children to learn concepts, discover efficient procedures, reason mathematically, and become better problem solvers.[2]

This section addresses the following teaching strategies, and elucidates how these can be best employed in the context of teaching geometry and measurement:

- Have High Expectations for All Students
- Base Practice on Educational Research
- Integrate Content Areas
- Incorporate Academic Standards
- Collaborate with Others
- Promote Cooperative Learning
- Use Technology as a Tool
- Use Inquiry-Based Learning
- Promote Mathematical Reasoning
- Promote Problem Solving
- Use Hands-On Activities to Model Topics
- Integrate Assessment and Instruction
- Reflect on Teaching and Learning
- Include Strong Academic Content
- Cluster Concepts

---

[1] John Sutton and Alice Krueger, *EDThoughts: What We Know about Mathematics Teaching and Learning* (Aurora, Co.: Mid-Continent Research for Education and Learning, 2002), p. 26.
[2] Sutton and Krueger, *EDThoughts.*

Have High Expectations for All Students

The Equity Principle of the NCTM *Principles and Standards for School Mathematics* states that: "All students, regardless of their personal characteristics, backgrounds, or physical challenges, must have opportunities to study—and support to learn— mathematics. Equity does not mean that every student should receive identical instruction; instead, it demands that reasonable and appropriate accommodations be made as needed to promote access and attainment for all students."[3]

Teachers share a responsibility to provide and support learning environments that respond to the unique educational needs of every student. School programs need to ensure that achievement will not depend on a student's race or ethnicity, gender, economic status, or physical or learning disability. Opportunity and access are not enough; teachers must also focus on each student's learning style. By using a broad range of instructional strategies, it is possible to address the educational needs of a greater number of students. These strategies may include:

- assessing and identifying the learning styles of each student
- addressing different student learning styles
- encouraging classroom participation of underrepresented students
- challenging each student
- engaging each student in higher-order thinking skills
- encouraging diverse student cooperation
- encouraging the use of inclusive language in the classroom
- requiring each student to master the same core curriculum
- accommodating students with special needs.

By varying instructional strategies and presenting content in a range of formats— including lecture, discussion, small group and individual work, books, video, computer software, or the Internet—a teacher can better meet the needs and address the learning styles of individual students.

---

[3] National Council of Teachers of Mathematics, *Principles and Standards for School Mathematics* (Reston, Va.: National Council of Teachers of Mathematics, 2000), p. 12.

Base Practice on Educational Research

Incorporating research results and findings is a way to profit from the work of others and to keep the quality of teaching fresh and challenging—for the teacher as well as the students. Knowing the latest research helps a teacher to avoid poor practices and to plan lessons and activities utilizing best practices. Research indicates that students—particularly females and minorities—benefit from cooperative learning.[4] Furthermore, calling on boys more than girls, or asking more challenging questions of white students than non-whites, sends the message that the teacher does not expect a certain group to do well in mathematics.[5]

For more information about integrating research, see Chapter 1. For details about effective teaching with multicultural perspectives and minority students, see page 19.

The use of calculators and computer software

Findings show that when students are allowed to use calculators for routine calculations in problem solving, they are better able to focus on problem-solving processes and strategies and are less likely to be distracted by or anxious about the computations.[6]

Computer programs that allow students to investigate concepts (such as simulations and dynamic geometry software) improve students' conceptual understanding and mathematical reasoning. While these findings may go against some long-held beliefs, they can help a teacher to make informed decisions in appropriate uses—and pitfalls— of using technology to teach mathematics.

These topics are discussed in more detail on page 49.

---

[4] American Association of University Women, *How Schools Shortchange Girls*. (Washington, D.C.: American Association of University Women Education Foundation, 1992), pp. 32, 72; Lucille Croom, "Mathematics for All Students, Access, Excellence, and Equity," in *Multicultural and Gender Equity in the Mathematics Classroom: The Gift of Diversity*, ed. Janet Trentacosta (Reston, VA: National Council of Teachers of Mathematics, 1997), p. 7.
[5] David Sadker, "Gender Equity: Still Knocking at the Classroom Door," *Educational Leadership* 56, no. 7 (1999), p. 24.
[6] Sutton and Krueger, *EDThoughts*, p. 64.

Integrate Content Areas

The various content areas of mathematics are often interconnected, and a teacher should emphasize these connections within the curriculum and in lessons. A coherent curriculum supports students in integrating various mathematics concepts and seeing how ideas build  upon and connect with each other. This makes it possible for students to develop and deepen their understanding and their skills.[7]

The learning of mathematics also becomes more meaningful for students when it makes sense to them in contexts beyond individual lessons. Mathematics should be connected in three ways: within mathematical concepts, with other disciplines, and to real-world situations. All of these, in different ways, help students to establish a framework of strategies that students can call upon in order to solve new problems and learn new concepts and algorithms.

Teachers should work collaboratively to develop and teach integrated or thematic units that span more than one discipline—not only mathematics and science or computers, but mathematics and language arts, social studies, physical education, or fine arts instruction. The only limit is the time, knowledge, and imagination of the team of teachers.[8]

*For an example of how to integrate content areas, see the lesson plan **How Close Is Our Estimate?** on page 95. To enhance students' understanding of multiplication, use the lesson plan **Visualizing Multiplication** on page 159.*

Incorporate Academic Standards

By actively addressing standards, whether at the state or national level, a teacher sets strong expectations for all students. Standards offer a teacher a detailed guide of the content and learning experiences that he or she should be providing students. How a teacher makes use of a standards-based curriculum is of the highest importance. Essential elements that a teacher must include when implementing a standards-based curriculum through instruction are:

- classroom discourse and writing to learn mathematics
- presenting mathematics skills in a problem-solving context
- applying concepts to real-life situations

---

[7] William Schmidt, Richard Houang, and Leland Cogan, "A Coherent Curriculum: The Case of Mathematics," *American Educator* 26, no. 2 (summer 2002): p. 19.

[8] The following articles provide more examples of how to integrate content areas: Deborah A. Moore and Maria C. Schwarz, "Fishy Fun under the Sun, A Week of Geometry Connections," *Mathematics Teaching in the Middle School* 9, No. 2 (October, 2003), pp. 78–82; and Jennifer Suh et al., "Junior Architects: Designing Your Dream Clubhouse Using Measurement and Geometry," *Teaching Children Mathematics* 10, no. 3 (November 2002), pp. 170–79.

- requiring students to justify their thinking
- expecting students to use multiple representations of concepts.[9]

Providing guidance for a teacher, standards indicate when students are developmentally ready to learn a concept, which topics to emphasize, and when students should master a concept or procedure. Standards are also useful when choosing activities and lessons; a teacher should alter or replace an activity that, while fun (for both students and the teacher), does not address any of the standards.

Integrating NCTM and state standards

All of the activities and lesson plans included in Chapter 4 incorporate NCTM and representative state standards. Appendix A of this document provides sample state standards for mathematics that pertain to the IMAGES content for geometry and measurement. Complete standards for these states are also available online; see page 210 for the Web sites.

Collaborate with Others

Students thrive in classrooms in which teachers have worked together to develop lessons and a community of learners.[10] Many of the strategies described here can be implemented

successfully only after months and, in many cases, years of experience. More experienced teachers have a wealth of knowledge gained from hard-won successes and painstaking challenges; it is their responsibility to share this resource with less-experienced teachers, just as it is the privilege of those newer to the profession to learn from the wisdom of those who know what it is to put theory into practice.

At the same time, young teachers often bring enthusiasm, ideas from leading educators, and a familiarity with recent educational research, which can benefit everyone in a school. Since every teacher has a unique teaching style and range of teaching and learning experiences, everyone benefits from collaboration. Teachers can learn from area business and industry volunteers who are willing to share how they use mathematics in the workplace. Higher education faculty in the mathematical sciences can also be a valuable resource.

---

[9] National Council of Teachers of Mathematics, *Principles and Standards for School Mathematics*, pp. 52–71.

[10] Jeremy Kilpatrick, et al., *Adding It Up: Helping Children Learn Mathematics* (Washington, D.C.: National Academy Press, 2001), pp. 344–45.

> **Lesson study: A model of collaboration**
>
> Lesson study is an innovative professional development method that uses teacher collaboration as its cornerstone. Through extensive team planning, observation, and systematic feedback, teachers work together to maximize each other's effectiveness in order to best benefit the students.
>
> To learn more about lesson study, see the lesson study page of the RBS Web site, http://www.rbs.org/lesson_study/.

Promote Cooperative Learning[11]

Cooperative learning is a valuable tool since students learn both from a teacher and from each other. Cooperative learning actively involves students in the learning process and encourages them to communicate mathematically. A teacher who promotes mathematical reasoning and problem solving also tends to create a classroom that is a supportive and collegial community of learners.

When a teacher poses challenging problems to a class, students benefit from working in small groups to explore and discuss ideas and then reporting their findings to the class. It is also effective to put students into groups, in which they compare and contrast the ways they approached problems and arrived at a solution. These strategies support the sharing of diverse kinds of thinking, place value on listening to and learning from others, and help students to develop ways to solve future problems. Cooperative learning also prepares students to work as a team, which is something that many employers will expect from them later, as employees.[12]

For examples of how to promote cooperative learning, see the lesson plans **Geoboard Squares** *on page 89 and* **Investigating Nets and Polyhedra** *on page 101.*

---

[11] For research in the area of cooperative learning, see: David Johnson and Roger Johnson, "The Internal Dynamics of Cooperative Learning Groups," in *Learning to Cooperate, Cooperating to Learn*, ed. R. Slavin et al. (New York: Plenum, 1985), pp. 103–22; Robert Slavin, "Cooperative Learning and Student Achievement," in *School and Classroom Organization*, ed. R. Slavin et al. (Hillsdale, N.J.: Lawrence Erlbaum, 1989), pp. 129–56.

[12] U.S. Department of Labor, The Secretary's Commission on Achieving Necessary Skills (SCANS), *What Work Requires of Schools: A SCANS Report for America 2000* (Washington, D.C.: U.S. Department of Labor, 1991). Available online at http://wdr.doleta.gov/SCANS/whatwork/whatwork.html.

Use Technology as a Tool

Technology provides a unique opportunity to improve student performance in mathematical reasoning and problem solving. When a teacher seeks the appropriate training and learns to use technology effectively, the focus in his or her classroom shifts away from teacher-centered instruction to a learning environment that is more student-centered and flexible.

Research suggests that with even eight hours of technology training, teachers are more likely to feel prepared and to use technology in class activities. Other studies have shown that instructional technology improves teaching programs in mathematics.[13] Research

further shows that technology positively affects students' learning, as teachers using technology were better equipped to adapt to their students' needs and interests.[14] Furthermore, some research suggests that the use of technology has an impact on students' attendance, time spent on task, and pro-social behavior.[15]

Still, teachers must control when and how students use technology in the classroom to ensure that it enhances teaching and learning. Specifically in geometry, using interactive software can enhance student development and understanding of two-dimensional shapes and their properties.[16] However, software programs that do not actively engage students can result in less learning than for students who do not use the software.[17] In addition, the possibilities for engaging students with physical challenges and other special needs increase dramatically with the use of technology.

Certain computer software offers immediate, personal feedback, as well as privacy, so that students can move at their own pace and either make repeated attempts at the same task, go back to simpler problems, or move swiftly ahead into more difficult subject matter without becoming discouraged, bored, or frustrated. This flexibility often leads to

---

[13] James Kulik, *Effects of Using Instructional Technology in Elementary and Secondary Schools: What Controlled Evaluation Studies Say, Final Report* (Arlington, Va.: SRI International, 2003).

[14] Brent G. Wilson and Karen Peterson, "Successful Technology Integration in an Elementary School: A Case Study," in *Practitioners Write the Book: What Works in Educational Technology*, Carolyn Lucas and Larry Lucas, eds. (Denton, Tex.: Texas Center for Educational Technology, 1995), pp. 201–67. Available online at http://carbon.cudenver.edu/~bwilson/peakview.html.

[15] Kathleen Cotton, "Computer-Assisted Instruction," *Northwest Regional Educational Laboratory School's Improvement Research Series (SIRS), Close-Up,* series 5, no. 10 (May 1991). Available online at http://www.nwrel.org/scpd/sirs/5/cu10.html.

[16] Michael T. Battista, "Learning Geometry in a Dynamic Computer Environment," *Teaching Children Mathematics* 8, no. 6 (February 2002): p. 333.

[17] In *Does It Compute? The Relationship between Educational Technology and Student Achievement in Mathematics* (Princeton, N.J.: Educational Testing Service, 1998), Harold Wenglinsky states that appropriate technology has a positive impact, but use of drill and practice software has either limited impact or a negative impact. See http://www.ets.org/research/pic/pir.html.

students who are persistent and effective in their problem solving and also willing to risk giving a wrong answer.

A classroom with five or more computers is an ideal environment for student collaboration and group investigations, which have a positive effect on students' attitudes and confidence.[18] The Internet, in particular, is an excellent tool for teachers and students to use to collect data, access information related to mathematics, and communicate with mathematicians as well as other students and teachers. The rapid pace of change in technology is a constant reminder that a teacher needs to be flexible and creative in keeping up with the developments that students will be asked to face in later years.

While there has been some controversy about the use of calculators in elementary school classrooms, there is substantial research indicating that calculators are a tool that supports student performance in mathematics.[19] Studies suggest that students who use calculators have better attitudes towards mathematics, are more proficient at mental arithmetic, and perform better in problem-solving situations.[20] Even on tests *without* calculators, students who are accustomed to using calculators on a daily basis in class have been shown to perform as well as or better than students who have not used calculators in an ongoing way.[21] If their use is carefully prescribed by the teacher, calculators can offer students a simple way to test their ideas and conjectures while avoiding tedious calculations.

*For an example of how to use technology as a tool, see the lesson plan **Sum of the Interior Angles of a Polygon** on page 135.*

Use Inquiry-Based Learning

The process of inquiry-based learning motivates students to learn new mathematical concepts. Teaching is most engaging for students when their own thoughts, opinions, and curiosities are addressed in the subject at hand. The best way to ensure that students feel they have a stake in their own learning is to create a classroom that values exploration, where teacher and students alike can support, discuss, and evaluate ways of thinking in an open and ongoing way.

---

[18] Jamie McKenzie, "Creating Technology Enhanced Student-Centered Learning Environments," *From Now On: The Educational Technology Journal* 7, no. 6 (1998). Available online at http://www.fno.org/mar98/flotilla.html#anchor275428.

[19] Kilpatrick et al., *Adding It Up*, p. 427; Aimee J. Ellington, "A Meta-Analysis of the Effects of Calculators on Students' Achievement and Attitude Levels in Precollege Mathematics Classes," *Journal for Research in Mathematics Education* 34, no. 5 (November 2003): pp. 456–57.

[20] Sutton and Krueger, *EDThoughts*, pp. 64–65.

[21] Ray Hembree and Donald J. Dessart, "Research on Calculators in Mathematics Education," in *Calculators in Mathematics Education. NCTM 1992 Yearbook*, ed. James T. Fey (Reston, Va.: 1992), pp. 24–26.

> ### *The difference between traditional and inquiry-based learning*
>
> In a traditional classroom, students first learn about discrete concepts and procedures, such as the perimeter and area of a rectangle. They would then learn how to use the formula "A = L x W" to find the area of a rectangle, given its length and width. Later, students would learn about the area of a triangle and how to find the area using a formula. Eventually, students apply this knowledge to determine the area of a figure composed of a rectangle and triangle.
>
> When a teacher uses inquiry-based learning, the process is reversed. The teacher presents a problem first, such as, "If you want to paint the front of a house, how much area must you paint?" Students then explore the problem and—with the teacher's guidance—discover that they need to understand how to cover an area with a standard-size unit. After solving the problem, students look for efficient procedures for finding the area and then develop formulas accordingly.

*For another example of how to use inquiry-based learning, see the **Reflections** lesson plan on page 113.*

Promote Mathematical Reasoning

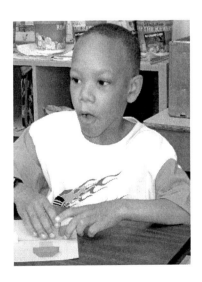

Critical thinking is a crucial component of learning, and mathematics offers a unique opportunity for students to exert control over their own thought processes. Students use mathematical reasoning during inquiry-based learning and problem solving. Inductive reasoning in mathematics supports students in learning to see patterns and make sense of a range of facts or concepts and the relationships between them. Students who engage in mathematical reasoning are better able to communicate their own understanding of mathematical concepts or ideas.[22]

Inductive reasoning tends to be the focus of elementary mathematics instruction, but teachers should also give students the opportunity to use deductive reasoning—that is, to use logic to show whether a pattern or relationship they discover in one instance is true in general. Facilitating discussions or written explanations in which students justify their thinking supports them in going beyond whether or not they got a correct answer.

*For an example of how to promote mathematical reasoning, see the **Find the Shape** lesson plan on page 85.*

---

[22] National Council of Teachers of Mathematics, *Principles and Standards for School Mathematics*, p. 188.

Promote Problem Solving

"Problem solving is…a process that should permeate the study of mathematics and provide a context in which concepts and skills are learned."[23] Through problem solving students experience the usefulness and power of mathematics in and outside of the mathematics classroom. Encouraging students to develop and apply a variety of problem-solving strategies will increase their ability to solve problems, which in turn builds confidence. A teacher should:

- use problems to introduce new concepts
- look to many sources to find problems, beyond what is offered in a textbook
- pose questions frequently
- encourage students to think for themselves
- present problems that are open-ended (whenever feasible), to allow for multiple problem-solving approaches.

An effective teacher is continually deciding the best way to support students in working through challenging tasks, without dominating the thinking process for them, so that the sense of discovery—and the challenge—is not lost. A teacher should allot time for students to develop approaches to a problem and to identify what tools will be most helpful to them. It is valuable for students to share with the class how they approach a problem and to compare and contrast those approaches. Instruction that promotes the solving of problems in this way aids students in conjecturing, testing and revising those conjectures as necessary, and reflecting on the results of their work.

*For an example of how to promote problem solving, see the **Geoboard Squares** lesson plan on page 89.*

Use Hands-On Activities to Model Concepts

It is critical that teachers make the link for students between an activity and the concept that it illustrates. A teacher should use hands-on activities to model concepts in geometry and measurement and to help students better understand the concepts of mathematics. Children grow to understand concepts when they have first experienced concepts on a concrete level. Manipulatives bring a range of senses into play. Students' long-term use of concrete instructional materials, at both the primary and secondary grade levels, supports achievement in mathematics.

However, using concrete materials and manipulatives

---

[23] National Council of Teachers of Mathematics, *Principles and Standards for School Mathematics*, p. 182.

also requires that a teacher frequently intervenes to help students connect the materials with the mathematics concepts.[24] By presenting an activity with various components (using manipulatives and technology to formalize the concept), a teacher addresses an array of learning styles and provides additional time for students to process a concept.

For a further discussion of these issues (and a suggestion for classroom use), see the **Concrete Representations** *section of Chapter 1, on page 11.*

Integrate Assessment and Instruction

Ongoing classroom assessment promotes the learning process. This is especially important given the rigorous standards of mathematics to which students are held. There are several ways that a teacher can incorporate assessment into instruction. Within a unit, assessment can reveal what a student or group of students knows, understands, and can do. A teacher must use both informal assessment (conversations with and observation of students in the classroom) and more formal means (tests, open-ended assessments, or projects) to create a profile of students' instructional needs and to assess the success of the instructional plan.

Within the classroom, a teacher can use assessment to address skills and knowledge that students already know or to determine areas where students need improvement. This requires that a teacher constructs or adapts problems that both promote learning and facilitate students' ability to work through misconceptions until they arrive at a clear understanding of mathematical concepts. Students' assessment and monitoring of their own learning is also valuable. Students can gain mastery of mathematics when they know what content is expected of them and how they need to represent that content. Assessment can support students in becoming more aware of their own responsibility for their academic success, for example, making a rubric to be used to evaluate a project helps students to produce a significantly better project.

A teacher should combine traditional modes of assessment with assignments that require open-ended answers and constructed responses. The latter encourage students to:
- incorporate higher-order thinking and skills into their solutions
- communicate their thinking
- explore various strategies to a solution
- apply their existing knowledge
- organize, analyze, and interpret information
- create a mathematical model
- make and test predictions.

For in-depth discussions of various assessment techniques, see Chapter 5.

---

[24] James Hiebert and Thomas P. Carpenter, "Learning and Teaching with Understanding," in *Handbook of Research on Mathematics Teaching and Learning*, Douglas A. Grouws ed. (New York: Macmillan, 1992), p. 70.

Reflect on Teaching and Learning

Metacognitive strategies—which essentially involve "thinking about thinking"—increase students' learning.[25] By helping students to reflect on and communicate what they learn and what is still unclear, teachers have a unique opportunity to aid their students. There are a number of ways to help manage or help students to manage their thinking by:

- making connections between new information and subject ideas already known
- choosing appropriate thinking strategies for a particular use
- planning, monitoring, and assessing how effective certain thinking processes are.

One way of accomplishing this kind of reflection is through the use of student-created portfolios. Even the process of selection that goes into making portfolios helps the student to build self-awareness and ultimately gives the student more control over her or his own learning. By shifting the focus of the teacher's role from instructor to facilitator of learning, the process gives students the responsibility to determine what they need to know. These portfolios support students in looking at mathematics in different ways and in seeing value in mathematics.

Writing is another way to encourage students to analyze, communicate, discover, and organize their growing knowledge. Facilitating classroom dialogues and other interactions and helping students to develop reasoning skills make it possible for students to evaluate their own and others' thinking.

Teacher reflection: A vignette about perimeter and area

During a class discussion of the relationship between perimeter and area, several students in Janet's class stated that increasing the perimeter would have to increase the area. None of the other students questioned these statements. That evening, Janet reflected on why her students developed this misconception. In reviewing the activities that she had asked the students to do prior to the discussion, she discovered that in every instance when the student increased the perimeter the area also increased. The students were justified in assuming this would always happen. She had decided that during the discussion she needed to do more than state that increasing the perimeter did not always increase the area. The students' belief structure had to be challenged by examples that did not fit their misconception.

(continued on next page)

---

[25] Kilpatrick et al., *Adding It Up*, p. 118.

Teacher reflection (continued)

After looking at several options, Janet decided to have the students work in groups using a geoboard. She would ask students to use Pick's theorem[26] to find as many triangles as they could with area equal to one. For each triangle, the students would measure the sides and calculate the perimeter. She would then ask them to create a table showing the perimeter and area of each triangle found, arranging the table from smallest perimeter to largest perimeter. She would then ask them to reflect on the relationship between perimeter and area, asking, "Does increasing the perimeter always yield a larger area?"

Student reflection: A sample math journal entry

At first my team did not see how we could make any triangle with area equal to 1, except for a right triangle with legs of length 2 and 1. When the teacher pointed out that the key to finding the area using Pick's theorem was the number of geoboard pins on the boundary of the triangle and the number of geoboard pins interior to the triangle, we focused on the pins instead of the triangle.

We were now able to find many triangles with area equal to 1. To my surprise, the perimeters of some of these triangles were much more than the perimeter of the first triangle. When we were working with rectangles, if we increased one of the sides of the rectangle, both the perimeter and the area increased. Maybe this only works with rectangles. At least I now know it does not work with triangles. If I get time tomorrow I may try to find some quadrilaterals with area equal to 1 and see if all of them have the same perimeter.

---

[26] Pick's theorem states that the area (A) of a polygon where each vertex is on a pin of a geoboard can be found by the formula $A = B/2 + I - 1$, where B is the number of boundary points and I is the number of interior points.

Include Strong Academic Content

A teacher should create any lesson or unit out of the best academic content available. In many instances this may mean that what the teacher includes in a lesson must go beyond specific skills to a broader mathematical context, with "real-world" and even interdisciplinary uses and applications. Studies have revealed that teachers who have a stronger background and broader experiences more effectively convey concepts to their students and are better able to make connections between those concepts for their students.[27]

Cluster Concepts

When students learn concepts and relationships in isolation, they often forget these ideas or are slow in making the connections among them.[28] A thinking process called "clustering," used to group, unify, integrate, and/or make connections among concepts, is something that students and adults use routinely, often without even realizing it.[29] A teacher can use this approach to cluster mathematical ideas, concepts, relationships, and objects in order to reveal common characteristics. This presentation in turn helps students to categorize and classify those ideas or objects and to remember properties and attributes, which makes the learning more meaningful.

> *Clustering quadrilaterals*
>
> Some students can best understand quadrilaterals when the teacher presents them as a unifying concept. In the process of clustering, a teacher guides students in studying, comparing, and classifying *all* quadrilaterals according to their attributes—not only the square and the rectangle, but the plain quadrilateral, the rhombus, the parallelogram, the trapezoid, and the isosceles trapezoid. This enables students to have a better sense of four-sided figures, their properties, and characteristics, so they can eventually internalize the idea and even develop a hierarchy of quadrilaterals based on properties.

---

[27] Sutton and Krueger, *EDThoughts*, p. 84.

[28] Robert Reys et al., *Helping Children Learn Mathematics*, 7th ed. (New York: John Wiley & Sons, 2001), p. 33–34.

[29] Ashish Ranpura, "How We Remember, and Why We Forget," *Brain Connection* (June 2000). Available only online at http://www.brainconnection.com/topics/?main=fa/memory-formation3.

Other ideas for clustering in geometry and measurement

- special lines in triangles such as medians, perpendicular bisectors, altitudes, and bisectors of angles
- special lines of circles
- the classification of Platonic solids
- the relationship of various types of tessellations
- proportionality
- Archimedean solids
- inscribed and circumscribed geometric figures
- the classification of angles
- nets of specific solids, such as cubes, pyramids, etc.
- the relationship between area and perimeter of quadrilaterals, triangles, circles, etc.
- the symmetry of geometric figures in two and three dimensions
- the similarity and congruency of polygons
- the relationship between surface area and volume.

Instructional Activities and Lesson Plans

Chapter 4

Learning with understanding is essential to enable students to solve the new kinds of problems they will inevitably face in the future.

—NCTM *Principles and Standards for School Mathematics*[1]

"Teaching mathematics is a complex endeavor, and there are no easy recipes."[2] In designing activities and lesson plans, teachers must work carefully to develop students' understanding of mathematics concepts. Teachers should also strive to represent those concepts in real-life problem-solving situations and authentic settings to which children can relate.

In this section is a complete alphabetical listing of the instructional activities and lesson plans referred to in the Content Strands sections of IMAGES. Teachers should always remember to reinforce the connection between the activity or lesson plan and the concept of geometry and measurement it models.

The use of these activities and lessons requires flexibility; the appropriate grade level of each is ultimately the teacher's decision, as in some instances older students would benefit from activities suggested for a younger level, and vice versa. Frequently, activities and lessons will overlap two or more content strands.

Lessons within this document address the five process standards presented in the NCTM *Principles and Standards for School Mathematics*: problem solving, reasoning, representation, connections, and communication.[3] The activities included also exemplify assessment strategies and best practices for teaching, which are both outlined in greater detail in other chapters.

---

[1] National Council of Teachers of Mathematics, *Principles and Standards for School Mathematics* (Reston, Va.: National Council of Teachers of Mathematics, 2000), p. 21.

[2] National Council of Teachers of Mathematics, *Principles and Standards for School Mathematics*, p. 17.

[3] National Council of Teachers of Mathematics, *Principles and Standards for School Mathematics*, pp. 52–71.

Instructional Activities

Listings as they appear here include links to relevant Web sites and children's literature titles. *All Web sites were current at the time of publication.*

Note: The 💻 symbol indicates that this activity includes a link to an online resource. The 📖 symbol indicates that the activity includes a reference to children's literature.

Area & Perimeter (grades 4–5)
Have students construct various two-dimensional shapes with K'NEX™ rods and connectors (or straws and gumdrops). Using K'NEX™, describe the perimeters in terms of rod colors and numbers, such as, "The perimeter of a square is four yellow rods." (Using straws, cut ones of different colors to various lengths.) Have students construct a square with a perimeter of eight yellow rods (or straws of a certain color) and then find its area.

Bubble Mania (grades 3–5) 💻
Have students create soap bubble prints to explore the concepts of diameter, circumference, and area of a circle. This activity is available online at the PBS site (http://www.pbs.org/teachersource/mathline/lessonplans/pdf/esmp/bubblemania.pdf), along with other outstanding measurement and geometry activities.

Build a Shape (grades 3–5)
Have students use 10 cubes to build a three-dimensional shape and draw the shape on graph paper showing how it would look from the front, back, side, top, and bottom. Have students try to match each other's drawings with the appropriate shapes.

Building Vocabulary (grades 4–5)
Have students make a word bank, looking for common roots in such words as "polygon," "polyhedron," "octagon," "octahedron," "dodecagon," "icosahedron." Have students use word roots to write definitions of words.

The Button Box (grades K–3) 📖
Read the book *The Button Box*.[4] Have students organize a box of buttons by different attributes (number of holes, color, size, thickness), describing the attributes used.

---

[4] Margarette S. Reid, *The Button Box* (Glenview, Il.: Scott Foresman, 1990).

Calendar Locations (grades 1–3)
Have students use a calendar to locate relative positions on a plane. Ask students such questions as, "What is the date of the Wednesday in the third week of the month?"

Centimeter by Centimeter or Inch by Inch (grades 3–5) 💻📖
Read the book *Inch by Inch*.[5] Have students make a meter stick (or one-foot ruler) by cutting out and pasting 10-centimeter strips (or one-inch strips) onto a strip of cardboard, using alternating colors for each 10-centimeter strip (or one-inch strip). Use the meter stick (or one-foot ruler) to measure objects in the classroom. For fourth and fifth grade students specify an appropriate degree of accuracy. This activity is adapted from one available at http://mathforum.org/paths/measurement/inchbyinch.html.

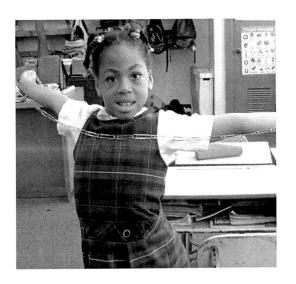

Comparing Lengths of Arms with Links (grades K–3) 📖
Put students in pairs and give each pair a package of commercially available links or large paper clips. Have each child use the links to make a chain as long as his or her arm. Have students in each pair compare the chains to determine whose arm-chain is longer (or shorter). Have students use the arm-chains to measure objects in the classroom. Have students compare their results to reveal that, when measuring with non-standard units, the same object can be equal to different numbers of arm-chains. Have students read the book *How Big Is a Foot?*[6]

Connect the Dots (grades 3–4)
Give a sheet of dot paper to groups of two or three students. Write the names of various polygons on slips of paper and put them in an envelope. Have each group of students select a slip of paper and take turns making one line segment on the dot paper (connecting two dots) in order to make their shape. As students complete a shape, have them put their initials in the center of the shape.

Coordinate Games (grades 4–5)
Have students play games such as *Battleship, Coordinate Tic-Tac-Toe, Hurkle*[7] or *Grid Football*.[8]

---

[5] Leo Lionni, *Inch by Inch* (New York: Mulberry Books, 1960).
[6] Rolf Myller, *How Big Is a Foot?* (New York: Atheneum Books for Children, 1972).
[7] Jean Kerr Stenmark, Virginia Thompson, and Ruth Cossey, *Family Math* (Berkeley, Ca.: Lawrence Hall of Science, 1986), pp. 196–200.
[8] Donovan A. Johnson, *Activities in Mathematics: Second Course—Graphs* (Glenview, Il.: Scott Foresman, 1971), pp. 13–14.

Creating Nets (grades 4–5) 💻
Have students build shapes (rectangular prisms) with wooden cubes and then create nets (two-dimensional paper that is folded to make three-dimensional objects) to wrap the shapes. Use the nets to discuss surface area. Visit http://mathworld.wolfram.com/Cube.html to see all the possible nets for a cube.

Creating Pentominoes (grades 4–5)
Have students use square tiles to create as many different pentomino pieces as possible. Have them record their results on graph paper or square dot paper. Have students work together to find the 12 different pentomino shapes. Help students to see that, by rotating or flipping some shapes, some that they have found are not different but congruent.

Creating Tessellations (grades 1–5) 💻
Give each student half of a 3-by-5-inch index card. Have students cut out a shape from one edge of the index card and then tape that shape onto the opposite edge of the card. This new shape will tessellate the plane. Have students experiment with this process to create various tessellations and color in their tessellations. Display the tessellations on a bulletin board. Connect this activity to the art of M. C. Escher.[9] For more information, visit http://www.iproject.com/escher/teaching/teaching.html.

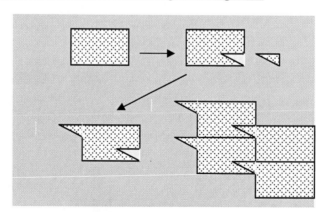

Creating Tessellations

---

[9] See M. C. Escher and Michael Solomon Sachs, *The Pop-Up Book of M. C. Escher* (Petaluma, Ca.: Pomegranate Artbooks, 1991); Bruno Ernst, *The Magic Mirror of M. C. Escher* (Suffolk: Tarquin Publications, 1985); Doris Schattschneider and Wallace Walker, *M. C. Escher Kaleidocycles* (Suffolk: Tarquin Publications, 1997); and Betty K. Zurstadt, "Tessellations and the Art of M. C. Escher," *Arithmetic Teacher* 31 (January 1984): pp. 54–55.

Creating Tilings (grades K–5)

Have students create tilings with pattern block pieces (triangle, square, rhombus, trapezoid, hexagon) and draw their tilings on triangle dot paper. Have upper-level students discuss why certain shapes will tile and why others will not.

Creative Writing Activity (grades 4–5) 📖

Have students read books such as *Sir Cumference and the First Round Table*[10] or *Sir Cumference and the Dragon of Pi*[11] and write a story using as many geometry vocabulary words as possible.

Describe the Shape (grades K–2) 💻📖

Help students learn to identify geometric shapes (triangle, square, rhombus, trapezoid, and hexagon) using pattern blocks, a pattern block applet, or triangle grid paper. Make connections to *The Shape of Me and Other Stuff*[12] and *The Shapes Game*.[13] This activity and related materials are available at http://www.mathforum.org/varnelle/kgeo.html.

Describing Attributes of Shapes (grades K–3)

Have students examine and describe attribute blocks, noting shapes (square, rectangle, triangle, hexagon, circle), size (large, small), thickness (thin, thick), and color (blue, red, yellow). Place a block where students cannot see it and have students, one by one, ask "yes" or "no" questions in a circle. If the answer to a student's question is "yes," then he or she can continue to ask questions; if the answer is "no," then it is the next student's turn to ask a question. Continue until a student can fully describe the figure.

Determining the Appropriate Unit of Measure (grades 1–3)

Give students different measuring tools, such as a 12-inch ruler, 10-centimeter strip or centimeter ruler, measuring tape, yardstick, and meter stick. Have students measure various objects around the classroom, including tables, windows, and the width of the room. Discuss with the students which tools and units are easier to use for measuring the different objects.

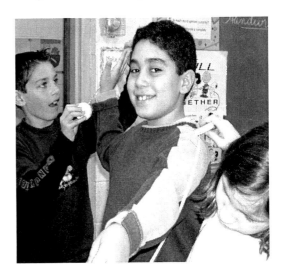

---

[10] Cindy Neuschwander, *Sir Cumference and the First Round Table: A Math Adventure* (Watertown, Mass.: Charlesbridge Publishing, 1997).

[11] Cindy Neuschwander, *Sir Cumference and the Dragon of Pi* (New York: Scholastic, 2000).

[12] Dr. Seuss, *The Shape of Me and Other Stuff* (New York: Random House, 1988).

[13] Paul Rogers, *The Shapes Game* (New York: Henry Holt, 1989).

Draw a Shape from Memory (grades K–5)

Show students a shape for a few seconds and have them try to draw the shape from memory. Have students show each other their drawings and discuss the characteristics of the shape in their drawings. Then show the original shape again. Start with simpler shapes and then draw more complex ones.

Finding Area with a Non-Standard Unit (grades 3–5)

Using overhead pattern blocks on the overhead projector, build an equilateral triangle with four green triangles. Tell students that each green triangle has an area of one square unit and ask them to determine the area of the larger equilateral triangle. Build the same triangle with a red trapezoid and a green triangle and ask students for the area of that triangle. Build other shapes with the pattern blocks and have students find the area for each of those. Have students record their work on grid or dot paper, coloring the shapes appropriately and recording the area of each shape.

Finding Perimeter with a Non-Standard Unit (grades 3–4)

Using overhead pattern blocks on the overhead projector, demonstrate that, if each side of a triangle is one unit, the distance around the triangle is three units. Have students find the perimeter of the other pattern block pieces. Have students make drawings on grid or dot paper, coloring the shapes appropriately and recording the perimeter of each shape. To go further, have students make different shapes with the pattern blocks, draw them on the dot or grid paper, and then identify the perimeter of each shape. This activity can also be done with straws and gumdrops or K'NEX™ rods and connectors.

Fixed Perimeter (grades 3–5)

Cut a piece of ribbon that measures about 10.5 yards. Tie the ends of the ribbon together so the perimeter of the loop of ribbon is 10 yards. Put the ribbon on the floor. Have three students take hold of the ribbon and make an equilateral triangle. Use chalk to trace the triangle. Add another student to the group and have the group make a square. Using a different color of chalk, trace the square. Make sure that the students measure the sides of the shapes to show that the perimeter is the same. Ask whether the equilateral triangle or square appears to have the larger area. Continue making regular polygons with the same perimeter. Encourage students to draw conclusions about what happens to the area of shapes if the perimeter is constant. Additional questions could include:

- Of all possible triangles with fixed perimeter, which one has the largest area? *(the equilateral triangle)*
- Of all possible rectangles with fixed perimeter, which one has the largest area? *(the square)*
- What is the relationship between perimeter and area? *(If the perimeter is fixed, a regular polygon will have the largest area of any polygon with that many sides.)*

For a related activity, see **Using the Geometer's Sketchpad® to Explore Area and Perimeter** *on page 14.*

Footprints in the Sand (grades K–2) 📖

Have students use blocks of various shapes to make impressions in the sand. Have students identify the shapes and match the blocks to the impressions. Read this poem as part of the activity:

> A monster made these footprints
> While we were all asleep.
> What funny shapes these prints are,
> And they're not very deep.
> I think the monster fooled us
> And used our blocks instead;
> And you can figure out which blocks
> If you just use your head.[14]

Geoboard Polygons (grades 1–4)

Have students duplicate a shape on a geoboard and then break the larger shape into smaller shapes (a rectangle into two squares or triangles; a trapezoid into three triangles or two triangles and a rectangle). Give students an irregular shape and have them find as many triangles, squares, or rectangles as possible.

Geo-Dot Paper (grades 3–5)

Have students draw different quadrilaterals on dot paper and then compare their shapes with a partner. Have students note the properties that the shapes have in common; encourage students to turn (rotate) or flip their papers as they make comparisons. Have them also show congruent and similar shapes on the dot paper and show translations by indicating the direction of the translation with an arrow.

Go-Together Rules (grades 3–4)

Prepare "Go-Together" rules for students to complete, such as "All _____ have _____" or "No _____ have _____." Have students make up rules for each other to complete.

Graphing Points on a Line (grades 2–4) 💻

Have students identify points on a number line. This activity, available at http://mathforum.org/cgraph/cplane/line.html, also includes negatives, scale, a glossary, and links.

---

[14] Miriam Leiva, ed., *Geometry and Spatial Sense* (Reston, Va.: National Council of Teachers of Mathematics, 1993), p. 6.

How Many Square Feet in a Square Yard? (grades 4–5)
Put nine one-foot squares of linoleum squares together to form a square. Use a yardstick to measure the side of the larger square and to demonstrate that there are three feet in one yard. Students will see that nine square feet are equal to one square yard.

I Have, Who Has (grades 2–5)
Prepare a series of cards that each contains a statement and a question—one card for each student. The statement acknowledges that the student "has" a certain geometric shape; the question describes characteristics of another shape. The first card should have only a question, to begin the game. For example:

[Card 1:]	Who has a figure with three sides?
[Card 2:]	I have a triangle. Who has the name of two figures that have the same size and shape?
[Card 3:]	I have congruent figures. Who has a figure with five sides?

(Note that the cards given to students do not identify order). The last card should answer a question and state: "This is the end of the game." Distribute one card to each student. Whoever has the card with just a question begins the game, and other students listen, process, and respond in turn.

Inching Along (grades K–2) 🖥️📖
Read the book *Inch by Inch*.[15] Have students measure objects using non-standard units, such as "inch worm" packing peanuts. This and other measurement activities are available online at http://eduref.org/cgi-bin/lessons.cgi/Mathematics/Measurement.

Is My Hand Bigger or Smaller Than Yours? (grades K–3)
Put students in pairs and have partners help draw around each other's hands. Have students compare the area of each partner's hand by placing one hand on top of the other to see which hand overlaps the other or has the larger area. Have students compare hands to find the hand with the smallest or largest area.

Lighting the Perimeter (grades 4–5) 🖥️
Have students use their knowledge of perimeter to determine the number of lights needed to decorate the outside of a building or other structure, such as a bridge. Take a digital photo of the structure; print the photo on regular-size paper and distribute to students. Assign a scale, such as one inch on the photograph equals one foot of the actual structure. Have students measure the perimeter of the structure on the photograph and use the scale to determine the actual perimeter. Have students determine how many feet of a string of lights would be needed to trace the entire perimeter. This activity was adapted from one at http://www.educationworld.com/a_tsl/archives/01-1/lesson0031.shtml.

---

[15] Lionni, *Inch by Inch*.

Line Symmetry (grades K–3)
Have students use pattern blocks, a pattern block applet, or paper folding to show lines of symmetry. Make connections to the books *What Is Symmetry?*[16] and *The Butterfly Alphabet*.[17] This activity is available at http://www.mathforum.org/varnelle/kgeo.html.

Measuring Desktops with Hands (grades 1–3)
Have students trace their hands and then cut out the tracings. Have each student use the cutout of his or her hand to measure the area of desktop. Emphasize that, since area is the region covered with the same hand, students might need numerous copies of the same hand to cover a desktop. Have students explore measuring parts of the desk that are not covered by a complete hand.

Mini-Metric Olympics (grade 5)
Familiarize students with metric units by having them estimate and measure in a "Metric Olympic" setting that includes six activities: paper plate discus, paper straw javelin, cotton ball shot-put, right-handed marble grab, left-handed sponge squeeze, and big foot contest. This activity[18] is available at the AIMS (Activities Integrating Math and Science) Web site at http://www.aimsedu.org/Activities/middle.html.

Mixed-up Pictures (grades K–2)
Show students "mixed-up" pictures, in which some items are upside-down and some are right-side-up, and have students identify the proper orientation for each item.

Nature Walk (grades K–3)
Read the book *If You Look Around You*.[19] Take students on a nature walk and have them identify various shapes in nature. Take photographs for a bulletin board display or have students draw sketches of what they find.

Number Line Message (grades 1–3)
Have students place specially chosen letters above numbers on the number line and have them read the message that appears. For example, if they place A at 2 and 12, D at 11, H at 1 and 7, I at 10, L at 9, O at 8, P at 3 and 4, and Y at 5 and 13, the message is:

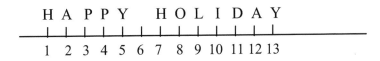

H A P P Y   H O L I D A Y

1 2 3 4 5 6 7 8 9 10 11 12 13

---

[16] Mindel Sitomer and Harry Sitomer, *What Is Symmetry?* (New York: Thomas Y. Crowell, 1970).

[17] Kjell B. Sandved, *The Butterfly Alphabet* (New York: Scholastic Inc., 1999).

[18] John Campopiano et al., *Math + Science: A Solution* (Fresno, Ca.: AIMS Educational Foundation, 1987).

[19] Fluvio Testa, *If You Look Around You* (New York: Dial Books for Young Readers, 1983).

Origami (grades 2–5) 🖥

Have students use origami to explore spatial relations and to investigate shapes and their properties.[20] Have younger students do easier foldings, such as a cup, boat, pigeon, or swan. As students fold, introduce important mathematical terms like *diagonal* and *midpoint* and discuss the various shapes that are created, such as triangles and squares. Have upper-grade elementary students do more detailed foldings, such as a frog that jumps or a box without a top.[21] Explore concepts of similarity, congruence, and classification of triangles. Different shapes appear as students fold, such as right isosceles triangles, squares, rectangles, and trapezoids. Give students printed directions for folding to help develop visualization and spatial reasoning skills; directions for simple foldings are usually included with origami paper. There are many inexpensive origami books available and numerous Web sites devoted to origami (see the Origami USA home page at http://www.origami-usa.org/).

Paper-Penny Boxes (grades 3–5) 📖

Have students explore the concept of volume by building a paper box that will hold 100 pennies. This activity[22] is based on the Newberry Medal Award book *The Hundred Penny Box*.[23] Have students discuss the strategies that they used to build their boxes.

Pattern Block Shapes (grades 2–3)

Introduce the pattern block shapes with students. Give students time to play with and become familiar with the shapes. Observe whether students sort the blocks by color or shape or use them to make designs or patterns. Work to develop the relationships between the different pattern block shapes by having students create one shape by using other shapes. Ask, "Can you use the triangles to make a hexagon?" and "Can you make the red trapezoid with any of the other figures?" Have students draw and color their shapes on triangle grid paper. When students have discovered how the various shapes are related, have them make a figure or picture with the shapes. Then have them draw the figure on the triangle grid paper and give a verbal explanation of the picture and the shapes they used.

See "Pattern Block Program" under Web sites on page 216.

---

[20] Rebecca Robichaux and Paulette R. Rodrigue, "Using Origami to Promote Geometric Communication," *Mathematics Teaching in the Middle School* 9, no. 4 (December 2003): pp. 222–29.

[21] Diane Downie et al., *Math for Girls and Other Problem Solvers* (Berkeley, Ca.: Lawrence Hall of Science, 1981), pp. 92–93.

[22] J. Hillen, "Paper-Penny Boxes," *AIMS Newsletter* 6, no. 6 (January 1992): pp. 30–34.

[23] Sharon Bell Mathis, *The Hundred Penny Box* (New York: Viking Press, 1986).

Pentomino Boxes (grades 4–5)
Have students try to visualize which of the 12 pentomino pieces can be folded to make a box without a top. Have students make the pentomino pieces on one-inch square grid paper and fold to confirm their conjectures.

Pentomino Pieces (grades 3–5)
Have students determine which pentomino pieces have line symmetry or rotational symmetry. Have students draw the pentominoes on graph paper or square dot paper and indicate the line of symmetry. Have younger students make paper pentominoes and fold to find lines of symmetry or use a mirror or Mira™.

Pi Day (grade 5) 🖥📖
Celebrate Pi Day, March 14 (also the birthday of Albert Einstein and Waclaw Sierpinski) with your students. Start the day with a reading of the book *Sir Cumference and the First Round Table*.[24] Have students search the Internet for information about Pi or direct them to appropriate Web sites such as http://www.joyofpi.com/, which includes basic information about Pi, Pi history, fun with Pi, Pi links, and more. Visit the Web site of the Goudreau Museum of Mathematics in Art and Science (New Hyde Park, NY), http://www.mathmuseum.org/, for information about their annual Pi Day Contest. A "Pi Trivia Game" is available at http://eveander.com/trivia/. As of February 2004, Pi Day greeting cards were available at http://www.bluemountain.com/kwsearch.pd?strSearch=pi+day&btnsearch.x=17&btnsearch.y=6. Attractive Pi t-shirts are available online at http://www.scienceteecher.com.

The Plane (grades 4–5) 🖥
Help students learn to plot points on the coordinate plane. Define terms such as line, plane, axis, and quadrant. The version of this activity available at http://mathforum.org/cgraph/cplane/plane.html includes the plane, finding points, graphing points, scale, glossary, links, and a "for grownups" section.

Platonic Solids (grades 4–5)
Discuss the Platonic solids (cube and regular tetrahedron, octahedron, dodecahedron, and icosahedron) and develop the concepts of edges, faces, and vertices—noting that all faces are regular polygons. Use nets to construct the shapes. Make a chart to determine the relationship between the number of edges, vertices, and faces (Euler's formula).

Playground Grids (grades 4–5)
Mark off a grid with X- and Y-axes on the playground. Have students walk to points on the grid by traveling along the grid lines, starting from (0,0) and following directions to the appropriate locations. Have students start at other points on the grid and describe how they could get to a different location. In a classroom with square floor tiles, have students move around the room following verbal directions to reinforce the concept of coordinates.

---

[24] Neuschwander, *Sir Cumference and the First Round Table: A Math Adventure*.

Plotting Pictures (grades 4–5)

Have students plot and connect sets of coordinates that result in various shapes, such as a sailboat, a chimney, or a palm tree.[25] For example, if students plot and connect the points (1,2), (2,3), (3,3), (4,2), (3,1), and (2,1), it forms a hexagon. Have students draw shapes on graph paper and then list the coordinates; give other students the coordinates for these designs to graph.

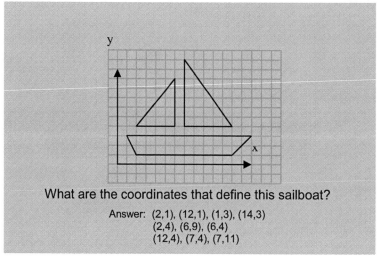

What are the coordinates that define this sailboat?

Answer: (2,1), (12,1), (1,3), (14,3)
(2,4), (6,9), (6,4)
(12,4), (7,4), (7,11)

Pumpkin Pi (grade 5)

Give each student a small pumpkin and have students measure the circumference of the circle at the middle of the pumpkin using a tape measure or string. Cut horizontally through the center of each pumpkin so students can measure the diameter. Record the circumferences and diameters on a chart on the overhead or on large paper. Have students calculate the quotient of the circumference divided by the diameter. Record the quotients in the chart and find the average, so students can see that their results approximate pi.

Regular Polygons (grades 4–5)

Have students use flexible straws (or K'NEX™) to make regular polygons by placing the short end of the flexible straw into the long end (this will ensure that all sides will be of equal length). Have students attempt to make each interior angle the same measure so that the resulting shapes are regular polygons. Discuss the attributes of the shapes.

---

[25] Jane Coultas, James Swalm, and Roslyn Wiesenfeld, *Strategies for Success in Mathematics* (Austin, Tex.: Steck-Vaughn, 1995); Donovan A. Johnson, *Activities in Mathematics: Second Course—Graphs* (Glenview, Il.: Scott Foresman, 1971), pp. 15–18.

Rope Polygons (grades 3–5)

Have three students make a triangle using rope or string. Have other students direct the three students to move to create different types of triangles (right, equilateral, isosceles). Have students create other polygons and determine how many students are needed for each polygon.

Scale Drawings (grades 4–5)

Use scale drawings to develop the concept of similarity. Have students make scale drawings of their classroom so they can see the relationships between sizes and shapes. One square on the graph paper can represent one square floor tile or a one-foot by one-foot square students make. Have students measure the lengths of sides of objects in the room and the corresponding sides of the scale drawing of the object. Ask, "What is the ratio of the measures of corresponding sides in each instance?" (All ratios should be equal or almost equal.) Have students look at the interior angles of a two-dimensional representation of an object in the room and the corresponding interior angles of the scale drawing of the object. (The corresponding angles should have the same measure.)

Shape Journals (grades 2–4)

Have students name a polygon on each page of their journal (include the different types of triangles and quadrilaterals) and then draw it. Have students look in magazines to find a picture of an object that closely resembles the polygon (a stop sign is an octagon; a candy bar is a rectangle), cut it out, and paste it into the journal.

Shape People (grades K–3)

Have students use different polygons and circles to create a shape person. Connect this with language arts by having each student write a story about his or her person.

Shape Puzzles (grades 3–5)

Enlarge and cut out the shapes below. Put the pieces into an envelope and draw the final shape on the outside of the envelope. Have students arrange the pieces into the shape shown on the envelope. Have students make shape puzzles for others to solve.

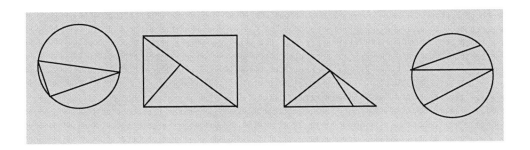

Simply Symmetrical (grades 1–5) 💻

This activity is available at the Web site of the U.S. Department of Education, http://www.ed.gov/pubs/parents/Math/mathhome.html. Adaptations of this for the classroom are:

- Explore your classroom for symmetrical designs and see how many of them students can find. Have students look for both reflection and rotation symmetry.
- Find pictures of objects with reflection symmetry. Cut the picture of the object along the line of symmetry and paste it onto a blank piece of paper. Have students draw the missing half of the object.
- Have students write their names in large block letters and look for lines of symmetry in the letters. Find out who has a name with the most letters that have reflection symmetry or if anyone has a name with all letters having reflection symmetry ("BOB"). Ask if any students have letters in their names with rotation symmetry (H, I, N, O, S, X, Z).

Traveling on a Grid (grades 2–3)

Have students use large block graph paper to draw city streets and buildings. Have students describe how many blocks you would have to travel east-west (left-right) or north-south (up-down) to move from one building to another. Have students draw their own cityscapes and list distances from one location to another.

Tree Measurement (grades 4–5) 💻

Working in pairs with string and a ruler, students learn a method for measuring the height of a tree that is too tall to measure directly and are introduced to the concept of circumference. This activity is available at http://eduref.org/cgi-bin/lessons.cgi/Mathematics/Measurement.

Using Geometric Software to Explore Triangles (grade 5)

Have students use dynamic geometric software (such as the Geometer's Sketchpad®) to draw a triangle. Have students measure the interior angles and the lengths of the sides. Grab a vertex of the triangle and move the vertex to create a new triangle. Have students create an equilateral triangle, isosceles triangle, scalene triangle, acute triangle, obtuse triangle, and right triangle. Lead students to discover the triangle inequality property—that the sum of the lengths of any two sides must be larger than the length of the third side. Have students determine that the sum of interior angles of a triangle is always 180 degrees.

Using Maps (grades 3–5)

Make copies of road maps (from an atlas or from various Web sites) for students. Have students measure the distances between cities and describe the directions from one city to another. Have students find the shortest distance between two cities by traveling on roads.

"Who Am I" Riddles (grades 2–4)

Prepare "Who Am I" riddles for students to solve, such as: "I am a polygon; I have four sides of equal length, but the four angles are not of equal measure. Who am I?" Have students make up riddles and share them with each other.

Winter Shapes (grades K–3)

Cut various two-dimensional shapes from construction paper and have students use the shapes to make all the winter objects they can think of, such as trees from triangles, snowmen from circles, and houses from rectangles and triangles. Make these objects the focus of the class bulletin board.

Writing Stories (grades 1–5)

Have students write stories using as many geometric terms as possible. Encourage them to be creative. Suggest a general topic or theme for their story or relate them to what you are teaching in language arts, science, or social studies.

Lesson Plans

The lesson plans in this section are intended to support teachers as they are thinking about the methods they use in order to meet the individual needs of their students. Lessons should be planned to engage students and to connect the activities with the mathematics content.
Each lesson should have a clear goal, and every part of that lesson—from the opening activity to the final summary—should be goal-focused, helping to move students toward a clearer understanding of the concepts at hand. These lessons are designed to: actively engage students, make use of real-world situations, and connect the mathematics concepts with the concepts that students have already learned. We encourage you to build on these plans and tailor them to the needs of your students.

(continued on next page)

Lesson plan	Grade Level	Content Strand	Topic	Page
Reflections	5	transformational geometry	reflections and glide reflections	113
Rep Tiles	3	visualization and spatial reasoning; 2- and 3-D geometry; transformational geometry; measurement	tessellating; tiling to create similar shapes	121
Rep Tiles	4–5	visualization and spatial reasoning; 2- and 3-D geometry; transformational geometry; measurement	tessellating; tiling to create similar shapes	127
Sum of the Interior Angles of a Polygon	4–5	2- and 3-D geometry; measurement	finding the sum of the interior angles of a polygon	135
Tiling the Plane	2–3	2- and 3-D geometry; transformational geometry; visualization and spatial reasoning	determining which pattern blocks tessellate	145
Tiling the Plane	5	2- and 3-D geometry; transformational geometry; visualization and spatial reasoning	determining which pattern blocks tessellate	149
Traveling around Our Town	1–2	coordinate geometry	tracing paths on a grid	155
Visualizing Multiplication	3–5	measurement; visualization and spatial reasoning	using an area model for multiplication	159

Can You Build It?

Lesson Topic
Perimeter

Grade
3

Lesson Length

40 minutes

NCTM Standards Addressed

- Understand measurable attributes of objects and the units, systems, and processes of measurement.
- Recognize the attributes of length.
- Understand how to measure using nonstandard units.
- Apply appropriate techniques, tools, and formulas to determine measurement.
- Measure with multiple copies of units of the same size.
- Use repetition of a single unit to measure something larger than the unit.

Sample State Standards Addressed

- Compare measurable characteristics of different objects of the same dimensions (e.g. area, length, perimeter).
- Determine the measurement of objects with standard and non-standard units.
- Use concrete objects to determine area and perimeter.

Student Objectives

Students will:
- use non-standard units (pattern blocks) to measure perimeter
- build a shape that satisfies given characteristics.

Grouping for Instruction

- Whole group for opening and closure
- Pairs for activities

Overview of Lesson

Students explore the concept of perimeter in terms of distance traveled by a ladybug around a shape. Students design a figure and measure its perimeter. Students make a shape that satisfies several characteristics.

Background Information

Students should be able to measure by repeating the use of a non-standard unit.

Materials and Equipment

- Pattern blocks (overhead and student set)
- Plain paper
- Overhead projector

Procedure

A. Motivation and introduction

1. Put an orange square pattern block on the overhead. Say: "Let's suppose that a ladybug is going to walk around the square. To go all the way around, the ladybug would walk four units. Each side of a square (or of a triangle) will represent one unit of measurement."
2. Put two orange squares together to form a rectangle. Ask: "If the ladybug walks around this rectangle, how far will it walk?"
3. Solicit answers from students. (Correct response: six units)
4. Say: "Today we are going to explore how far a ladybug will walk in going around objects made with the pattern blocks. This distance around is called the perimeter."

B. Development (including discussion points and feedback)

1. Have students work in pairs.
2. Give each pair a set of pattern blocks, a piece of paper, and a pencil.
3. Demonstrate how to measure a ladybug's distance around a red trapezoid.
4. Put three pattern blocks together, namely: a red trapezoid, a green triangle, and a blue rhombus.
5. Demonstrate how to trace the shape with its component parts.
6. Ask: "How far will the ladybug travel in its journey around this shape?"
7. Instruct students: "Build any shape made up of four pattern blocks."
8. Instruct students: "Now, trace around the shape and its parts."
9. Instruct students: "Give your picture to your partner and ask the partner to determine how many units the ladybug will travel in going around the shape."
10. Give students time to work and to share their responses with their partners.
11. Call on a few students to share with the class. (Possibly collect the students' work for assessment.)
12. Say: "I'm going to see what good detectives you are. I am going to give you some clues and you are to build the shape that satisfies all the clues."
13. Put four red trapezoids on the overhead projector.
14. Say: "Use four red trapezoids to build a large trapezoid. How many units will the ladybug travel to go around the large trapezoid?"

15. Observe as students work. Have students share answers and explain how they arrived at their answers.
16. Put one green triangle, one blue rhombus, and two red trapezoids on the overhead projector.
17. Say: "Use one green triangle, one blue rhombus, and two red trapezoids to make a large triangle with a perimeter of nine units."
18. Observe as students work. Have students share responses. Look for alternate ways of doing this problem.
19. Say: "Build a large square. In your large square, there are four red trapezoids and one orange square. What is the perimeter of the large square?"
20. Say: "Build a large triangle. There are five green triangles, three red trapezoids, and one blue rhombus. What is the perimeter of the large triangle?"
21. Observe as students work. Have students share responses.

C. Summary and closure

Ask the class: "What have we done today?" Build on student responses. Emphasize that <u>perimeter</u> is the distance around an object.

D. Assignment

Draw any shape made of no more than nine pattern blocks. Find the perimeter of the shape in terms of units a ladybug would walk.

Think about: When a praying mantis walks around a large square made of four trapezoids and a square, the mantis walks four big units. How many big units would the praying mantis walk around the shape you made?

Assessment

- Observe students as they draw shapes and determine the distance around them.
- Collect the drawing made for the assignment.

Can You Name That Shape?

Lesson Topic ———————————— **Grade** ————
Polygons   2-4

Lesson Length ———————————————————————

80 minutes

NCTM Standards Addressed ————————————————

- Build and draw geometry objects.
- Recognize, name, build, draw, compare, and sort shapes.
- Describe attributes and parts of shapes: circle, rectangle, square, triangle, parallelogram (sides and vertices); locate interior (inside) and exterior (outside) angles.
- Identify right angles in polygons.
- Develop vocabulary and concepts related to two- and three-dimensional geometric shapes.

Sample State Standards Addressed ——————————

- Name and label geometric shapes in two and three dimensions (e.g., circle/sphere, square/cube, triangle/pyramid, rectangle/prism).
- Build geometric shapes using concrete objects (e.g., manipulatives).
- Construct two- and three-dimensional shapes and figures using manipulatives, geoboards, and computer software.
- Identify properties of geometric figures (e.g., parallel, perpendicular, similar, congruent, symmetrical).

Student Objectives ——————————————————

Students will:
- Construct polygons
- Identify attributes of two-dimensional shapes
- Name common shapes
- Draw two-dimensional shapes
- Sort two-dimensional shapes

Grouping for Instruction ————————————————

- Individual students for building shapes, drawing shapes, and making a shape poster
- Whole class for shapes round-robin

Overview of Lesson

Students use K'NEX™ materials to build, investigate, and draw two-dimensional shapes (polygons). The class will combine the shapes they have built and draw from the pile to begin a round-robin activity to name and determine the attributes of a selection of the shapes. Individual students will return to their desks with a single shape to draw on poster paper. Students will include lists of: names, attributes, and real world examples of their shapes.

Background Information

Students should have had exposure to basic shape names and have some knowledge of attributes.

Materials and Equipment

- K'NEX™ Math Manipulatives sets
- Large easel or chart paper (one page per student)
- Crayons to share
- Rulers

Procedure

A. Motivation and introduction

1. Introduce K'NEX™ rods and connectors to students.
2. Provide time for creative exploration and play with the materials.
3. Select a student's model or creation that is a polygon. Instruct students that the rods represent sides and the connectors represent vertices.

B. Development (including discussion points and feedback)

1. Instruct each student to build three to four different polygons.
2. Have students take their shapes to an open area in the classroom. Have students stand in a circle and place their shapes in the circle.
3. Select a student to pick up someone's shape (other than his or her own) that he/she can name.
4. Have the student name the shape. Pass the shape to the person on the right.
5. Have that person give one of the following:
   - attribute of the shape
   - another name for the shape
   - a real world example of the shape (limit to three per shape).

6. The shape continues moving to the right in round-robin style until students are stumped.

7. The next student picks a new shape.
8. Continue for about 15 to 20 minutes. Students will learn from each other's observations and the quality of responses will improve as the activity continues.
9. Tell students that they will each complete this activity with a single shape on their own.
10. Give a shape from the floor to each student along with a large sheet of paper.
11. Instruct students to:
    - lay the shape at the top of the page.
    - use pencil point to make a dot on the paper below the circular opening in each K'NEX™ Connector (vertex) of their shape. Their pencil point will fit nicely in the opening in each connector.
    - remove the shape and use a ruler to draw the shape by connecting the dots.
    - use crayons to color the sides of the shapes.
    - place three titles below their shape leaving room below them for lists.
        - Names
        - Attributes
        - Real-world examples
    - begin their posters.
12. Have students share their posters with others and discuss lists.
13. Select a few posters and review them with the class.
14. Ask students to question entries of which they are unsure.

C. Summary and closure

1. Ask students to write three things that they learned today.
2. Have them share their statements with another student or students in their group.
3. Have students share with the class.

D. Assignment

Have students use other resources (text, Internet, library) to find three things to add to their lists during the next class session.

Assessment

Place K'NEX™ two-dimensional shapes at locations around the room and have students move from station to station. Provide questions at each station, for example,
- How many vertices does the shape have?
- List three attributes of the shape.
- List two names for the shape.
- Does the shape have any right angles? How many?

Find the Shape

Lesson Topic

Using ordered pairs to identify, locate, and plot points on the coordinate plane

Grades

4–5

Lesson Length

40 minutes

NCTM Standards Addressed

- Describe location and movement using common language and geometric vocabulary.
- Make and use coordinate systems to specify locations and to describe paths.

Sample State Standards Addressed

- Locate and identify points on a coordinate system.

Student Objectives

Students will:
- identify points on the coordinate plane using ordered pairs
- plot ordered pairs on the coordinate plane
- use properties of shapes to identify polygons such as triangles and quadrilaterals (square, rectangle, parallelogram, trapezoid).

Grouping for Instruction

- Whole class for motivation, introduction, summary, and closure
- Pairs for activities

Overview of Lesson

Students play a game similar to the game *Battleship*. They identify ordered pairs and plot ordered pairs in the first quadrant. (This lesson can be extended to include the entire coordinate plane.)

Background Information

Students should have some familiarity with the first quadrant of the coordinate plane and with identifying and plotting ordered pairs (mastery is not expected). Students should also be familiar with polygons such as triangles and quadrilaterals and their geometric properties.

Materials and Equipment

- Square grid paper
- Colored pencils
- Overhead projector

Procedure

A. Motivation and introduction

1. Ask students if they have ever played the game *Battleship*. If a student is familiar with the game, have him or her tell the class about the game. Tell the students that today we are going to play a game similar to *Battleship*.
2. On the overhead projector or on large graph paper draw the first quadrant of the coordinate plane. Have individual students plot a point and then identify the ordered pair. Do this a few times; if no one selects the origin (0,0), then put a point there and ask students to identify the coordinates.
3. On a different graph draw a few polygons such as a triangle, square, rectangle, parallelogram, and isosceles trapezoid. Ask students to identify the shapes and name coordinates of the vertices.

B. Development (including discussion points and feedback)

1. Divide the class into pairs. Instruct students in each pair to move their desks so that they are facing each other. Each pair should place a pile of books between them so that they cannot see their partners' papers.
2. Distribute to each student a sheet of paper that has a graph of the first quadrant on the upper half of the paper and also on the lower half of the paper.
3. Have each student draw a polygon (triangle, square, rectangle, parallelogram, or isosceles trapezoid) on the top grid. Discuss some of the properties of shapes that might help students identify the shapes.
4. Ask each student to try to guess what shape his or her partner drew. To do this, the students in each pair take turns asking whether or not their partner's shape has a point plotted at a specific location (ordered pair). When a student names a point, that point is plotted on the bottom grid. If the point is plotted on the partner's grid, then the student should put a dot there; if it is not, then the student should put an "X" at the point. (This allows students to keep track of their guesses.) When a student thinks that he or she

knows the partner's shape, he or she should identify the shape and call out all the ordered pairs.
5. Repeat as time allows.

C. Summary and closure

1. Ask students what mathematics they did today.
2. Ask students to share some of the strategies that they used to figure out their partners' shapes. Encourage them to talk about the properties of shapes that helped them to do this.
3. Have students plot and connect points that either spell out a message (such as "THE END") or make a picture such as (1,2), (2,3), (3,3), (4,2), (3,1), and (2,1), which makes a hexagon.

D. Assignment

Have students draw a picture on graph paper (first quadrant only) and then identify the coordinates that would be connected to draw the picture.

Assessment

- Observe the students during the activity to make sure they are playing the game correctly and to see whether they are just making random guesses or are actually using their knowledge of ordered pairs and properties of shapes to find their partners' shapes.
- Make notes of students' ability and insight into plotting points and developing strategies.

Geoboard Squares

Lesson Topic

Squares and patterns

Grades

2–3

Lesson Length

50 minutes

NCTM Standards Addressed

- Make and test conjectures about geometric properties and relationships and develop logical arguments to justify conclusions.
- Build and draw geometric objects.
- Create and describe mental images of objects, patterns, and paths.
- Relate ideas in geometry to ideas in number and measurement.

Sample State Standards Addressed

- Compare measurable characteristics of different objects on the same dimensions (e.g., time, temperature, area, length, weight, capacity, perimeter).
- Determine the measurement of objects with non-standard and standard units (e.g., U.S. customary and metric).
- Name and label geometric shapes in two and three dimensions (e.g., circle/sphere, square/cube, triangle/pyramid, rectangle/prism).
- Build geometric shapes using concrete objects (e.g., manipulatives).
- Draw two- and three-dimensional geometric shapes and construct rectangles, squares, and triangles on the geoboard and on graph paper satisfying specific criteria.

Student Objectives

Students will:
- create squares of different sizes on a geoboard
- find and describe a pattern
- use the pattern to determine the number of squares possible on a 10-by-10 geoboard.

Grouping for Instruction

- Whole class for launch and closure
- Small groups of four or five for the investigation

Overview of Lesson

Students create squares with a horizontal base (and vertical sides) on a geoboard. They are guided to find a pattern to the number of such squares that can be created on a geoboard of various sizes (one-by-one, two-by-two, etc.). Students then use the pattern to predict how many such squares can be created on a four-by-four (five pin) geoboard. Their result can be tested using the geoboard. They then make a conjecture concerning how many such squares can be created on a 10-by-10 (11 pin) geoboard.

Background Information

Students should have played with a geoboard prior to this investigation. Students need to know what a square is and the concept of dimensions (length and width). They need to be familiar with the square numbers so they can recognize the pattern. (This could be accomplished prior to this lesson by using multi-link cubes to create representations of squares and being guided to discover that each square number is the sum of one or more consecutive odd numbers starting at one. For example, $9 = 1 + 3 + 5$.) Students need to be able to find larger square numbers.

Materials and Equipment

- At least one geoboard and rubber bands for each team
- Geoboard for overhead projector
- Overhead projector

Procedure

A. Motivation and introduction

1. Ask students: "Have any of you ever seen a ceramic tile floor?" (Wait for response.) Say: "Ceramic tiles are very hard. If the number of tiles needed to tile a floor does not fit perfectly you must break tiles to make them fit. This sometimes results in tiles that cannot be used because they do not break as planned. If possible, you want to tile the floor without having to break tiles to make them fit. In our next investigation we will look at how we can determine the number of different sized tiles you will need to tile various sizes of square rooms. We will simulate this situation using the geoboards. Since we may decide to tile only part of the floor and use hardwood flooring for the remainder of the room, we will also consider squares that do not tile the floor perfectly."
2. Demonstrate how to create a square on an overhead geoboard.
3. Discuss the concepts of vertical and horizontal and state: "Since we want to tile the floor, we will only use square tiles with a horizontal base and vertical sides."
4. Put on the overhead projector a square composed of 16 small squares. Ask: "How many squares do you see?" (A student will probably say 16.) Say: "If we use small tiles it

would take 16 small tiles to cover the floor. This will require a lot of work. Could we use larger squares?"

5. Place a colored two-by-two square over the transparency of the four-by-four grid. Show how sliding the two-by-two square around the grid shows other two-by-two squares "hidden" on the grid. Ask: "Do you see how you could use this approach to find the number of squares of various dimensions that could be created on the grid?"

6. Say: "Let's explore in teams and see if we can find a rule that can be used to determine the number of squares that can be made."

B. Development (including discussion points and feedback)

1. Place the students in heterogeneous cooperative groups of four or five students.
2. Assign a task to each person in a team (leader, recorder, reporter, etc.).
3. Distribute and discuss the project on geoboards and squares (Worksheet: Geoboards and Squares, page 92).
4. Ask each team to complete this project. Circulate among the groups, guiding them to complete the project.
5. Ask each group to report to the class what they did and what conjecture they made. Say: "Did you find any connections between this project and anything we learned earlier?" Generate discussion on how square numbers were used in this investigation.

C. Summary and closure

1. Ask students to complete a one-minute paper stating one thing they learned from this lesson.
2. Ask some students to share their responses.
3. Ask students which size squares could be used to completely cover the four-by-four geoboard. Have them explain their reasoning.

D. Assignment

Ask the students to consider how many rectangles could be formed on a four-by-four geoboard. They should bring their answers and how they found their answers to the next class.

Assessment

*   Observe the students during the group project. Use note cards or adhesive notes to record how they are working in their group and whether the students made a connection to the previous work on square numbers.
*   Grade the group work sample, the performance (presentations), or the homework.
*   Ask students to respond about what they learned or what they found difficult about the project in their mathematics journal.

Worksheet: **Geoboards and Squares**

Problem Statement: Let the distance between pins on a row or column be 1. Then the dimensions of your geoboard are 4-by-4. How many squares with horizontal and vertical sides can you make on the geoboard? On a 10-by-10 geoboard?

1. **Define (understand) the problem.**

   Restate this problem in your own words.

2. **Devise a plan.**

   This is a very difficult problem. Create a similar, simpler problem. State the problem in the space below.

   Solve your similar, simpler problem.

   It may help to solve several similar, simpler problems and look for a pattern. Use part of your geoboard to find the number of different size squares with vertical and horizontal sides and total number of such squares for the different size geoboards shown in the table. Complete the table.

3. Carry out the plan.

Complete the table:

Geoboard Size	Square Dimensions				Totals
	1-by-1	2-by-2	3-by-3	4-by-4	
1-by-1	1	-------------	---------------	---------------	1
2-by-2					
3-by-3					

Describe any patterns you found.

Use the patterns to find the total number of squares with vertical and horizontal sides that you can form on your 4-by-4 geoboard.

Use the patterns to find the total number of squares with vertical and horizontal sides that you can form on a 10-by-10 geoboard.

4. Looking back

How could you convince someone that your answer is correct?

What have you learned about problem solving from this investigation?

How Close Is Our Estimate?

Lesson Topic ——————————— Grade ————

Estimation and measurement   5

Lesson Length ————————————————

50 minutes

NCTM Standards Addressed ————————————

- Understand measurable attributes of objects and the units, systems, and processes of measurement.
- Understand such attributes as length, area, and volume.
- Understand the need to measure with standard units.
- Develop strategies for estimating the perimeter, area, and volume.

Sample State Standards Addressed ————————

- Select and use appropriate instruments and units for measuring quantities (e.g., perimeter, area, volume).
- Estimate, refine, and verify specified measurements of objects.
- Add and subtract measurements.

Student Objectives ——————————————

Students will:
- estimate perimeter, area, and volume
- measure perimeter and area using nonstandard units of measurement
- add and subtract non-standard units of measurement.

Grouping for Instruction ——————————————

- Individually
- Groups of three or four

Overview of Lesson ——————————————————

Students use non-standard units to explore the concepts of perimeter, area, and volume. Students estimate measures of perimeter, area, and volume of their classroom. Students add and subtract units of measurement.

Background Information ——————————————

Students should be able to add mixed numbers and simplify the sum.

Materials and Equipment ——————————————

- Box of tennis balls
- Pieces of rope that are the length of five tennis balls
- Grids with measurements that are five-tennis-balls by five-tennis-balls
- Estimation sheets (one for each student)
- Chalk or masking tape for marking regions on the floor

Procedure ——————————————————————

A. Motivation and introduction

1. Say: "Today I am going to have you investigate the dimensions of our classroom. But first I'm going to let you estimate the dimensions to see how close you can come."
2. Give each student a questionnaire (Worksheet A: How Big Is Our Classroom?, page 98). Tell students they have two minutes to complete the questionnaire.
3. After two minutes, collect the questionnaires.
4. Explain that today's lesson involves an investigation of distance around (perimeter), region covered (area), and space filled (volume).

B. Development (including discussion points and feedback)

1. Divide the class into heterogeneous groups of three or four students, and number the groups one, two, three, etc.
2. Explain that each group should:
   - estimate the number of tennis balls it will take to go around the classroom, to cover the floor, and to fill the classroom
   - use the tennis balls to measure.
3. Give each group a questionnaire (Worksheet B: How Big Is Our Classroom?, page 99).
4. Tell the students they have five minutes to complete the questionnaire and that every student in each group should be involved in the process.
5. Observe the students as they work. Note students' interaction and reasoning.
6. Collect the questionnaires after five minutes.

7. Explain: "Now that we have thought about this and made an estimate, we are going to figure out a way to measure the class using tennis balls."

8. Give a set of three tennis balls to half of the groups (the odd-numbered groups). Give ropes that are five-tennis-balls long to the other half of the groups (even-numbered groups).

9. Assign groups one and two the task of measuring the front wall, groups three and four the task of measuring the back wall, etc. Instruct the students with tennis balls to measure to the nearest half of a ball and those with ropes to measure to the nearest fifth of a rope.

10. Compile the results from the class.

11. Discuss the methods used to measure. Discover what efficient methods can be used and how accurate the measurements are.

12. Have the groups that measured with tennis balls use the ropes and the groups with the ropes use the tennis balls.

13. Having previously divided the classroom into sections, assign the groups the task of measuring the area of a section of the classroom in tennis balls or in five-by-five tennis-ball grids.

14. Once all measurements are taken, compile the results.

15. Discuss the methods of finding the area of sections. Ask: "How many tennis balls are in one of the grids? How many tennis balls would be in a 12-ball by 12-ball grid?"

C. Summary and closure

1. Say: "Today we measured the perimeter and area of the floor of our classroom with non-standard units of measurement. If you were going to buy carpet for our classroom, would you give the salesman the measurements in tennis balls?" (Responses)

2. Say: "What kinds of measurement would you give the salesman?" (Responses)

3. Say: "How exact would these measurements have to be?" (Responses)

4. Develop a discussion of non-standard and standard units of measurement and the need for exact measurement at critical times.

D. Assignment

"Describe how you would determine the number of tennis balls it would take to fill our classroom. You must write at least four sentences telling the procedures."

Assessment

Most of the assessment for this lesson is embedded in the activities. Each student has individually filled out a questionnaire. Each group has completed a questionnaire. Each student can now be asked to answer the questions: "How would you estimate the perimeter of our classroom in feet? How would you estimate the area of our room in square yards?"

Worksheet A   Name _____

HOW BIG IS OUR CLASSROOM?

You have 2 minutes to **estimate** different measurements in our classroom. You are to work by yourself and put down your best guess.

1. How many tennis balls would it take to go around our classroom? _____
    (The balls are lined up around the edges of our classroom; each ball touches the next ball.)

2. How many tennis balls would it take to cover the floor of our classroom? _____
    (The balls touch each other.)

3. How many tennis balls would it take to fill our classroom? _____

Worksheet B

Names of Group Members:

_____

_____

_____

_____

HOW BIG IS OUR CLASSROOM?

You have 5 minutes to **estimate** different measurements in our classroom. You are to work as a group to determine the best estimate.

1. How many tennis balls would it take to go around our classroom? _____
    (The balls are lined up around the edges of our classroom; each ball touches the next ball.)

2. How many tennis balls would it take to cover the floor of our classroom? _____
    (The balls touch each other.)

3. How many tennis balls would it take to fill our classroom? _____

4. Explain how your group decided on the best estimates. Your explanation should contain at least two sentences.

Investigating Nets and Polyhedra

Lesson Topic ──────────── Grade ───────

Three-dimensional shapes and their nets   5

Lesson Length ────────────────────────

50 minutes

NCTM Standards Addressed ──────────────

- Make and test conjectures about geometric properties and relationships and develop logical arguments to justify conclusions.
- Build and draw geometric objects.
- Create and describe mental images of objects, patterns, and paths.
- Identify and build a three-dimensional object from two-dimensional representations of that object.
- Identify and draw a two-dimensional representation of a three-dimensional object.

Sample State Standards Addressed────────

- Describe in words how geometric shapes are constructed.
- Construct two- and three-dimensional shapes and figures using manipulatives, geoboards, and computer software.

Student Objectives ──────────────────

Students will:
- create a net for a given polyhedron
- determine the corresponding polyhedron for a given net.

Grouping for Instruction ──────────────

- Whole class for launch and closure
- Small groups of four or five for the investigation

Overview of Lesson ──────────────────

Students will investigate several polyhedra (cube, tetrahedron, and one of their choosing) and their corresponding nets. Given a polyhedron, students must find at least one net. Given a net, they must visualize the solid the net will produce.

Background Information

Students need to be familiar with putting together and taking apart Polydrons™ or Klikko™ pieces and the concepts of square, triangle, pentagon, hexagon, and congruence.

Materials and Equipment

- Classroom set of Polydrons™ or Klikko™
- Masking tape for each team
- 500 one-inch cardboard or cardstock squares
- Grid paper for each team
- Overhead projector

Procedure

A. Motivation and introduction

1. Define the term *polyhedron* as a closed three-dimensional surface formed by polygons. Consider objects in your own home and write down a list of polyhedra (the plural of polyhedron). Show students examples of polyhedra. (Wait.)
2. Show the students a cube made from Polydrons™ or Klikko™ pieces and say: "For example, a cube is a polyhedron with each face being a square. Notice that the surface of squares divides space into three regions—the region inside the surface, the surface itself, and the region outside the surface."
3. Say: "Look around you. Do you see any polyhedra in this room?" Ask students to explain why they think an object qualifies as a polyhedron. Allow other students to question whether an object is a polyhedron.
4. Say: "Consider objects in your home. What are some polyhedra in your home?" List several on the overhead projector.
5. Help students find one net of the cube. Show them how you can create a "T" with the Polydrons™ or Klikko™ pieces used to create a cube. Say: "This is one net of the cube. It consists of faces of the Polydrons™ or Klikko™ pieces where each face is connected to at least one other face along one entire side. Do you think there are any other nets of the cube?"
6. Say: "Let's investigate nets of some polyhedra."

B. Development (including discussion points and feedback)

1. Place the students in heterogeneous cooperative groups of about four students each.
2. Assign a task to each person in a team (leader, presenter, recorder, materials person).
3. Ask the teams to complete the worksheet "Investigating Nets and Polyhedra" (page 105).

4. Circulate among the groups, guiding them to complete the project and observing students' participation, interactions, and understanding.
5. Ask each group to report on one net they found for the cube or another polyhedron.
6. Make sure each student understands the concept of a net. Ask questions such as "What makes this a net?" and "Why is this disconnected set of squares not a net?" and "Could you have a net of the cube that contained only five squares? Explain your reasoning."
7. Fold a cloth net around a pyramid with a square base made with Polydrons™ or Klikko™ pieces to emphasize the relationship between a figure and its net.

C. Summary and closure

1. Ask each group to work together to write three statements about what they did today and why it is important.
2. Have each group share one statement, and continue going around the room from group to group until all points are made.
3. Summarize by emphasizing:
   - the definition of a net
   - that there are a number of different nets for a given polyhedron
   - that nets of different polyhedra are different.

D. Assignment

Give each student a net for a prism on a sheet of paper. Have them cut out the net and create the corresponding prism. Invite them to decorate their prism.

Assessment

- Observe the students during the group project.
- Record how they are working in their group and whether the students can visualize a net from the solid and the solid from a net.
- Grade the group project and the presentations (if they are more formal than implied in the project).
- Grade the homework.

Extensions

1. A cube is an example of a **prism**—a polyhedron formed by congruent polygons for the base and top and parallelograms for each side face. Use the Polydrons™ or Klikko™ pieces to create three other prisms.
2. The tetrahedron is an example of a **pyramid**—a polyhedron formed with a polygon for the base and sides formed of triangles that meet at a single point (called the **apex**) off the plane containing the base. Use the Polydrons™ or Klikko™ pieces to create three other pyramids.
3. The cube has six faces, eight corners (called **vertices**), and twelve edges. The mathematician Leonhard Euler (pronounced "oiler") discovered a relationship between

the faces, vertices, and edges of any polyhedron. Use the Polydrons™ or Klikko™ pieces to create other polyhedra. Create a table showing the number of faces, vertices, and edges for each polyhedron. Look for a pattern in the table. Create a formula that relates the faces, vertices, and edges.

4. A **Platonic solid** is a polyhedron in which each face is a regular polygon, the faces are all congruent, and each vertex has the same number of polygons meeting at the vertex. There are five Platonic solids. Find them. Create a net for each Platonic solid.

5. Use the Internet to find information on the **Archimedean solids**. Find a net for each of the Archimedean solids. How do the Archimedean solids differ from the Platonic solids?

6. Research kaleidocycles. Use an M. C. Escher tessellation to create a kaleidocycle. Describe the polyhedron used and any transformations Escher used in creating the tessellation.

Worksheet: **Investigating Nets and Polyhedra**

Each team has been given a cube made using Polydrons™ or Klikko™ pieces. If you take apart the cube while keeping each square attached to the entire side of at least one other square and then lay the resulting figure flat, you will have a **net** for the cube consisting of the six square faces of the cube. Below is one example of a net for the cube.

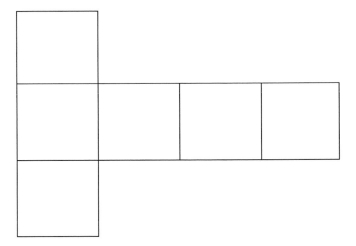

1. Find as many nets as you can that can be used to create a cube. If you are not sure if a particular net can be used to create a cube, make the net using the cardboard squares and masking tape and then try to fold the net into a cube. Sketch all the nets of the cube your team found on the grid paper provided.

2. Show a net of six squares that cannot be used to create a cube.

3. A regular tetrahedron is a polyhedron formed by four equilateral triangles. Create a regular tetrahedron using the Polydrons™ or Klikko™ pieces.

4. Find a net for the regular tetrahedron. Sketch the net in the space below.

5. Create a net that can be used to create a polyhedron. Sketch the net in the space below. Trade nets with another team. Can you predict what the resulting polyhedron will look like? Describe or sketch the polyhedron you predict will result next to the net. Test your prediction by using the Polydrons™ or Klikko™ pieces to create the polyhedron. Were you correct?

It's a 3-D World Out There!

Lesson Topic
Polyhedra

Grade
2–4

Lesson Length

80 minutes

NCTM Standards Addressed

- Build and draw geometric objects.
- Recognize, name, build, draw, compare, and sort shapes: sphere (ball), cone, cylinder (can), pyramid, prism (box), cube.
- Describe attributes and parts of shapes; identify faces, edges, vertices (corners).
- Develop vocabulary and concepts related to two- and three-dimensional geometric shapes.

Sample State Standards Addressed

- Name and label geometric shapes in two and three dimensions (e.g., circle/sphere, square/cube, triangle/pyramid, rectangle/prism).
- Build geometric shapes using concrete objects (e.g., manipulatives).
- Construct two- and three-dimensional shapes and figures using manipulatives, geoboards, and computer software.
- Identify properties of geometric figures (e.g., parallel, perpendicular, similar, congruent, symmetrical).

Student Objectives

Students will:
- Construct polygons
- Identify attributes of three-dimensional shapes
- Name common three-dimensional shapes
- Draw three-dimensional shapes
- Sort three-dimensional shapes.

Grouping for Instruction

- Groups of three students to build, draw, and make a poster of assigned three-dimensional shapes.
- Whole class for three-dimensional shapes round-robin.

Overview of Lesson

Students use K'NEX™ materials sets to build, investigate, and draw three-dimensional shapes (polyhedra). The class will combine the shapes they have built and draw from the pile to begin a round-robin activity to name and determine the attributes of a selection of the shapes. Individual students will return to their desks with a single shape to draw on poster paper. Students will include lists of: names, attributes, and real world examples of their shapes.

Background Information

Students should have had exposure to basic three-dimensional shape names and have some knowledge of attributes.

Materials and Equipment

- K'NEX™ Math Manipulatives sets
- Large easel or chart paper (one page/student)
- Crayons to share
- Rulers

Procedure

A. Motivation and introduction

1. Introduce K'NEX™ rods and connectors to students.
2. Provide time for creative exploration and play with the materials.
3. Select a student's model or creation that is a polyhedra. Instruct students that the rods represent edges of three-dimensional shapes and the connectors represent vertices.

B. Development (including discussion points and feedback)

1. Assign a shape from the list below to each of the groups for building:
   - cube
   - square pyramid
   - rectangular prism
   - triangular pyramid
   - triangular prism
   - hexagonal prism
   - octagonal prism.

2. Have students take their shapes to an open area in the classroom. Have students stand in a circle and place their shapes in the circle.
3. Select a student to pick up someone's shape (other than his or her own) that he or she can name.
4. Have the student name the shape. Pass the shape to the person on the right.
5. Have that person give one of the following:
    - attribute of the shape
    - another name for the shape
    - a real world example of the shape (limit to three per shape).
6. The shape continues moving to the right in round-robin style until students are stumped.
7. The next student picks a new shape.
8. Continue for about 15 to 20 minutes. Students will learn from each others' observations and the quality of responses will improve as the activity continues.
9. Tell students that they will each complete this activity with a single shape on their own.
10. Give a shape from the floor to each group of students along with a large sheet of paper.
11. Instruct students to:
    - make a two-dimensional line drawing of the three-dimensional shapes they have been assigned
    - use crayons to color the edges of the shapes
    - place three titles below their shape leaving room below them for lists
        - Names
        - Attributes
        - Real-world examples
    - begin their posters by listing information in the three categories on their paper.
12. Have students share their posters with others and discuss lists.
13. Select a few posters and review them with the class.
14. Ask students to question entries of which they are unsure.

C. Summary and closure

1. Ask students to write three things that they learned today.
2. Have them share their statements with another student or students in their group.
3. Have students share with the class.

D. Assignment

Have students use other resources (text, Internet, library) to find three things to add to their lists during the next class session.

Assessment

- Provide each group of students with a sheet of easel or chart paper.
- Section the paper as shown below.
- Each individual member of the group is to sit in front of one of the sections of the paper.
- Each student is to list information he or she has learned about the shape.
- After a given amount of time, each group is to discuss the information they have listed and place a group listing of what they have learned in the square at the center of their page.

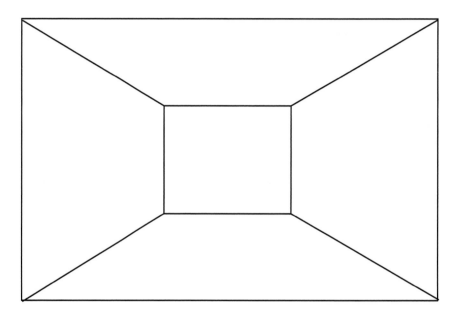

Reflections

Lesson Topic   Grade

Reflections and glide reflections   5

Lesson Length

50 minutes

NCTM Standards Addressed

- Explore congruence and similarity.
- Make and test conjectures about geometric properties and relationships and develop logical arguments to justify conclusions.
- Predict and describe the results of sliding, flipping, and turning two-dimensional shapes.
- Describe a motion or a series of motions that will show that two shapes are congruent.
- Understand such attributes as length, area, weight, volume, and size of angle and select the appropriate type of unit for measuring each attribute.
- Understand that measurements are approximations and understand how differences in units affect precision.
- Select and apply appropriate standard units and tools to measure length, area, volume, weight, time, temperature, and the size of angles.

Sample State Standards Addressed

- Select and use appropriate instruments and units for measuring quantities (e.g., perimeter, volume, area, weight, time, temperature).
- Select and use standard tools to measure the size of figures with specified accuracy, including length, width, perimeter, and area.
- Estimate, refine, and verify specified measurements of objects.
- Construct two- and three-dimensional shapes and figures using manipulatives, geoboards, and computer software.
- Represent and use the concepts of line, point, and plane.
- Analyze simple transformations of geometric figures and rotations of line segments.
- Identify properties of geometric figures (e.g., parallel, perpendicular, similar, congruent, symmetrical).

Student Objectives

Students will:
- create a reflection of a polygon using a Mira™
- discover that a line connecting a vertex of a polygon and the corresponding vertex of its reflection is perpendicular to the line of reflection
- discover that the line of reflection bisects a line connecting a vertex of a polygon and the corresponding vertex of its reflection
- discover that a shape and its reflection across a line are congruent
- be able to create a glide reflection of a shape
- discover that a shape and its glide reflection are congruent
- recognize that a glide reflection is a combination of a reflection and a translation.

Grouping for Instruction

- Whole class for launch and closure
- Small groups of four or five for the investigation

Overview of Lesson

Students use a Mira™ to investigate reflections and glide reflections. Students are guided to discover that these transformations are rigid transformations—a reflection or a glide reflection is congruent to the original shape. Students use measurement to discover properties of a shape and its reflection.

Background Information

Students should have been given time to play with a Mira™ prior to starting this lesson. Students need to know how to measure angles using a protractor and how to measure lengths fairly accurately using a ruler. They should be familiar with the concepts of perpendicular lines and the midpoint of a line segment.

Materials and Equipment

- A classroom set of Miras™
- A full-length mirror
- A classroom set of pattern blocks
- An overhead set of pattern blocks
- An overhead projector
- Blank paper
- Rulers
- Protractors
- Transparency of a picture of footprints in the sand

Procedure

A. Motivation and introduction

1. Have several students stand in front of the full-length mirror. "What do you notice about <Josh> and his reflection?"
2. Place a transparency with a line on the overhead. Place an overhead triangle pattern block on one side of the line. Ask a student to place a triangle pattern block showing in the position and orientation it would be if the triangle were "flipped" (reflected) over the line.
3. Ask the class if the student placed the triangle correctly. Ask respondents to explain the reasons for saying the student is or is not correct.
4. Show an overhead transparency of a picture of footprints in the sand. Ask a student to place the transparency with a line so the footprints are equally spaced on each side of the line.
5. Ask the students if the right footprint is a reflection of the left footprint. Get them to explain that it is not a reflection because it is not directly across the line from the left footprint. Explain that a glide reflection is a slide or translation followed by a reflection. Ask a student to show the slide/translation followed by a reflection.
6. Ask the students to look around the room. Is anyone wearing any clothing that includes a reflection or glide reflection? How about a translation?
7. Ask why reflections or glide reflections might be used in clothing.

B. Development (including discussion points and feedback)

1. Place the students in heterogeneous cooperative groups of about four students each.
2. Assign a task to each person in a team (leader, recorder, reporter etc.).
3. Distribute the worksheet "Pattern Blocks, Mira, and Reflections" (page 117).
4. Ask the teams to complete the "Pattern Blocks, Mira, and Reflections" project.
5. Circulate among the groups, guiding them to complete the project, and observing how students work.

C. Summary and closure

1. Ask each group to work together to summarize the concepts that they discussed today, what these concepts mean, and why they are important.
2. Have each group share one statement, and continue going around the room from group to group until all points are made.
3. Guide the discussion to include:
   - translation
   - reflection (flip)
   - line of reflection

- glide reflection
- image
- similar
- congruent.

D. Assignment

Ask each student to find a household item such as a tie or a quilt that shows a reflection or glide reflection. Have them draw a sketch of the pattern. Show the line of reflection on the sketch.

Assessment

Observe the students during the group project. Record how they are working in their group and whether the students can visualize a net from the solid and the solid from a net. You can either grade the group project, the presentations (if they are more formal than implied in the project), or the homework.

Worksheet: **Pattern Blocks, Mira™, and Reflections**

1. Draw a line down the center of a blank sheet of paper. Place the Mira™ on the line. Place a red trapezoid on one side of the Mira™. Using a pencil draw the perimeter of the trapezoid. Make sure the trapezoid stays in this spot as you draw its reflection. Looking through the Mira™ draw the perimeter of the reflection of the trapezoid. Remove the Mira™ and pattern block leaving the drawing of the original figure, the line of reflection, and the drawing of the figure's reflection. Label the original figure's vertices as shown below. Label the corresponding vertices on the reflection as A', B', C', and D'.

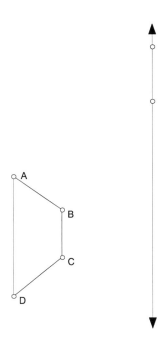

2. Draw the line segment AA' on your sheet. Using your protractor, measure the angle formed by the line of reflection and the line segment AA'. What did you discover?

3. Let A″ be the point of intersection of the line of reflection and the line segment AA'. Using your ruler, measure AA″ and A″A'. What did you discover about the lengths of these two segments?

4. Draw the line segment BB'. What is the angle formed by this line segment and the line of reflection?

5. Compare the length of BB' and the distance from B to the line of reflection. What did you discover?

6. Does the same pattern hold for CC'?   For DD'?

   State the pattern in your own words.

7. Are the reflection of the original trapezoid and the original trapezoid **similar** (the same shape)? How do you know?

8. Are the original trapezoid and the reflection of the original trapezoid **congruent** (the same shape and size)? How do you know?

9. On the same sheet of paper create a **glide reflection** (a slide parallel to the line of reflection followed by a flip across the line of reflection) of the original trapezoid by translating the original figure up 2 inches and then reflecting the trapezoid. Is this new figure similar to the original? Justify your answer.

10. Are the original figure and its glide reflection congruent? Justify your answer.

11. Label the vertices of the trapezoid formed by the glide reflection W, X, Y, and Z with W corresponding to A in the original trapezoid, X to B, etc. Draw the line segments AW, BX, CY, and DZ. Does the line of reflection bisect each line segment? How do you know?

12. The reflection of a shape is often called a "flip" of the shape. Why do you think a reflection is often called a flip?

13. The points A′, B′, C′, and D′ are called the **images** of the points A, B, C, and D, respectively. What will be true about a point F that is on the line of reflection and its image F′?

14. If a point G is 1 inch from the line of reflection, how far will its reflection be from the line of reflection?

Rep Tiles

Lesson Topic —   Grade —

Creating similar shapes using a single shape   3

Lesson Length

60 minutes

NCTM Standards Addressed

- Identify, compare, and analyze attributes of two- and three-dimensional shapes and develop vocabulary to describe the attributes.
- Investigate, describe, and reason about the results of subdividing, combining, and transforming shapes.
- Explore congruence and similarity.
- Make and test conjectures about geometric properties and relationships and develop logical arguments to justify conclusions.
- Predict and describe the results of sliding, flipping, and turning two-dimensional shapes.
- Build and draw geometric objects.
- Use geometric models to solve problems in other areas of mathematics, such as number and measurement.
- Understand such attributes as length, area, weight, volume, and size of angle and select the appropriate type of unit for measuring each attribute.
- Explore what happens to measurements of a two-dimensional shape such as its perimeter and area when the shape is changed in some way.

Sample State Standards Addressed

- Compare measurable characteristics of different objects on the same dimensions (e.g., time, temperature, area, length, weight, capacity, perimeter).
- Construct two- and three-dimensional shapes and figures using manipulatives, geoboards, and computer software.
- Determine the measurement of objects with non-standard and standard units (e.g., U.S. customary and metric).
- Use concrete objects to determine area and perimeter.
- Name and label geometric shapes in two and three dimensions (e.g., circle/sphere, square/cube, triangle/pyramid, rectangle/prism).
- Build geometric shapes using concrete objects (e.g., manipulatives). Predict how shapes can be changed by combining or dividing them.

Student Objectives

Students will:
- develop a deeper understanding of similarity
- review names of geometric figures
- make predictions about what happens to the perimeter of a shape when it is used to create a similar figure.

Grouping for Instruction

- Whole class for launch and closure
- Small groups of four to six for the investigation

Overview of Lesson

Students use pattern blocks of one shape at a time to try to create a similar shape. They then compare the perimeter of the new figure with the perimeter of the original shape and look for a pattern. The pattern is used to predict what will happen with other shapes.

Background Information

Students should have played with pattern blocks prior to starting this lesson. Students should be familiar with basic shapes and understand that the name of the shape remains the same even if the orientation changes. Students need to know how to find the perimeter of basic shapes. Familiarity with tilings of the plane would be beneficial. Students need some facility with a ruler.

Materials and Equipment

- Set of overhead pattern blocks
- A set of pattern blocks for each team
- A classroom set of rulers
- A classroom set of calculators

Procedure

A. Motivation and introduction

1. Use an overhead set of pattern blocks to show that four squares can be combined to create a new square that is similar to the original square. Explain: "Because the squares can be combined to create a similar square, we say the square is a 'rep tile' (for repeating tile). In fact, it is a rep-4 tile because it requires four squares to make a similar square."

2. Remind students that for two shapes to be similar, corresponding angles must be congruent (the same measure) and corresponding sides must be proportional. Ask: "Is this true for the original square and the larger square just formed? Explain."

3. Use six overhead squares to create a rectangle. Ask: "Is the larger shape similar to the original square? Why or why not?"

4. Ask: "Do you think other pattern blocks are rep tiles? How could you test your conjecture?"

5. Suggest that the students work on this problem in teams.

B. Development (including discussion points and feedback)

1. Place the students in heterogeneous cooperative groups.
2. Assign each student a task (leader, reporter, recorder, etc.).
3. Distribute the worksheet "Rep Tiles" (page 125).
4. Ask the teams to complete the investigation.
5. Circulate among the teams, guiding the students to complete the project.
6. Ask questions that will help students understand that they may have to rotate or flip the pattern blocks to make a similar shape.
7. Make sure each team compares the perimeters of the similar shapes.
8. Ask each team to report on one part of the investigation.
9. Ask questions to assess whether the students understand the concepts of perimeter and similarity, and the patterns discovered:
   - "If these shapes are similar, what must be true about the corresponding angles?"
   - "What does it mean for corresponding sides to be proportional?"
   - "How did you find the perimeter?"
   - "Justify your pattern. How do you know it always holds?"
10. Encourage the students to question whether each team has in fact found a rep tile, whether each team found a pattern that always holds.
11. Ask the students to predict the perimeter of a rep tile made from a rectangle that is one inch by three inches. Have a student show the rep tile on the overhead and measure the perimeter to determine if the conjecture is accurate.

C. Summary and closure

1. Ask students to write three mathematics concepts that they explored today (area, perimeter, similarity, rep tiles, etc.)
2. Have some students share what they wrote. Explore students' understanding. (Did they learn what you wanted them to learn?)
3. Ask students why they think these concepts are important.

D. Assignment

Give examples of polygons that are not convex (as are all of the pattern blocks). Ask the students to find a non-convex polygon that is a rep tile for homework. Students should show a picture of their non-convex rep tile and how its similar shape was formed.

Assessment

- Observe the students during the investigation.
- Use anecdotal note cards to record your observations.
- Use prompting questions to help students find similar shapes and to understand what it means for shapes to be similar.
- Grade the group project, giving each team a group grade.
- Grade the homework, if you give them a rubric first.

Worksheet:

Rep Tiles
A Geometry Project Using Pattern Blocks

A **rep tile** is a polygon with the property such that you can put several of them together to form a larger version of the same polygon. For example, a square is a rep tile. Look at your pattern blocks. We say the square is a rep-4 tile because you can put 4 squares together to get a larger square.

1. In the space below trace the square pattern block and the larger square.

2. The perimeter of the small square is 4. What is the perimeter of the large square?

3. Fill in the perimeter for the large square (rep tile) in the table on the next page.

4. Which of the other pattern blocks are rep-4 tiles? Complete the table below by recording the name of each pattern block that is a rep-4 tile, the perimeter of the pattern block, and the perimeter of the larger similar figure you created.

Pattern Block Name	Perimeter of Pattern Block	Perimeter of Rep Tile
Square	4	

5. Refer to the table above. Do you see a pattern between the perimeter of the original pattern block and the perimeter of the rep-4 tile formed using this pattern block? Describe the pattern using your own words.

6. Suppose the perimeter of a polygon is 12 centimeters. If four of these polygons form a similar polygon, what is the perimeter of the new, larger polygon?

    Perimeter:

7. There is a triangle that is a rep-2 tile. Can you find it? Use what you have learned to sketch the triangle and the similar triangle formed using two of the original triangles. Find the perimeters of the two triangles.

Rep Tiles

Lesson Topic ——————————— Grades ——————

Creating similar shapes using a single shape   4–5

Lesson Length

50–75 minutes

NCTM Standards Addressed

- Identify, compare, and analyze attributes of two- and three-dimensional shapes and develop vocabulary to describe the attributes.
- Investigate, describe, and reason about the results of subdividing, combining, and transforming shapes.
- Explore congruence and similarity.
- Make and test conjectures about geometric properties and relationships and develop logical arguments to justify conclusions.
- Predict and describe the results of sliding, flipping, and turning two-dimensional shapes.
- Build and draw geometric objects.
- Use geometric models to solve problems in other areas of mathematics, such as number and measurement.
- Understand such attributes as length, area, weight, volume, and size of angle and select the appropriate type of unit for measuring each attribute.
- Explore what happens to measurements of a two-dimensional shape such as its perimeter and area when the shape is changed in some way.

Sample State Standards Addressed

- Construct two- and three-dimensional shapes and figures using manipulatives, geoboards, and computer software.
- Describe the relationship between the perimeter and area of triangles, quadrilaterals, and circles.
- Identify properties of geometric figures (e.g., parallel, perpendicular, similar, congruent, symmetrical).

Student Objectives

Students will:
- develop a deeper understanding of similarity
- review names of geometric figures

- make predictions about what happens to the perimeter and area of a shape when it is used to create a similar figure.

Grouping for Instruction

- Whole class for launch and closure
- Small groups of four to six for the investigation

Overview of Lesson

Students use pattern blocks of one shape at a time to try to create a similar shape. They then compare the perimeter and area of the new figure with the perimeter and area of the original shape.

Background Information

Students should be familiar with basic shapes and understand that the name of the shape remains the same even if the orientation changes. Students should be familiar with the concept of similarity. Students should know how to find the perimeter and area of basic shapes. Familiarity with tilings of the plane would be beneficial. Students need some facility with a ruler.

Materials and Equipment

- Pattern blocks and rulers for each team
- Overhead projector
- Pattern blocks for the overhead projector

Procedure

A. Motivation and introduction

1. Use an overhead set of pattern blocks to show that four squares can be combined to create a new square that is similar to the original square. "Because the squares can be combined to create a similar square, we say the square is a 'rep tile' (for repeating tile). In fact, it is a rep-4 tile because it requires four squares to make a similar square."
2. Remind students that for two shapes to be similar, corresponding angles must be congruent (the same measure) and corresponding sides must be proportional. Ask: "Is this true for the original square and the larger square just formed? Explain."
3. Use six overhead squares to create a rectangle. Ask: "Is the larger shape similar to the original square? Why or why not?" "Is this new figure a rep tile?"
4. Ask: "Do you think other pattern blocks are rep tiles? How could you test your conjecture?"
5. Suggest that the students work on this problem in teams.

B. Development (including discussion points and feedback)

1. Place the students in heterogeneous cooperative groups.
2. Assign each student a task (leader, recorder, reporter, etc.).
3. Distribute the worksheet "Rep Tiles" (page 131).
4. Ask the groups to complete the "Rep Tile" investigation.
5. Circulate among the teams, guiding the students to complete the project, and observing how students work and understand the concepts.
6. Ask questions that will help students understand that they may have to rotate or flip the pattern blocks to make a similar shape.
7. Make sure each team compares the perimeters of the similar shapes.
8. Make sure each team compares the areas of the similar shapes.
9. Ask each team to report on one part of the investigation.
10. Ask questions to assess whether the students understand the concepts of perimeter, area, similarity, and the patterns discovered. Examples are:
    - "If these shapes are similar, what must be true about the corresponding angles?"
    - "What does it mean for corresponding sides to be proportional?"
    - "How did you find the perimeter? The area?"
    - "Justify your pattern. How do you know it always holds?"
11. Encourage the students to question whether each team has in fact found a rep tile, and ask for the patterns found.
12. Have students develop equations for each pattern. (For a rep-4 tile, the perimeter of the larger shape is twice the perimeter of the original shape.)

C. Summary and closure

1. Ask students to write three mathematics concepts that they did today (area, perimeter, similarity, rep tiles, etc.).
2. Have some students share what they wrote. Explore students' understanding. (Did they learn what you wanted them to learn?)
3. Ask students why they think these concepts are important.

D. Assignment

Give examples of polygons that are not convex (as are all of the pattern blocks). Ask students to find a non-convex polygon that is a rep tile for homework. Students should show a picture of their non-convex rep tile and how its similar shape was formed.

Assessment

- Observe the students during the investigation. Take notes on individual students' ability to approach this task and their understanding of the concepts.
- Grade the group project, giving each team a group grade.
- Grade the homework, if you give them a rubric first.

Worksheet:

Rep Tiles
A Geometry Project Using Pattern Blocks

A **rep tile** is a polygon that will tile the plane. For example, a square is a rep tile. We say the square is a rep-4 tile because it requires 4 congruent squares to form a similar figure—in this case a larger square.

Recall:

- Two polygons are **congruent** if the corresponding sides are the same length and the measures of corresponding interior angles are the same.
- Two polygons are **similar** if the corresponding sides are proportional—the ratios of corresponding sides equal a constant k—and corresponding interior angles have the same measure.

1. Trace a square pattern block in the space to the right.

2. Measure the sides to find the dimensions of the square.

3. What is the perimeter of the square?

4. What is the area of the square?

5. Fill in the perimeter and area of the square (columns 2 and 4) on the first row of the table on the next page.

6. Use four squares to create a larger square and trace the larger square in the area to the right.

7. Find the perimeter and area of the larger square.

8. Fill in the perimeter and areas of the rep tile (columns 3 and 5) on the first row of the table on the next page.

9. Explore to determine which of the other pattern blocks are rep-4 tiles. Complete the table on the next page by recording the name of each pattern block that is a rep-4 tile and the perimeters and areas of the original polygon and similar polygon.

Pattern Block Name	Perimeter of Pattern Block	Perimeter of Rep Tile	Area of Pattern Block	Area of Rep Tile
Square				

10. Refer to the table above. Look for a pattern between the perimeter of the original pattern block and the perimeter of the rep-4 tile formed using this pattern block. Describe the pattern using your own words.

11. Describe the pattern using an equation.

12. Refer to the table above. Look for a pattern between the area of the original pattern block and the area of the rep-4 tile formed using this pattern block. Describe the pattern using your own words.

13. Describe the pattern using an equation.

14. Suppose the perimeter of a polygon is 12 centimeters and its area is 10 square centimeters. If four of these polygons form a similar polygon, what is the perimeter and area of the new, larger polygon?

Perimeter:

Area:

15. Suppose it requires 9 copies of a polygon to form a similar polygon. What do you think would have to be true about the relationship between the **perimeter** of the original polygon and the perimeter of the larger, similar polygon made using 9 of the original polygon?

16. Suppose it requires 9 copies of a polygon to form a similar polygon. What do you think would have to be true about the relationship between the **area** of the original polygon and the area of the larger, similar polygon made using 9 of the original polygon?

17. Check your conjectures by using 9 squares to create a square and then measuring to find the perimeter and area.
    - Were you correct?
    - Do you want to revise your conjectures?
    - If you want to change your conjecture, what new conjecture would you make?

18. Notice that the perimeter of a similar shape requiring 4 polygons has a perimeter 2 times the perimeter of the original polygon and an area 4 times the area of the original polygon. Also, the perimeter of a similar shape requiring 9 polygons has a perimeter 3 times the perimeter of the original polygon and an area 9 times the area of the original polygon. Suppose it requires 16 polygons to make a similar shape. What must be true about the perimeter and area of the similar shape? Explain how you know this.

19. There is a triangle that is a rep-2 tile. What is it? Use what you have learned to sketch the triangle and the similar triangle formed using two of the original triangles. Find the area and perimeter of the two triangles.

20. Can you find a polygon that is a rep-3 tile? Show it and the similar polygon formed in the space below. Find the perimeter and area of each figure.

21. Can you find a rep-5 tile? Show it and the similar polygon constructed in the space below.

The Sum of the Interior Angles of a Polygon

Lesson Topic

Decomposing polygons into triangles to find a formula for the sum of the interior angles of a polygon with n sides.

Grades

4–5

Lesson Length

50–75 minutes

NCTM Standards Addressed

- Investigate, describe, and reason about the results of subdividing, combining, and transforming shapes.
- Make and test conjectures about geometric properties and relationships and develop logical arguments to justify conclusions.
- Use geometric models to solve problems in other areas of mathematics, such as number and measurement.
- Understand such attributes as length, area, weight, volume, and size of angle and select the appropriate type of unit for measuring each attribute.
- Explore what happens to measurements of a two-dimensional shape such as its perimeter and area when the shape is changed in some way.
- Recognize geometric ideas and relationships and apply them to other disciplines and to problems that arise in the classroom or in everyday life.

Sample State Standards Addressed

- Give formal definitions of geometric figures.
- Identify properties of geometric figures (e.g., parallel, perpendicular, similar, congruent, symmetrical).

Student Objectives

Students will:
- see how all polygons can be decomposed into triangles
- discover the sum of the measures of the interior angles of a triangle
- review names of geometric figures
- find a rule for determining the number of triangles that a polygon with n sides can be decomposed into by drawing diagonals from a single vertex

- find a rule for finding the sum of the measures of the interior angles of a polygon with *n* sides
- learn to use the Geometer's Sketchpad® to explore polygons and make and test conjectures.

Grouping for Instruction

- Whole class for launch and closure
- Small groups of four to six for the investigation

Overview of Lesson

Students use the Geometer's Sketchpad® software to create and dynamically manipulate triangles, measure interior angles, and find their sum. They then repeat the process for quadrilaterals and pentagons. Students make a conjecture and investigate this conjecture using paper and pencil. Students discover a relationship between the number of sides of a polygon and the number of triangles that the polygon can be decomposed into by drawing diagonals from a single vertex. They also discover a relationship between the number of triangles in the decomposition and the sum of the interior angles. Students find a formula for the sum of the interior angles of a polygon and use the formula to solve a problem.

Background Information

Students should be familiar with basic shapes and their definitions and properties. Students should know the meaning of the terms diagonal and vertex. Students should be familiar with the concept of a variable. Students must know how to use a mouse.

Materials and Equipment

- For each team
  - Blank paper
  - Rulers
  - Calculators
  - Computer with the Geometer's Sketchpad® software loaded on the computer
- Overhead projector for the computer

Procedure

A. Motivation and introduction

1. Introduce the students to the Geometer's Sketchpad®. Show them how to get on the computer and how to start Geometer's Sketchpad®.
2. Show students on the overhead projector how to draw and label points, undo a construction, and start a new sketch. Have them construct several points.

3. Use the overhead projector to show students how to select points and construct line segments. Have the students do this on their computers.
4. Show students how to select the vertices of an angle and use Geometer's Sketchpad® to measure the angle. Have the students do this on their computers.
5. Have the students create a triangle. Ask them to guess the sum of the interior angles of their triangles. Have them measure the three angles. Ask: "Will this (180°) be the sum for every triangle? How could you test this conjecture?"
6. Show students how to select a vertex of the triangle and drag the vertex to create other triangles. Have them do this with their triangle. Ask: "What is the sum of the interior angles of this new triangle? Does your conjecture seem to hold?"
7. Ask: "Do you think the sum of the interior angles will stay the same, increase, or decrease if you create a polygon with more sides?" "How could you determine if you are correct?"
8. Suggest that the students work on this problem in teams.

B. Development (including discussion points and feedback)

1. Place the students in heterogeneous cooperative groups of about four students.
2. Assign each student a task (leader, recorder, reporter, etc.).
3. Distribute the worksheet "The Sum of the Interior Angles of a Polygon" (page 139).
4. Ask the teams to complete the investigation.
5. Circulate among the teams, guiding the students to complete the project, and observing the participation of students in the groups and their understanding of the mathematics concepts.
6. Ask questions to ensure that students know how to round off the sum of the interior angles to a whole number of degrees.
7. Make sure each team knows how to drag a vertex and that they know why showing that the conjecture holds for many different polygons of the same type implies that the conjecture is true, but is not a proof.
8. Help teams to decompose polygons into triangles. Guide them to discover a pattern to the number of triangles.
9. Guide students to find a relationship between the number of triangles in a polygon and the sum of the interior angles of that polygon.
10. Guide students to discover a rule for determining the sum of the interior angles of a polygon based on the number of its sides.
11. Lead students to see that a 20-sided polygon must have 20 interior angles. Ask: "In a 20-sided polygon, if each angle has the same measure, what must be the measure of each one, given the total (sum) of all the interior angles?"
12. Ask each team to report on how to determine the sum of the interior angles of a particular polygon (quadrilateral, pentagon, etc.). Ask them to explain how they discovered the rule they are using. Encourage different approaches.

13. Ask questions to assess whether the students understand the concepts of vertex, decomposition, and making and testing conjectures.
    - "What makes a point on a polygon a vertex?"
    - "If I add a triangle to a polygon, is that a decomposition? Why or why not?"
    - "How did you come up with your conjecture?"
    - "What makes you think your conjecture is reasonable?"
14. Ask all students if they could understand the team presenting their conjecture. That is, make sure all students are comfortable expressing the patterns in words.
15. Show equations for each pattern for a polygon with n sides. [For a polygon with n sides the number of triangles T is $T = n - 2$. For a polygon that can be decomposed into T triangles, the sum S of the interior angles is $S = 180\,T$ degrees. The sum of the interior angles of a polygon with n sides is $S = 180\,(n - 2)$].

C. Summary and closure

1. Ask teams to discuss and agree upon two things that they learned (did) today.
2. Have teams report out and share what they learned. Guide responses to summarize the following:
    - The sum of the interior angles of a triangle is 180°.
    - Polygons can be decomposed into triangles.
    - Any given polygon may be decomposed into $n - 2$ triangles (where n is the number of sides of the polygon).
    - The sum(s) of the interior angles of a polygon of n sides is $S = 180\,(n - 2)$.
    - We learned how to navigate on the Geometer's Sketchpad®.

D. Assignment

Ask the students to determine the measure of each interior angle of a regular pentagon and a regular hexagon. If students are familiar with tilings of the plane, ask them, "Which of these regular polygons will tile the plane?" Ask them to justify their conclusions.

Assessment

- Observe the students during the investigation.
- Grade the group project, giving each team a group grade.
- Grade the homework, if you give them a rubric first.

Worksheet:

The Sum of the Interior Angles of a Polygon:
A Geometer's Sketchpad® Investigation

Start the Geometer's Sketchpad® program. Click on "File|New Sketch."

> **To create points:** Click on the "Draw Point" icon. Draw three points for the vertices of the triangle.
>
> **To select points:** Click on the Select or Translate arrow icon. Click on the first point. While holding down the shift key, click on the other points. All should now be highlighted, with a circle around each point.
>
> **To draw line segments:** Make sure the vertices were selected in the order you want the line segments drawn. Click on "Construct|Segment."
>
> Create a triangle using Geometer's Sketchpad®.

1. Measure each of the interior angles of the triangle you created.
   - Select the 3 vertices so the second vertex is at the angle you want to measure.
   - Click on "Measure|Angle."
   - Repeat this for the other 2 angles.

2. Find the sum of the measures of the interior angles. Round the answer to the nearest degree. What is the sum of the interior angles of the triangle?

3. Select a vertex of the triangle and hold down the mouse button while moving the mouse in order to drag the vertex to a new location. Find the sum of the interior angles for this new triangle, rounded to the nearest degree.

4. Repeat this several more times. What did you discover? What is always the sum of the interior angles of any triangle? Why can you feel comfortable making this assertion?

Click on "File|Close|Don't Save."

Sum of the Interior Angles of a Quadrilateral (4-sided, closed figure)

5. Using Geometer's Sketchpad®, draw 4 points in a clockwise direction for the 4 vertices of a quadrilateral. Select the 4 vertices in this order and construct the sides of the quadrilateral. Find the measure of each interior angle as shown above. Find the sum of the measures of the interior angles. Round the sum to the nearest degree.

6. Select a vertex of the quadrilateral and hold down the mouse button while moving the mouse in order to drag the vertex to a new location. Find the sum of the interior angles for this quadrilateral, rounded to the nearest degree.

    Repeat this several more times. What did you discover?

7. In turn, select different vertices and drag them to create new quadrilaterals. What is the sum of the interior angles for each of these new quadrilaterals?

8. What is always the sum of the interior angles of any quadrilateral? Why can you feel comfortable making this assertion?

Click on "File|Close|Don't Save."

Sum of the Interior Angles of a Pentagon (5-sided, closed figure)

9. Create a pentagon. Find the measures of each of the 5 interior angles. Find the sum of these measures, rounded to the nearest degree. What is the sum?

10. Select and drag a vertex of the pentagon to create a new pentagon. What is the sum of the interior angles for this pentagon?

    Repeat this several times. What is the sum of the interior angles for any pentagon? Why can you feel comfortable making this assertion?

11. Look at the sum of the interior angles for a triangle, a quadrilateral, and a pentagon. Do you see a pattern to these sums? Describe the pattern.

12. Use the pattern to predict the sum of the interior angles of a hexagon (6-sided, closed figure).

13. Draw a hexagon and find the sum of the interior angles. Was your conjecture correct?

Click on "File|Close|Don't Save."

A More Formal Justification of Our Findings

We will attempt to find a rule for finding the sum of the interior angles of a polygon with a certain number of sides. Refer to the polygons in the table below. Notice that each polygon can be divided into triangles by drawing straight lines from a single vertex to other vertices. Recall that the sum of the interior angles of a triangle is 180°.

14. Complete the table below. Draw additional figures as needed.

# sides (*n*)	# triangles	sum of the interior angles
3	1	180°
4	2	360°
5		
6		
7		

15. Describe in your own words the pattern between the number of triangles that can be formed in this way and the number of sides of the original polygon.

16. If a polygon has 9 sides, how many triangles can be formed in this manner?

17. Describe in your own words the pattern between the number of triangles and the sum of the interior angles. That is, what must you do to the number of triangles in the convex polygon to obtain the sum of the interior angles in each instance?

18. If a polygon has 9 sides, what will be the sum of its interior angles?

19. Describe in your own words how you found the sum of the interior angles for a convex polygon with 9 sides.

20. Use the pattern you just found to find the sum of the interior angles of a 20-sided polygon.

21. What is the measure of each interior angle of a regular 20-sided polygon? (A **regular polygon** is a polygon with all sides **congruent** [same length] and all interior angles **congruent** [same measure]).

Explain how you found this answer.

Tiling the Plane

Lesson Topic

Tiling the plane with pattern blocks

Grades

2–3

Lesson Length

30 minutes

NCTM Standards Addressed

- Recognize, name, build, draw, compare, and sort two- and three-dimensional shapes.
- Investigate and predict the results of putting together and taking apart two- and three-dimensional shapes.

Sample State Standards Addressed

- Name and label geometric shapes in two and three dimensions (e.g., circle/sphere, square/cube, triangle/pyramid, rectangle/prism).
- Build geometric shapes using concrete objects (e.g., manipulatives).
- Draw two- and three-dimensional geometric shapes and construct rectangles, squares, and triangles on the geoboard and on graph paper satisfying specific criteria.

Student Objectives

Students will:
- develop a deeper understanding of tessellations (tiling the plane)
- review names of geometric figures.

Grouping for Instruction

- Whole class for launch and closure
- Small groups of four to six for the investigation

Overview of Lesson

Students use pattern blocks and triangular grid paper to review shape names, be introduced to the concept of a tiling of the plane, and determine which pattern blocks will tile the plane.

Background Information

Students should be familiar with basic shapes and understand that the name of a shape remains the same even if its orientation changes.

Materials and Equipment

- Pattern blocks for each team
- Pattern blocks for the overhead projector
- Triangular grid paper for each student
- Triangular grid paper for the overhead projector
- Overhead projector

Procedure

A. Motivation and introduction

1. Ask students: "Have you ever seen a floor or a wall where the blocks are in a pattern? Where?"
2. Use an overhead set of pattern blocks to show that the equilateral triangle will cover the overhead screen with no overlapping and no spaces between the triangles.
3. State that this is an example of a tessellation—a tiling of the plane.
4. Show an overhead transparency in which regular pentagons only partially cover the screen (there are gaps between the pentagons). Ask: "Is this a tiling of the plane? Why or why not?"
5. Show an attempt at a tiling in which the polygons overlap. "Is this a tiling of the plane? Why or why not?"
6. Show the students a copy of the triangular grid paper on the overhead projector. Show how to place the triangle and the trapezoid on the paper and "line up" the sides with the sides of the triangles on the grid paper.
7. Ask: "The triangle tessellates or tiles the plane. Do you think other pattern blocks will tile the plane? How could you test your conjecture?"
8. Suggest that the students work on this problem in teams.

B. Development (including discussion points and feedback)

1. Place the students in heterogeneous cooperative groups of about four students.
2. Assign each student a task (leader, recorder, reporter, materials person, etc.).
3. Have the materials persons for each group come up and get for their group the pattern blocks, the triangular grid paper, and the investigation worksheet: "Pattern Blocks, Triangle Grid Paper, and Tilings" (page 148).
4. Ask the teams to complete the investigation.
5. Circulate among the teams, guiding the students to complete the project.
6. Ask questions that will help students understand that they may have to rotate or flip the pattern blocks to make them tile the plane.

7. Ask each team to report on one pattern block that tiles the plane and show a sample of the tiling.
8. Ask questions to assess whether the students understand what a tiling is.
   - "Do you agree that this is a tiling?" (EPR: thumbs up to show agreement, thumbs down to show disagreement)
   - "Why is this a tiling?" or "Why is it <u>not</u> a tiling?"
   - "If the pieces overlap, is it still a tiling?"
9. Encourage the students to comment on the reports and to question whether each team has in fact found a tiling.
10. Have the materials person collect all materials.

C. Summary and closure

1. Ask groups to collaborate to write:
   - One sentence on what we learned (did) today.
   - Two places where tessellations (tilings) may be seen in nature or used in a real-life situation.
2. Have groups share their responses and build on their responses to summarize the following:
   - A tessellation or tiling of a plane occurs when a figure is able to cover a plane completely with no gaps and no overlaps.
   - Tessellations are found in nature and in real-life in a honeycomb, patterns in floors, walls, buildings, works of art, etc.

D. Assignment

Give examples of polygons that are not convex (as are all of the pattern blocks). Ask the students to create a non-convex polygon that will tile the plane for homework. Students should color in a sheet of triangular grid paper to show the polygon they used. (That is, they will have to use different colors for adjacent polygons.)

Assessment

- Observe the students during the investigation.
- Grade the group project, giving each team a group grade.
- Grade the homework, if you give them a rubric first.

Worksheet: **Pattern Blocks, Triangle Grid Paper, and Tilings**

1. Refer to the triangle grid paper provided. This paper shows one way that the green equilateral triangle pattern block could be used to **tile the plane** (completely cover an infinite plane with one or more figures). Using the triangle grid paper and the pattern blocks, show how you could tile the plane with the blue **rhombus** (a 4-sided figure with all sides the same length). Use different colors to show the tiling.

2. Using the triangle grid paper and the pattern blocks, show how you could tile the plane with the **regular hexagon** (a 6-sided figure with all sides the same length and all interior angles the same measure) pattern block. Use different colors to show the tiling.

3. Using the triangle grid paper and the pattern blocks, show how you could tile the plane with the **trapezoid** (a 4-sided figure in which two opposite sides are parallel and the other pair of opposite sides are not parallel) pattern block. Use different colors to show the tiling.

4. Using the triangle grid paper and the pattern blocks, show how you could tile the plane using two different pattern blocks. Show your tiling using different colors.

5. Can you tile the plane with a different pattern block? Convince me you are correct.

Tiling the Plane

Lesson Topic

Tiling the plane with pattern blocks

Grade

5

Lesson Length

50 minutes

NCTM Standards Addressed

- Recognize, name, build, draw, compare, and sort two- and three-dimensional shapes.
- Investigate and predict the results of putting together and taking apart two- and three-dimensional shapes.
- Predict and describe the results of sliding, flipping, and turning two-dimensional shapes.
- Select and apply appropriate standard units and tools to measure length, area, volume, weight, time, temperature, and the size of angles.

Sample State Standards Addressed

- Give formal definitions of geometric figures. Construct two- and three-dimensional shapes and figures using manipulatives, geoboards, and computer software.
- Create an original tessellation.
- Represent and use the concepts of line, point, and plane.
- Analyze simple transformations of geometric figures and rotations of line segments.

Student Objectives

Students will:
- develop a deeper understanding of tessellations (tiling the plane)
- review names of geometric figures.

Grouping for Instruction

- Whole class for launch and closure
- Small groups of four to five for the investigation

Overview of Lesson

In this lesson students will use pattern blocks and triangular grid paper to review shape names, be introduced to the concept of a tiling of the plane, and determine which pattern blocks will tile the plane. This information will be used to determine the measures of the interior angles of the regular pattern blocks that will tile the plane.

Background Information

Students should have had an opportunity to play with pattern blocks prior to starting this lesson. Students should be familiar with basic shapes and understand that the name of a shape remains the same even if its orientation changes. Students may or may not be familiar with the word "tessellation" or the concept of tiling.

Materials and Equipment

- A set of overhead pattern blocks
- A classroom set of pattern blocks
- Several sheets of triangular grid paper per student
- Triangular grid paper for the overhead projector
- Overhead projector
- Examples of M.C. Escher's art that use tessellations.

Procedure

A. Motivation and introduction

1. Ask students if they know what a tessellation is. Same for a tiling. Ask where they might have seen a tessellation or tiling.
2. Use an overhead set of pattern blocks to show that the equilateral triangle will cover the overhead screen with no overlapping and no spaces between the triangles.
3. State that (or ask if) this is an example of a tessellation—a tiling of the plane.
4. Show an overhead transparency in which regular pentagons only partially cover the screen (there are gaps between the pentagons). Ask: "Is this a tiling of the plane? Why or why not?"
5. Show an attempt at a tiling in which the polygons overlap. Ask: "Is this a tiling of the plane? Why or why not?"
6. Show the students a copy of the triangular grid paper on the overhead. Show how the triangle and the trapezoid can be placed on the paper and have the sides "line up" with sides of the triangles on the grid paper.
7. State: "The triangle tessellates or tiles the plane. Do you think other pattern blocks will tile the plane? How could you test your conjecture?"
8. Suggest that the students work on this problem in teams.

B. Development (including discussion points and feedback)

1. Place the students in heterogeneous cooperative groups of about four students.
2. Assign each student a task (leader, recorder, reporter, materials person, etc.).
3. Have the materials persons for each group come up and get for their group the pattern blocks, the triangular grid paper, and the investigation worksheet: "Pattern Blocks, Triangle Grid Paper, and Tilings" (page 153).
4. Ask the teams to complete the investigation.
5. Circulate among the teams, guiding the students to complete the project, and observing the groups' approaches and individual students' participation and understanding of the process and concepts.
6. Ask questions that will help students understand that they may have to rotate or flip the pattern blocks to make them tile the plane.
7. Ask each team to report on one pattern block that tessellates the plane, and show a sample of a tessellation.
8. Ask questions to assess whether the students understand what a tessellation is.
   - "Do you agree that this is a tessellation?" (EPR: thumbs up to show agreement, thumbs down to show disagreement.)
   - "Why is this a tessellation?"
   - "If the pieces overlap, is it still a tessellation?"
9. Encourage the students to question whether each team has in fact found a tiling.
10. Show examples of some of the tilings of M. C. Escher on the overhead projector, if possible. Ask the students if they can recognize which shape Escher used with each tiling and how he used that shape.
11. Ask the students if Escher used rotations or flips in creating the tiling.
12. Tell students that they should try this. Perhaps one day they might be an artist like M.C. Escher and design tessellations.

C. Summary and closure

1. Ask groups to collaborate to write:
   - One sentence on what we learned (did) today.
   - Two places where tessellations (tilings) may be seen in nature or used in a real-life situation.
2. Have groups share their responses and build on their responses to summarize the following:
   - A tessellation or tiling of a plane occurs when a figure is able to cover a plane completely with no gaps and no overlaps.
   - Tessellations are found in nature and in real life in a honeycomb, patterns in floors, walls, buildings, works of art, etc.

D. Assignment

Give examples of polygons that are not convex (as are all of the pattern blocks). Ask the students to create a non-convex polygon that will tile the plane for homework. Students should be encouraged to create a picture using their tiling using M. C. Escher as an inspiration. Have the class develop a rubric for assessing the assignment.

Assessment

- Observe the students during the investigation using a checklist to note what students know and any areas that need to be addressed again.
- Grade the group project, giving each team a group grade.
- Have students assess the tilings they created for homework using a rubric the class developed.
- Give students practice in assessing their own work using the rubric.

Worksheet:

Pattern Blocks, Triangle Grid Paper, and Tessellations

1. Refer to the triangle grid paper provided. This paper shows one way that the green equilateral triangle pattern block could be used to **tessellate (tile) the plane** (completely cover an infinite plane with one or more figures). Using the triangle grid paper and the pattern blocks, show how you could tessellate the plane with the blue **rhombus** (a 4-sided figure with all sides the same length). Use different colors to show the tessellation.

2. Using the triangle grid paper and the pattern blocks, show how you could tessellate the plane with the **regular hexagon** (a 6-sided figure with all sides the same length and all interior angles the same measure) pattern block. Use different colors to show the tessellation.

3. Using the triangle grid paper and the pattern blocks, show how you could tessellate the plane with the **trapezoid** (a 4-sided figure in which two opposite sides are parallel and the other pair of opposite sides are not parallel) pattern block. Use different colors to show the tessellation.

4. Using the triangle grid paper and the pattern blocks, show how you could tessellate the plane using two different pattern blocks. Show your tessellation using different colors.

5. Can you tessellate the plane with a different pattern block? Convince me you are correct.

6. How many equilateral triangles meet at a point when they are used to tile the plane?
    Since the total of all the angles around the point is 360 degrees, what must be the measure of one angle of the equilateral triangle?

7. What is the measure of each angle of the regular hexagon? How do you know?

Traveling around Our Town

Lesson Topic   Grades

Tracing a path on a grid from one location to another   1–2

Lesson Length

30 minutes

NCTM Standards Addressed

- Describe, name, and interpret relative positions in space.
- Describe, name, and interpret direction and distance in navigating space and apply ideas about direction and distance.
- Find and name locations with simple relationships such as "near to" and in coordinate systems such as maps.

Sample State Standards Addressed

There are generally no mathematics standards listed for these grade levels.

Student Objectives

Students will:
- specify locations on a grid
- use words such as right, left, up, and down to describe locations on a grid
- identify and describe paths from one location on a grid to another.

Grouping for Instruction

- Whole class and partners for motivation and introduction and for summary and closure
- Small groups for creating the grids and identifying paths

Overview of Lesson

Students learn to specify locations on a grid by using the words *right*, *left*, *up*, and *down*. They also find and describe different paths from one location to another.

Background Information

Students should be familiar with the words *up*, *down*, *right*, and *left*.

Materials and Equipment

- Square grid paper (one-inch)
- Small stickers with pictures of houses or other types of buildings
- Colored pencils for students to draw houses if stickers are not available
- Square grid paper for the overhead projector
- Overhead projector
- Grid paper of Our Town (page 158)

Procedure

A. Motivation and introduction

1. Ask each student to describe to a partner how he or she walks to school or the bus stop.
2. On an overhead projector show one-inch grid paper or hang large grid paper on a bulletin board. At an intersection of two lines on the grid paper, show a house and then ask one student to describe how he or she walked to school (or the bus stop) and then place a picture of a school (or the bus stop) at the intersection of two lines.
3. Identify and practice the directional words that students use such as up, down, right, left, or across. List all of these words on the chalkboard. Suggest these words to the students to help them describe their walks if necessary.

B. Development (including discussion points and feedback)

1. Divide the class into heterogeneous groups of three to four students. Distribute a piece of one-inch grid paper and four stickers to each group. Instruct students to place stickers of different buildings at the intersections of lines on the grid to create their "town." (Make sure that they understand that the intersection is the place where two lines cross each other. Illustrate this.)
2. Tell student groups to describe how to travel from one location to another. Each student should write down a description for three different trips on the grid (traveling to and from different buildings or structures). Students should share what they have written with the other members of their group.
3. On the grid paper on the overhead projector, the teacher should show the "town" of one group. Select two buildings and ask students to find as many different paths as they can to travel from one building to another. Use colored pens to show the different paths on the overhead grid paper.
4. Have each group select two buildings in its town and find as many different paths as possible.

5. Have each group show its town to the class.
6. Ask students to share the words that they used to describe how they moved from one location to another. Again, list these words for the students to see (left, right, up, down).

C. Summary and closure

1. Ask students to talk with a partner and write down three things they learned (did) today.
2. Ask several students to share their responses, and build on their responses to include:
   - Used directional terms: up, down, left, right
   - Located buildings on grid
   - Identified and described paths to go from one house to another.
3. Ask students why it would be important for them to know this.

D. Assignment

Give students the worksheet "Our Town" (page 158). Tell students to write out directions for traveling from school to the city. Tell students to find as many possible paths as they can from the church to the school.

Assessment

- Observe the students during the activity to make sure they are using the directional/positional terms correctly.
- Check homework to determine whether each individual child understands the terms and can trace paths from one location to another.

Worksheet:　　　　**Our Town**

1. Write out the directions for traveling from school to the city.

2. Find and trace as many paths as you can from the church to the school.

Visualizing Multiplication

Lesson Topic

Area model for multiplication

Grades

3–5

Lesson Length

50 minutes

NCTM Standards Addressed

- Identify, compare, and analyze attributes of two- and three-dimensional shapes and develop vocabulary to describe the attributes.
- Investigate, describe, and reason about the results of subdividing, combining, and transforming shapes.
- Make and test conjectures about geometric properties and relationships and develop logical arguments to justify conclusions.
- Build and draw geometric objects.
- Understand such attributes as length, area, weight, volume, and size of angle and select the appropriate type of unit for measuring each attribute.
- Describe location and movement using common language and geometric vocabulary.
- Make and use coordinate systems to specify locations and to describe paths.
- Use geometric models to solve problems in other areas of mathematics, such as number and measurement.
- Recognize geometric ideas and relationships and apply them to other disciplines and to problems that arise in the classroom or in everyday life.

Sample State Standards Addressed

- Select and use appropriate instruments and units for measuring quantities (e.g., perimeter, volume, area, weight, time, temperature).
- Develop formulas and procedures for determining measurements (e.g., area, volume, distance).
- Construct two- and three-dimensional shapes and figures using manipulatives, geoboards, and computer software.

Student Objectives

Students will:
- represent multiplication of a two-digit number by a two-digit number as the area of a rectangle with dimensions of the two factors

- find patterns for the number of different base ten blocks in a rectangle representing a product
- use the patterns to find such products mentally.

Grouping for Instruction

- Whole group for launch and closure
- Small groups for the investigation of transformations

Overview of Lesson

Students use base ten blocks to represent whole numbers. For example, 123 can be represented by one flat (one hundred), two longs (two tens) and three units (three ones). Remind the students that one interpretation of multiplication is the area model. Show students how to measure a length and width of a rectangle that correspond to the two factors of a product of two two-digit numbers. They then determine which base ten blocks will fill in the corresponding rectangle. They use the values of the blocks to determine the product. Students record the results of several products done in this manner in a table and look for patterns. The students then use the patterns to find several products mentally.

Background Information

Students should have used base ten blocks to represent numbers prior to this investigation and be familiar with the names for the different blocks. They should feel comfortable using a ruler to measure in centimeters. They should be able to draw perpendicular lines. Students need to have a solid understanding of place value up to hundreds.

Materials and Equipment

- Overhead projector and transparencies
- Overhead base ten blocks
- A classroom set of base ten blocks
- Rulers
- Calculators

Procedure

A. Motivation and introduction

1. Tell students: "You are familiar with multiplying one-digit numbers such as five times six. Today we are going to look at multiplying a two-digit number by a two-digit number."
2. State: "Recall that the product of five and six can be interpreted as the area of a rectangle with dimensions five and six." Illustrate this on the overhead projector.

3. Ask: "How could we use the area model to find the product (13)(34)?"
   (Take some students' suggestions.)
4. Say: "If we represent 13 using base ten blocks it would be one long and three units. If you create a train with a long and 3 units, how long is the train?" Illustrate this on the overhead projector.
5. Ask: "How would you represent 34 using base ten blocks?" (Wait for responses.)
   "If you create a train with these base ten blocks, how long is the train?"
6. Put a transparency on the overhead that has a rectangle 13 centimeters by 34 centimeters. "The rectangle on this transparency is 13 centimeters by 34 centimeters. Notice that three flats fit in the area of this rectangle." Ask:
   • "What is the value of three flats?" (Wait for responses.)
   • "How many longs will fit in the remaining area?"
   • "Can I trade in some longs for a flat? How many do I need?"
   • "What is the total value of the flats and longs?"
   • "How many units will fit in the remaining area?"
7. Ask: "What is the value of all the base ten blocks needed to cover the area of the rectangle? That is, what is the product of 13 and 34?"
8. Ask: "Do you think there are patterns when multiplying a two-digit number by a two-digit number? Let's find out."

B. Development (including discussion points and feedback)

1. Place the students in heterogeneous cooperative groups of about four students each.
2. Assign a task to each person in a team (leader, recorder, reporter, materials coordinator).
3. Ask the teams to complete the worksheet, "Multiplication Using Base Ten Blocks" (page 163).
4. Circulate among the groups, guiding them to complete the project and observing student interaction and understanding.
5. Have each team report to the class what they learned from the lesson.

C. Summary and closure

1. Ask students to write two statements in their math journal about what they learned today.
2. Have several students share and build on other students' responses.
   Guide students to observe the following:
   • used base ten blocks to show the multiplication of a two-digit number by a two-digit number
   • showed multiplication as the area of a rectangle
   • found patterns for determining the number of squares in a rectangle representing a product.

3. State: "Consider the product of 25 and 32. If you create a rectangle to represent this product, what dimensions should you use?"

    - "When you create this rectangle, how many flats will fit inside the rectangle? How do you know?"
    - "How many vertical longs will fit inside the remaining area of the rectangle formed? How do you know?"
    - "How many horizontal longs will fit inside the remaining area of the rectangle formed? How did you determine this?"
    - How many units will fit inside the remaining area of the rectangle formed? How can you find this number from the original product?
    - Can someone explain why these patterns hold?

D. Assignment

Ask someone in your house to give you an example of a problem where you would have to multiply two two-digit numbers to solve the problem. Use what you learned in this lesson to find the product mentally. Check your answer with a calculator.

Assessment

- Observe the students during the group work.
- Use a checklist to record any students who do not have the necessary background, so this can be rectified.
- Give each team a group grade on the project.
- Ask the students to explain in their mathematics journal what they learned during the lesson and any concepts that are still unclear.
- Ask students to explain how they could use the area of a rectangle to find the product of six and thirty-five.

Worksheet:

Multiplication Using Base Ten Blocks:
Using Geometry to Visualize Multiplication

Example: We can represent the product of 13 and 34 as shown below. We can use trading to get the correct final answer. The procedure is as follows.

34 cm

13 cm

1. Measure 13 centimeters vertically. (The length of the rectangle equals the first factor.)
2. Measure 34 centimeters horizontally starting at the top of the vertical line. (The width of the rectangle equals the second factor.)
3. Use as few base ten blocks as possible to fill in the rectangle.
4. The sum of the values of these base ten blocks is the desired product.

1. Use this technique to find the following products. Fill in the following table for each product.

Problem	# Flats	# Vertical Longs	# Horizontal Longs	# Units	Product
13 x 34	3	4	9	12	442
12 x 23					
31 x 25					
16 x 13					

2. Refer to the table. How could you find the number of flats in the rectangle from the original problem?

3. Refer to the table. How could you find the number of vertical longs in the rectangle from the original problem?

4. Refer to the table. How could you find the number of horizontal longs in the rectangle from the original problem?

5. Refer to the table. How could you find the number of units in the rectangle from the original problem?

Exercise: Use the pattern you just discovered to find the following products mentally.

6. 31 x 22

7. 41 x 12

8. 52 x 45

9. 28 x 36

10. Why does this work?

Assessment

Chapter 5

Assessment should enhance mathematics learning and support good instructional practice.

*—Measuring What Counts: A Conceptual Guide
for Mathematics Assessment* [1]

More than giving grades and ranking students, assessment is the gathering of evidence—about a student's knowledge of, ability to use, and disposition towards a subject—and then making inferences from this evidence. A teacher can use assessment as a tool to make instructional decisions, to support and enhance students' learning, and to answer the question: "How do I know what my students know?" The best instruments for assessment also increase students' knowledge and understanding.

Teachers need to strive to make assessment an ongoing, daily aspect of the teaching process, rather than an occasional interruption. Assessment should be appropriate to the conceptual levels/objectives of the lesson and be aligned with standards and with the instruction itself. For example, if students use manipulatives during instruction, then they should use them during the assessment as well.

Building an accurate picture of student performance in the classroom requires integrating a number of different ways to assess students' performance:

- **Formative** assessments help the teacher understand what the students know, do not know, and might need in terms of instruction. Ideally, these assessments are going on all the time as the teacher uses the feedback to enable students to learn better.
- **Summative** assessments, such as graded work, attempt to measure the quality of students' performance or to summarize student learning at some point in the course of a class.
- Assessments should be both **formal** (planned in advance with specific goals in mind) and **informal** (recording observations in the course of regular teaching).
- Assessments can be done **before**, **during**, and/or **after** a lesson.

---

[1] National Academy Press, *Measuring What Counts: A Conceptual Guide for Mathematics Assessment* (Washington, D.C.: National Academy Press, 1993), p. 6

Assessment standards are criteria for judging the quality of assessment practices. These embody a vision of assessment that is consistent with the curriculum and teaching standards derived from shared principles of mathematics, cognition, and learning.[2]

This section addresses the following assessment techniques and gives examples for how they are best represented in geometry and measurement:[3]

- Observation
- Questioning
- Interviewing
- Performance Tasks
- Self-Assessment and Peer Assessment
- Work Samples
- Portfolios
- Writings
- Teacher-Designed Written Tests
- Achievement Tests

Assessment terms that appear in this section in bold are also compiled in Appendix C.

---

[2] National Council of Teachers of Mathematics, *Assessment Standards for School Mathematics* (Reston, Va.: National Council of Teachers of Mathematics, 1995), p. 87.

[3] These 10 assessment techniques are also discussed in Robert Reys et al., *Helping Children Learn Mathematics*, 6th ed. (New York: John Wiley & Sons, 2001), pp. 53–67.

Observation

Observation is a direct means for learning about students, including what they do or do not know and can or cannot do. This information makes it possible for the teacher to plan ways to encourage students' strengths and to work on their weaknesses.

Observation is most effective when it follows a systematic plan. This might involve, for instance, seeing and recording which students use physical materials, which do most of the problems mentally, which use thinking strategies, and which rely on memorized facts.[4] It may be helpful at times to focus on observing one student within the context of a group setting.

Observation tools are instruments and techniques that help teachers to record useful data about students' learning in a systematic way. Some observation tools include:

Anecdotal notes: Short notes written during a lesson, as students either work in groups or individually, or after a lesson.

Anecdotal notebook: A notebook where a teacher records his or her observations. An index on the side, organized by either student name or behavior, is helpful.

Anecdotal note cards: An alternative system to an anecdotal notebook, in which the teacher records observations using one card per child. One way to facilitate this process is to select five children per day for observation. The cards can be kept together on a ring.

Labels/adhesive notes: Like note cards, the use of these small adhesive notes frees the teacher from having to carry a notebook around the classroom. After the observation is complete, the teacher can adhere the notes into his or her filing system.

> *Sample observations*
>
> A checklist of possible behaviors to observe in students:
>
> ___ names/identifies two-dimensional shapes
> ___ sorts two-dimensional shapes using attributes
> ___ identifies two-dimensional shapes in nature
> ___ uses correct terminology to describe two-dimensional shapes
> ___ uses concrete objects to join two shapes to make a new shape
> ___ can use attributes to create shapes on a geoboard

---

[4] Reys et al., *Helping Children Learn Mathematics*, p. 54.

Questioning

Questioning is a way of teaching that
actively invites students to convey what they
are thinking. Good questions, prepared
before a lesson, will help a teacher determine
whether students use varied approaches to a
problem and how well students can explain
their own thinking. This process
complements observation.

Another important aspect of questioning is
waiting for students to respond. While the
average time teachers wait for responses is
less than three seconds, teachers should allow
for more time for students to think through
their responses.

Think-alouds are a teaching/assessment strategy in which one verbalizes his
or her thought process. A teacher should incorporate this into the daily practice
of teaching, modeling it first, and then encouraging students to try it as well.
Think-alouds can be especially helpful in revealing how a student arrived at
a particular answer.

Probing questions are a teaching/assessment strategy that provides insight
into the mental processes a student is using by engaging him or her in
conversation about the subject. The goal of the questions is to deepen the
student's understanding of the content.

> ### *Sample probing questions*
>
> - How did you know that?
> - What strategy did you use?
> - Does that remind you of another problem we solved?
> - Can you show us how you did that?
> - Is there another explanation?
> - Can that be done another way?
> - What if I changed [some element of problem]?

Prompting questions are a process by which a teacher supports a student by giving hints that point the student toward appropriate strategies to use to solve a problem or to clarify his or her response. Prompting questions go far beyond simply making statements to students in the form of a question. It is important that teachers not "funnel," by either answering the question themselves or changing the question to one that requires little thought to respond.

Sample prompting questions

- Remember when we did [a past problem]?
- How would you begin this problem?
- What do you think this relates to?
- What are you thinking about this problem?

It is important that a teacher directs questions to all students in a classroom. Research has indicated that teachers often pose more challenging questions to male students[5] and then allow more wait time when they ask more difficult questions of male students.[6] While male students have been shown to benefit from this increased interaction with teachers, female and minority students suffer in terms of confidence and achievement.[7]

Interviewing

Interviewing is an interaction in which a teacher presents a student with a planned sequence of questions and listens for answers. These exchanges can be a rich source of information about how the child is constructing concepts or using procedures, and they give the teacher direction for modifying instruction.

Interviewing is also beneficial when done student-to-student or within a group of students. The teacher should assign one student the role of interviewer, one the role of interviewee, and any others the role of observers. In student-student interviews, the teacher needs to provide leading

---

[5] Jeremy Kilpatrick et al., *Adding It Up: Helping Children Learn Mathematics* (Washington, D.C.: National Academy Press, 2001), p. 343.

[6] Gila C. Leder, "Mathematics and Gender: Changing Perspectives," in *Handbook of Research on Mathematics Teaching and Learning*, ed. Douglas A. Grouws (New York: Macmillan, 1992), p. 611.

[7] Leder, "Mathematics and Gender," p. 611; Myra Sadker and David Sadker, *Failing at Fairness: How America's Schools Cheat Girls* (New York: Charles Scribner's Sons, 1994), pp. 57–58.

questions and guidelines for interviews, including what to look for. The teacher can also play the role of observer, using observation strategies to gain insight into students' understanding.

> ### Sample interview [8]
> (grades 3–5)
>
> Display a collection of either two- or three-dimensional shapes. Select one shape that has something in common with more than one shape in the collection. Ask the student to select a shape that is like your shape in some way and to explain the choice. Observe whether or not the student uses visual cues or is able to use attributes. Ask the student to select another shape that is like your shape in some way and to justify that choice.

Performance Tasks

Performance tasks are open-ended, multi-step problems that require students to apply information, understanding, and previous knowledge to create their own learning activity. These tasks should be designed carefully, both to engage students' intellect and to incorporate sound and significant mathematics. Ideally, performance tasks offer students time to investigate and grapple with a problem and to devise their own responses and explanations for how they arrived at an answer. It may be helpful to start with

simpler tasks and work up to longer, more complex ones. Assigning students to work on performance tasks in pairs or groups of four will enrich the teacher's observations and notes about strategy, results, and attitude.

Teachers often evaluate performance tasks using a **rubric**, which is a hierarchy of performance standards and expectations. Whether task-specific or general, the rubric makes it possible to determine a student's score based on overall performance on a task, as opposed to simply the number of correct or incorrect items. A sample rubric could

---

[8] This sample is based on an activity in John A. Van de Walle, *Elementary and Middle School Mathematics: Teaching Developmentally*, 3rd ed. (New York: Addison Wesley Longman, 1998), p. 350.

consist of a scale of three to six points that are used to rate performance. Rubrics can be shared with students to help to engage and empower them in the learning process.

Sample performance task
(grades 4–5)

Materials:
Pattern blocks, paper, and colored pencils or crayons

Directions:
1. If the area of the green triangle is one square unit, find the area of the blue rhombus, the red trapezoid, and the yellow hexagon.
2. Use your pattern blocks to create two different designs with an area that is exactly 15 square units. Draw your patterns on the paper provided.
3. Write three observations about each of your designs.

Sample rubric for this task:

Points Performance
5: The student correctly determines that the area of the blue rhombus is two square units, the area of the red trapezoid is three square units, and the area of the yellow hexagon is six square units. The two designs have an area of exactly 15 square units, and the student's observations use correct geometric terms.
4: One of the areas is incorrect or the student uses a geometric term incorrectly.
3: Two or three mistakes are made in determining areas or using geometric terminology.
2: Four mistakes are made in determining areas or using geometric terminology.
1: Five or more mistakes are made in determining areas or using geometric terminology.
0: No work is shown or the work is not on task.

Self-Assessment and Peer Assessment

Self-assessment is the process by which students evaluate their own work, given criteria established by the teacher. This is important because, ultimately, the responsibility for learning belongs to the student. A teacher might ask students to validate their thinking on certain problems or to explain how they arrived at a particular solution. It is important that a teacher asks about correct answers as well as incorrect ones, in order to support the idea that students have control of the subject and that questioning is not related to students' mistakes or failure. Student self-assessment helps to build students' self-esteem, and it helps them to see how incorrect answers can be valuable in the process of arriving at correct solutions.

Sample self-assessment

After students complete a mathematical problem or investigation, ask them to evaluate how they felt about their work by writing "yes," "no," or "not sure," in response to all of the following questions. Be sure to explain that there are no correct or incorrect responses.

I understood the directions to the problem. _____

I found an answer to the problem. _____

I could explain this problem to another student. _____

I enjoyed solving this problem. _____

I thought the problem was too hard. _____

I thought this problem was too easy. _____

I thought this problem was just right. _____

I never saw this kind of problem before. _____

This problem reminds me of other problems I have solved. _____

I would like to do more problems like this one. _____

Peer assessment is a group activity in which students listen to, discuss, and analyze each others' strategies for solving problems. Peer assessment makes it possible for students to see different ways to proceed and to make judgements about which way makes the most sense, which seems easier, and which leads to stumbling blocks. Observing these discussions will benefit the teacher in learning about the students.

Work Samples

Work samples include projects, written assignments, and other student products that the teacher collects and evaluates. Scoring, which involves judgement, and analyzing the work make it possible to learn about student performance.

> ### *Possible work samples*
>
> - problems students have solved
> - charts students have constructed
> - journal entries
> - written passages in which students explain the process by which they solved a problem, how to approach a problem, and/or how a problem is related to other activities in mathematics
> - students' evaluation of "error patterns" in problems
> - problems students have constructed themselves.

Portfolios

A **portfolio** is a collection of a student's work over a period of time (a term, a year), which can be used for assessment by both the teacher and by the student. It can include special problem-solving tasks, writings, investigations, projects, and reports—even photographs of students working individually, in a group, or on a project. These items can be presented not only on paper but also on audio- or videotapes and/or computer disks.

By dating each of the entries, the student (and the teacher) can use the portfolio to see the growth of a body of work. Portfolios can be "learner-managed" (organized by the student), teacher-managed, or both, although a teacher of lower grade levels should give students specific directions as to how to organize their portfolios. It can also be valuable to give a student a portfolio project over consecutive years, in order to observe the evolution of that student's understanding.

Writings

Students' writing, such as a journal or items included in a portfolio, is a valuable means of assessment. Writing projects can be as simple as asking students to describe what they learned in a particular day, what they like about mathematics, or what they did or did not understand about an assignment. A letter to a friend about mathematics class or a poem about triangles is a creative tool by which a teacher can assess students' knowledge of and attitudes about mathematics in general.

Journal writing is a series of writings in which a student reflects on his or her learning. Since journals can include diagrams, graphs, labels, and symbols, journal writing can be a more inclusive form of communication than an oral response. In many cases writing also deepens students' understanding because it requires them to organize their thoughts differently.

A teacher must respect the privacy of what students write in journals. Because the journal is not only a forum for the teacher to respond to students as learners, but also a learning tool for the students themselves, the teacher should make it clear to students that their individual journal entries will not be graded.

Writing prompts are statements that provide students with a clear, well-defined purpose for a particular writing assignment.[9] A teacher needs to communicate clearly to students exactly what he or she expects in a response, such as whether it should include certain components or be a particular length.

> *Sample writing prompts*
> (grades 3–5)
>
> After reading *The Greedy Triangle* by Marilyn Burns,[10] give students the following prompts:
>
> - If I could be a shape, I would be a _____ because _____.
> - My favorite shape is _____ because _____.
> - Why was the triangle greedy?
> - Pick one of the shapes in the story and use your own words to describe it.
> - Write a letter to a classmate telling him/her how the greedy triangle changed shapes.

For examples of other writing-related instructional activities, see Chapter 4, especially **Building Vocabulary**, **Creative Writing**, **Pattern Block Shapes**, *and* **Writing Stories**.

---

[9] John A. Van de Walle, *Elementary and Middle School Mathematics: Teaching Developmentally,* 4th ed. (New York: Addison Wesley Longman, 2001), p. 74.
[10] Marilyn Burns, *The Greedy Triangle* (New York: Scholastic, 1994).

Teacher-Designed Written Tests

Teacher-designed written tests not only help determine a student's grades, but can also inform and guide a teacher's instruction. They do not provide a complete assessment of students' knowledge, but only one piece of the puzzle.

Students need to know *what* they are being assessed on as well as *how* they are being assessed. Teacher-made tests should be thoughtful and well-constructed and should include items at different levels on Bloom's taxonomy, such as knowledge and skill problems, selected-response problems, and constructed-response (or "open-ended") problems, which can be either brief or extended. It is helpful for a teacher to construct the test before teaching a unit in order to help clarify in his or her own mind what are the most important elements.

Achievement Tests

Nearly all teachers must administer standardized or state-wide tests at one time or another. While it is not always possible to receive the results in a timely enough fashion to make adjustments within the same school year, a teacher should look at incoming students' achievement test scores from previous years in order to identify strengths and/or weaknesses. By analyzing test results, a teacher can diagnose strengths and weaknesses of particular students and plan his or her teaching accordingly. An analysis of all test results for a particular grade can illuminate weaknesses in the curriculum that a teacher needs to address or areas that require greater emphasis. Teachers should make use of data from these assessments to help refine content as well as instructional strategies.

Criterion-referenced assessment is a test that measures student achievement against well-defined criteria for a specific learning objective or performance standard. An example of criterion-referenced assessment is the Pennsylvania System of School Assessment (PSSA).

Norm-referenced assessment is a test that measures a student's quantitative scores (such as how many items the student answered correctly) against a normal distribution of scores by other students of the same age or grade. This kind of testing is often used to rank students, measure their relative standing, and assess their general knowledge across broad areas. Examples of norm-referenced assessment are Terra Nova, the Iowa Test of Basic Skills, and SAT-9.

Resources

Given the relationship of the quality of the instructional materials to student achievement, it is important to pay sufficient attention to the selection of quality materials.

—EDThoughts[1]

IMAGES offers a range of tools for teachers to choose from, beyond content and curriculum. The "References" section serves as a bibliography for this volume; all sources listed in footnotes also appear there. Some of these sources are available free online; see the footnotes (or the Web version of IMAGES) for links.

Other sections in this chapter have been compiled by educators who have special experience with effectively incorporating literature, technology, multimedia, and manipulatives into instruction.

In this chapter, the reader will find:
- References
- Children's Literature
  - o Coordinate Geometry
  - o Measurement
  - o Transformational Geometry
  - o Two- and Three-Dimensional Geometry
  - o Visualization and Spatial Reasoning
  - o Multicultural
- Manipulatives
- Technology
    Software
    Web Sites
- Videos

---

[1] John Sutton and Alice Krueger, eds., *EDThoughts: What We Know about Mathematics Teaching and Learning* (Aurora, Co.: Mid-Continent Research for Education and Learning, 2002), p. 52.

REFERENCES

Ameis, Jerry A. *Mathematics on the Internet: A Resource for K–12 Teachers*. Upper Saddle River, N.J.: Merrill, 2000.

American Association for the Advancement of Science (AAAS). *Benchmarks for Science Literacy, Project 2061*. New York: Oxford University Press, 1993.

American Association of University Women (AAUW), *How Schools Shortchange Girls*. Washington, D.C.: AAUW Education Foundation, 1992, pp. 32, 72.

Baratta-Lorton, Mary. *Mathematics Their Way: An Activity-Centered Mathematics Program for Early Childhood Education*. Menlo Park, Ca.: Addison Wesley, 1976.

Baroody, Arthur J., and Bobbye H. Bartels. "Using Concept Maps to Link Mathematical Ideas." *Mathematics Teaching in the Middle School* 5, no. 9 (2000): pp. 604–9.

Bassarear, Tom. *Mathematics for Elementary School Teachers*. New York: Houghton Mifflin, 2001.

———. *Mathematics for Elementary School Teachers: Explorations*, 2nd ed. Boston: Houghton Mifflin, 2001.

Battista, Michael T. "Learning Geometry in a Dynamic Computer Environment." *Teaching Children Mathematics* 8, no. 6 (February 2002): pp. 333–39.

Battista, Michael T., et al. "Students' Spatial Structuring of Two-Dimensional Arrays of Squares." *Journal for Research in Mathematics Education* 29, no. 5 (1998): pp. 503–32.

Battista, Michael T., and Douglas H. Clements. "Using Spatial Imagery in Geometric Reasoning." *Arithmetic Teacher* 39, no. 3 (1991): pp. 18–21.

Beaumont, Vern, Roberta Curtis, and James Smart. *How to Teach Perimeter, Area, and Volume*. Reston, Va.: National Council of Teachers of Mathematics, 1986.

Bell, Clare V. "Learning Geometric Concepts through Ceramic Tile Design." *Mathematics teaching in the middle school* 9, no. 3 (November 2003): pp. 134–40.

Bendick, Jeanne, and Marcia Levin. *Take Shapes, Lines, and Letters: New Horizons in Mathematics*. New York: McGraw-Hill, 1962.

Bloomer, Anne, and Phyllis Carlson. *Activity Math: Using Manipulatives in the Classroom*. Reading, Mass.: Addison Wesley, 1993.

Braddon, Kathryn L., Nancy J. Hall, and Dale Taylor. *Math through Children's Literature: Making the NCTM Standards Come Alive.* Englewood, Co.: Teacher Ideas Press, 1993.

Buck, Donna Kay, and Francis Hildebrand. *Graphic Organizers for Mathematics: MATH-O-GRAPHS.* Pacific Grove, Ca.: Critical Thinking Press and Software, 1990.

Burns, Marilyn. *Math and Literature, K–3.* White Plains, N.Y.: Cuisenaire Co., 1992.

Campbell, Linda, Bruce Campbell, and Dee Dickinson. *Teaching and Learning through Multiple Intelligences*, 2nd ed. Boston: Allyn & Bacon, 1999.

Campopiano, John et al. *Math + Science: A Solution.* Fresno, Ca.: AIMS Educational Foundation, 1987.

Cloke, Gayle, Nola Ewing, and Dory Stevens, eds. "The Fine Art of Mathematics." *Teaching Children Mathematics* 8, no. 2 (2001): pp. 108–10.

COMAP, Inc. "The Constellations." *The Elementary Mathematician* 4, no. 3 (autumn 1990).

Conference Board of the Mathematical Sciences. *The Mathematical Education of Teachers*, pts. 1 and 2. Washington, D.C.: Mathematical Association of America, 2001.

Cotton, Kathleen. "Computer-Assisted Instruction." *Northwest Regional Educational Laboratory School's Improvement Research Series (SIRS), Close-Up,* series 5, no. 10 (May 1991). http://www.nwrel.org/scpd/sirs/5/cu10.html (accessed February 11, 2004).

Coultas, June, James Swalm, and Roslyn Wiesenfeld. *Strategies for Success in Mathematics.* Austin, Tex.: Steck-Vaughn, 1995.

Croom, Lucille. "Mathematics for All Students, Access, Excellence, and Equity." In *Muticultural and Gender Equity in the Mathematics Classroom: The Gift of Diversity*, p. 7. Ed. Janet Trentacosta. Reston, Va.: National Council of Teachers of Mathematics, 1997.

Crowley, Mary L. "The Van Hiele Model of the Development of Geometric Thought," in *Learning and Teaching Geometry, K–12*, pp. 1–16. Ed. Mary M. Lindquist. Reston, Va.: National Council of Teachers of Mathematics, 1987.

Cuevas, Gilbert J., ed. *Navigating through Geometry in Grades 3–5.* Reston, Va.: National Council of Teachers of Mathematics, 2004.

————, ed. *Navigating through Measurement in Grades 3–5*. Reston, Va.: National Council of Teachers of Mathematics, 2004.

CUPM Panel on Teacher Training. *Recommendations on the Mathematical Preparation of Teachers*. Washington, D.C.: Mathematical Association of America, 1983.

Curcio, Frances, ed. *Geometry in the Middle Grades*. Reston, Va.: National Council of Teachers of Mathematics, 1992.

De Klerk, Judith. *Illustrated Math Dictionary*. Parsippany, N.J.: Good Year Books, 1999.

Del Grande, John. "Spatial Sense." *Arithmetic Teacher* 37, no. 6 (1990): pp. 14–20.

De Villiers, Michael. "The Future of Secondary School Geometry." *Pythagoras* 44 (December 1997): pp. 37–54. http://www-didactique.imag.fr/preuve/Resumes/deVilliers/deVilliers98/deVilliers98.html (accessed February 11, 2004).

Downie, Diane, et al. *Math for Girls and Other Problem Solvers*. Berkeley, Ca.: Lawrence Hall of Science, 1981.

Ellington, Aimee J. "A Meta-Analysis of the Effects of Calculators on Students' Achievement and Attitude Levels in Precollege Mathematics Classes." *Journal for Research in Mathematics Education* 34, no. 5 (November 2003): pp. 433–63.

Ellison, Elaine, and Diana Venters. *Mathematical Quilts: No Sewing Required*. Emeryville, Ca.: Key Curriculum Press, 1999.

Ernst, Bruno. *The Magic Mirror of M. C. Escher*. Suffolk: Tarquin Publications, 1985.

Fennell, Francis, and David E. Williams, eds. *IDEAS from the Arithmetic Teacher: Grades 4–6, Intermediate School*. 2nd ed. Reston, Va.: National Council of Teachers of Mathematics, 1986.

Fine, Sue, and Greg Purcell. *Maths Plus for Victorian Schools: Working towards CSF Level 4, Assessment Tasks*. Syndey: Horwitz Martin, 1999.

Gardner, Howard. *Frames of Mind: The Theory of Multiple Intelligences*. New York: Basic Books, 1983.

Garfunkel, Solomon A., and Gail S. Young. *In the Beginning: Mathematical Preparation for Elementary School Teachers*. Lexington, Mass.: COMAP, Inc., 1992.

Gay, Geneva. "The Importance of Multicultural Education." *Educational Leadership* 61, no. 4 (December 2003/January 2004): pp. 30–35.

Ghyka, Matila. *The Geometry of Art and Life*. New York: Dover, 1977.

Granger, Tim. "Math Is Art." *Teaching Children Mathematics* 7, no. 1 (2000): pp. 10–13.

Great Source Education Group, Inc. *Math at Hand*. New York: Houghton Mifflin Co., 1999.

Greenes, Carole, ed. *Navigating through Geometry in Prekindergarten–Grade 2*. Reston, Va.: National Council of Teachers of Mathematics, 2001.

———, ed. *Navigating through Measurement in Prekindergarten–Grade 2*. Reston, Va.: National Council of Teachers of Mathematics, 2001.

Grouws, Douglas A., ed. *Handbook of Research on Mathematics Teaching and Learning*. New York: Macmillan, 1992.

Hanna, Gila. "Reaching Gender Equity in Mathematics Education." *The Educational Forum* 67, no. 3 (spring 2003): pp. 204–14. http://math.unipa.it/~grim/Jhanna (accessed February 11, 2004).

Helton, Sonia M. *Math Activities for Every Month of the School Year*. West Nyack, N.Y.: The Center for Applied Research in Education, 1991.

Hembree, Ray, and Donald J. Dessart. "Research on Calculators in Mathematics Education." In *Calculators in Mathematics Education: NCTM 1992 Yearbook*, pp. 24–26. Ed. James T. Fey. Reston, Va.: National Council of Teachers of Mathematics, 1992.

Hiebert, James, and Thomas P. Carpenter, "Learning and Teaching with Understanding," in *Handbook of Research on Mathematics Teaching and Learning*, ed. Douglas A. Grouws. New York: Macmillan, 1992: pp. 65–97.

Higginson, William, and Lynda Colgan. "Algebraic Thinking through Origami." *Mathematics Teaching in the Middle School* 6, no. 6 (February 2001), p. 343.

Hill, Jane M., ed. *Geometry for Grades K–6: Readings from the Arithmetic Teacher*. Reston, Va.: National Council of Teachers of Mathematics, 1987.

Hillen, J. "Paper-Penny Boxes," *AIMS Newsletter* 6, no. 6 (January 1992): pp. 30–34.

Hoffer, Alan R. *Mathematics Resource Project: Geometry and Visualization*. Palo Alto, Ca.: Creative Publications, 1977.

Houghton Mifflin Mathematics. *Scope and Sequence, Grades K–6*. New York: Houghton Mifflin, 2001.

Human Relations Media. *Exploring Perimeter, Area and Volume: The Zoo Design Challenge*. Mount Kenisco, N.Y.: Human Relations Media, 1993.

Immerzeel, George, and Melvin Thomas, eds. *IDEAS from the Arithmetic Teacher: Grades 1–4, Primary*. Reston, Va.: National Council of Teachers of Mathematics, 1982.

———, eds. *IDEAS from the Arithmetic Teacher: Grades 6–8, Middle School*. Reston, Va.: National Council of Teachers of Mathematics, 1982.

Jacobson, Cathy, and Richard Lehrer. "Teacher Appropriation and Student Learning of Geometry through Design." *Journal for Research in Mathematics Education* 31, no. 1 (January 2000): pp. 71–88.

Jensen, Robert J., ed. *NCTM Research Interpretation Project. Research Ideas for the Classroom: Early Childhood Mathematics*. New York: Simon & Schuster Macmillan, 1993.

Johnson, David, and Roger Johnson. "The Internal Dynamics of Cooperative Learning Groups." In *Learning to Cooperate, Cooperating to Learn*. Ed. R. Slavin et al. New York: Plenum, 1985, pp. 103–22.

Johnson, Donovan A. *Activities in Mathematics: Second Course—Graphs*. Glenview, Il.: Scott Foresman, 1971.

Johnson, Gretchen L., and R. Jill Edelson. "Integrating Music and Mathematics in the Elementary Classroom." *Teaching Children Mathematics* 9, no. 8 (April 2003): pp. 474–79.

Kami, Constance. *Young Children Reinvent Arithmetic: Implications of Piaget's Theory*. New York: Teachers College, 2000.

Kappraff, Jay. *Connections: The Geometric Bridge Between Art and Science*. New York: McGraw-Hill, 1991.

Kilpatrick, Jeremy, Jane Swanford, and Bradford Findell, eds. *Adding It Up: Helping Children Learn Mathematics*. Washington, D.C.: National Academy Press, 2001.

Krause, Marina C. *Multicultural Mathematics Materials*. 2nd ed. Reston, Va.: National Council of Teachers of Mathematics, 2000.

Krulik, Stephen. *A Mathematics Laboratory Handbook for Secondary Schools*. Philadelphia: W. B. Saunders, 1972.

Kuhns, Catherine L. "Building Mathematical Connections with *Village of Round and Square Houses*." *Teaching Children Mathematics* 10, no. 2 (October, 2003): pp. 120–24.[2]

Kulik, James. *Effects of Using Instructional Technology in Elementary and Secondary Schools: What Controlled Evaluation Studies Say, Final Report.* Arlington, Va.: SRI International, 2003.

Kulm, Gerald. *Mathematics Assessment: What Works in the Classroom.* San Francisco: Jossey-Bass, 1994.

Lappan, Glenda, et al. *Connected Mathematics Program.* White Plains, N.Y.: Dale Seymour Publications, 1998.

Leder, Gila C., "Mathematics and Gender: Changing Perspectives," in *Handbook of Research on Mathematics Teaching and Learning,* ed. Douglas A. Grouws. New York: Macmillan, 1992: p. 611.

Leiva, Miriam, ed. *Geometry and Spatial Sense.* Reston, Va.: National Council of Teachers of Mathematics, 1993.

Liedtke, Werner W. "Developing Spatial Abilities in the Early Grades." *Teaching Children Mathematics* 2, no. 1 (September 1995): pp. 12–19.

Lindquist, Mary Montgomery, ed. *Learning and Teaching Geometry, K–12.* Reston, Va.: National Council of Teachers of Mathematics, 1987.

Loveless, Tom, and Paul Diperna. *The Brown Center Report on American Education: How Well Are American Students Learning? Focus on Math Achievement.* Washington, D.C.: Brookings Institution, 2000.

Ma, Liping. *Knowing and Teaching Elementary Mathematics.* Mahwah, N.J.: Lawrence Erlbaum Associates, 1999.

Maislin, Seth, ed. *The Partners in Change Handbook: A Professional Development Curriculum in Mathematics.* Boston: Boston University, 1997.

Manouchehri, Azita, Mary C. Enderson, and Lyle A. Pagnucco. "Exploring Geometry with Technology." *Mathematics Teaching in the Middle School* 3, no. 6 (January 1998): pp. 436–42.

Mathematical Sciences Education Board and the National Research Council. *Measuring Up: Prototypes for Mathematics Assessment.* Washington, D.C.: National Academy Press, 1993.

---

[2] See Ann Grifalconi's *Village of Round and Square Houses* in the Children's Literature section, p. 194.

Miller, Don, and Anne McKinnon. *The Beginning School Mathematics Project: A Case Study of School-University Collaboration for Improving Children's Learning of Mathematics in the First Three Years of School.* Alexandria, Va.: Association for Supervision and Curriculum Development, 1995.

Millington, Jon. *Curve Stitching: The Art of Sewing Beautiful Mathematical Patterns.* Suffolk: Tarquin Publications, 1996.

Moore, Deborah A., and Maria C. Schwarz. "Fishy Fun under the Sun: A Week of Geometry Connections." *Mathematics Teaching in the Middle School* 9, no. 2 (October 2003): pp. 78–82.

Moore, Sara D., and William P. Bintz. "Teaching Geometry and Measurement through Literature." *Mathematics Teaching in the Middle School* 8, no. 2 (October 2002): pp. 78–84.

Moyer, Patricia S. "Patterns and Symmetry: Reflections of Culture." *Teaching Children Mathematics* 8, no. 3 (November 2001): pp. 140–44.

Murray, William D., and Rigney, Francis J. *Paper Folding for Beginners.* New York: Dover, 1960.

National Academy Press. *Measuring What Counts: A Conceptual Guide for Mathematics Assessment.* Washington, D.C.: National Academy Press, 1993.

National Center for Education Statistics. *Nation's Report Card.* 2003. http://nces.ed.gov/nationsreportcard (accessed February 10, 2004).

National Council of Teachers of Mathematics. *Assessment Standards for School Mathematics.* Reston, Va.: National Council of Teachers of Mathematics, 1995.

———. *Principles and Standards for School Mathematics.* Reston, Va.: National Council of Teachers of Mathematics, 2000.

National Science Teachers Association. *Atlas of Science Literacy, Project 2061.* Washington D.C.: American Association for the Advancement of Science, 2001.

Neumann, Maureen D. "The Mathematics of Native American Star Quilts." *Mathematics Teaching in the Middle School* 9, no. 4 (December 2003): pp. 230–36.

Owens, Douglas T., ed. *National Council of Teachers of Mathematics Research Interpretation Project: Research Ideas for the Classroom, Middle Grades Mathematics.* New York: Simon & Schuster Macmillan, 1993.

Palacios, Vicente. *Origami for Beginners.* New York: Dover, 1995.

Papert, Seymour. "Papert on Piaget." *Time* (March 29, 1999): p. 105. http://www.papert.org/articles/Papertonpiaget.html (accessed February 11, 2004).

Pappas, Theoni. *The Joy of Mathematics: Discovering Mathematics All around You.* San Carlos, Ca.: Wide World Publishing, 1989.

Paznokas, Lynda S. "Teaching Mathematics through Cultural Quilting." *Teaching Children Mathematics* 9, no. 4 (December 2003): pp. 250–56.

Pennsylvania Board of Education. "Academic Standards for Mathematics." *Pennsylvania Bulletin* 29, no. 3 (January 1999): pp. 427–41. http://www.pde.state.pa.us/ (accessed February 11, 2004).

Polonsky, Lydia, et al. *Math for the Very Young: A Handbook of Activities for Parents and Teachers.* New York: John Wiley and Sons, Inc., 1995.

Ranpura, Ashish. "How We Remember, and Why We Forget." *Brain Connection* (June 2000). http://www.brainconnection.com/topics/?main=fa/memory-formation3 (accessed February 11, 2004).

Renne, Christine G. "Is a Rectangle a Square? Developing Mathematical Vocabulary and Conceptual Understanding." *Teaching Children Mathematics* 10, no. 5 (2004): pp. 258–63.

Reys, Robert E., et al. *Helping Children Learn Mathematics.* 6th ed. New York: John Wiley & Sons, 2001.

———. *Helping Children Learn Mathematics.* 7th ed. Hoboken, N.J.: John Wiley & Sons, 2004.

Roberge, James J. "Tangram Geometry." *Mathematics Teacher* 70, no. 3 (1977): pp. 239–41.

Robichaux, Rebecca, and Paulette R. Rodrigue. "Using Origami to Promote Geometric Communication." *Mathematics Teaching in the Middle School* 9, no. 4 (December 2003): pp. 222–29.

Russell, Dorothy S., and Elaine M. Bologna. "Teaching Geometry with Tangrams." *Arithmetic Teacher* 30, no. 2 (1982): pp. 34–38.

Sachs, Leroy, ed. *Middle School Student Merit Awards.* Reston, Va.: National Council of Teachers of Mathematics, 1984.

Sadker, David. "Gender Equity: Still Knocking at the Classroom Door." *Educational Leadership* 56, no. 7 (1999): p. 24.

Sadker, Myra and David Sadker. *Failing at Fairness: How America's Schools Cheat Girls.* New York: Charles Scribner's Sons, 1994.

Schattschneider, Doris. *Visions of Symmetry.* New York: W. H. Freeman, 1992.

Schattschneider, Doris, and Wallace Walker. *M. C. Escher Kaleidocycles.* Suffolk: Tarquin Publications, 1997.

Schloemer, Cathy G. "Tips for Teaching Cartesian Graphing: Linking Concepts and Procedures." *Teaching Children Mathematics* (September 1994): pp. 20–23.

Schmidt ,William, Richard Houang, and Leland Cogan. "A Coherent Curriculum: The Case of Mathematics." *American Educator* 26, no. 2 (summer 2002): pp. 10–26, 47–48.

Selden, Annie, and John Selden, "The Role of Examples in Learning Mathematics." *The Mathematics Association of America Research Sampler 5* (February 20, 1998). http://www.maa.org/t_and_l/sampler/rs_5.html (accessed February 11, 2004).

Serra, Michael. *Discovering Geometry: An Inductive Approach.* 2nd ed. Berkley, Ca.: Key Curriculum Press, 1997.

Slavin, Robert. "Cooperative Learning and Student Achievement." In *School and Classroom Organization*, pp. 129–56. Ed. R. Slavin et al. Hillsdale, N.J.: Lawrence Erlbaum, 1989.

Sobel, Max A., and Evan M. Malestsky. *Teaching Mathematics: A Sourcebook of Aids, Activities, and Strategies.* Boston: Allyn and Bacon, 1999.

Stenmark, Jean Kerr, Virginia Thompson, and Ruth Cossey. *Family Math.* Berkeley, Ca.: Lawrence Hall of Science, 1986.

Suh, Jennifer, et al. "Junior Architects: Designing Your Dream Clubhouse Using Measurement and Geometry." *Teaching Children Mathematics* 10, no. 3 (November 2002): pp. 170–79.

Sutton, John, and Alice Krueger, eds. *EDThoughts: What We Know About Mathematics Teaching and Learning.* Aurora, Co.: Mid-Continent Research for Education and Learning, 2002.

Swenson, Karen A., and Marcia L. Swanson. *Student Resource Handbook: Mathematics for Elementary Teachers*, 5th ed. New York: John Wiley & Sons, 2000.

Taylor, Lyn, et al. "American Indians, Mathematical Attitudes, and the Standards." *Arithmetic Teacher* 38, no. 6 (February 1991): pp. 14–21.

Trentacosta, Janet, ed. *Multicultural and Gender Equity in the Mathematics Classroom: The Gift of Diversity.* Reston, Va.: National Council of Teachers of Mathematics, 1997.

Troutman, Andria P., and Betty K. Lichtenberg. *Mathematics: A Good Beginning.* Belmont, Ca.: Wadsworth/Thomson Learning, 2003.

Trussell-Cullen, Alan. *Assessment in the Learner-Centered Classroom.* Carlsbad, Ca.: Dominie Press, Inc., 1998.

U.S. Department of Education's Math and Science Education Expert Panel. *Exemplary and Promising Mathematics Programs.* Washington, D.C.: U.S. Department of Education, 1999. http://www.enc.org/professional/federalresources/exemplary/promising (accessed February 11, 2004)

U.S. Department of Education, National Center for Education Statistics. *Pursuing Excellence: A Study of U.S. Fourth-Grade Mathematics and Science Achievement in International Context.* Washington, D.C.: U.S. Government Printing Office, 1997.

————. *Pursuing Excellence: A Study of U.S. Eighth-Grade Mathematics and Science Teaching, Learning, Curriculum, and Achievement in International Context.* Washington, D.C.: U.S. Government Printing Office, 1996.

U.S. Department of Education, National Commission on Mathematics and Science Teaching for the 21st Century. *Before It's Too Late: A Report on the Nation.* Washington, D.C.: U.S. Government Printing Office, 2000. http://www.ed.gov/inits/Math/glenn/index.html (accessed February 11, 2004).

U.S. Department of Education, Office of the Secretary. *Back to School, Moving Forward: What 'No Child Left Behind' Means for America's Communities.* Washington, D.C., 2001.

U.S. Department of Labor, The Secretary's Commission on Achieving Necessary Skills, *What Work Requires of Schools: A SCANS Report for America 2000.* Washington, D.C.: U.S. Department of Labor, 1991. http://wdr.doleta.gov/SCANS/whatwork/whatwork.html (accessed February 11, 2004).

Van de Walle, John A. *Elementary and Middle School Mathematics: Teaching Developmentally.* 3rd ed. New York: Addison Wesley Longman, 1998.

————. *Elementary and Middle School Mathematics: Teaching Developmentally.* 4th ed. New York: Addison Wesley Longman, 2001.

Van Hiele, Pierre M. "Developing Geometric Thinking through Activities that Begin with Play." *Teaching Children Mathematics* 5, no. 6 (February 1999): pp. 310–16.

Vissa, Jeanne. "Coordinate Graphing: Shaping a Sticky Situation." *Arithmetic Teacher* 35, no. 3 (November 1987): pp. 6–10.

Weiss, Stefanie. "Howard Gardner: All Kinds of Smarts," *NEA Today* 17, no. 6 (March 1999): p. 42. http://www.nea.org/neatoday/9903/meet.html (accessed February 11, 2004).

Welchman-Tischler, Rosamond. *How to Use Children's Literature to Teach Mathematics.* Reston, Va.: National Council of Teachers of Mathematics, 1992.

Wenglinsky, Harold. *Does It Compute? The Relationship between Educational Technology and Student Achievement in Mathematics.* Princeton, N.J.: Educational Testing Service, 1998.

Wheeler, Ed R., and Jane Thompson Barnard. *Mathematics Activities for Teaching.* 10th ed. Dubuque, Ia.: Kendall/Hunt Publishing, 1999.

Wiest, Lynda R. "Multicultural Mathematics Instruction: Approaches and Resources." *Teaching Children Mathematics* 9, no. 1 (September 2002): pp. 49–55.

Willingham, Daniel T. *Cognition: The Thinking Anima.* New York: Prentice Hall, 2001.

Wilson, Brent G., and Karen Peterson. "Successful Technology Integration in an Elementary School: A Case Study." In *Practitioners Write the Book: What Works in Educational Technology*, pp. 201–67. Eds. Carolyn Lucas and Larry Lucas. Denton, Tex.: Texas Center for Educational Technology, 1995. http://carbon.cudenver.edu/~bwilson/peakview.html (accessed February 11, 2004).

Wright, Elena Dworkin, and Susan Shapero. *Round Table Geometry.* Watertown, Mass.: Charlesbridge, 1998.

Zaslavsky, Claudia. "Exploring World Cultures in Math Class." *Educational Leadership* 60, no. 2 (October 2002): pp. 66–69.

———. "Multicultural Mathematics Education for the Middle Grades." *Arithmetic Teacher* 38, no. 6 (February 1991): pp. 8–13.

Zurstadt, Betty K. "Tessellations and the Art of M. C. Escher." *Arithmetic Teacher* 31, no. 5 (January 1984): pp. 54–55.

CHILDREN'S LITERATURE

Children love to read and to have someone read to them. Many of the books that are linked with mathematics embody concepts that children need to learn. By integrating children's literature directly into the mathematics lesson, a teacher can help children to become excited about and to gain a deeper understanding of the mathematics they are learning.

The books are listed here by content strand, as well as multicultural or miscellaneous. The instructional activities section (in Chapter 4) provides a number of examples of how and where to integrate some of these books into mathematics instruction.

Coordinate Geometry

Anno, Mitsumasma. *Anno's Math Games*. New York, NY: Philomel, 1989.
[grades K–3]

———. *Anno's Math Games III*. New York, NY: Philomel, 1991.
[grades K–3; also measurement]

Ayres, Pam. *Guess Where?* Cambridge, Ma.: Candlewick Press, 1994.
[grades Pre-K–2]

Glass, Julie. *The Fly on the Ceiling: A Math Myth*. New York: Random House, 1998.
[grades K–2]

Murphy, Stuart. *Bug Dance*. New York: Harper Trophy, 2002.
[grades pre-K–1; directions; also visualization and spatial reasoning]

Penner, Lucille Recht. *X Marks the Spot*. New York: Kane Press, 2002.
[grades K–2]

Measurement

Adams, Pam. *Ten Beads Tall*. Wiltshire, U.K.: Child's Play (International) Ltd., 1990.
[grades pre-K–1]

Adler, David A. *How Tall, How Short, How Faraway*. New York: Holiday House, 1999.
[grades K–2]

Anastasio, Dina. *It's about Time*. New York: Grosset and Dunlap, 1993.
[grades K–3]

Anno, Mitsumasma. *Anno's Math Games III*. New York: Philomel, 1991.
[grades K–3; also coordinate geometry]

Axelrod, Amy. *Pigs Go to Market: Fun with Math and Shopping*. New York: Simon & Schuster Books for Young Readers, 1997.
[grades K–3; weights and measures]

Burns, Marilyn. *The I Hate Mathematics Book*. Boston: Little, Brown, and Co., 1975.
[grades 4–6; also two- and three-dimensional geometry]

———. *Spaghetti and Meatballs for All*. New York: Scholastic, 1997.
[grades K–3; area and perimeter]

Cave, Kathryn. *Just in Time*. London: Frances Lincoln, 1989.
[grades K–3; time]

Cohen, Don. *Calculus by and for Young People*. Champaign, Il.: The Mathman, 1989.
[grades 2 and up]

Friedman, Aileen. *A Cloak for the Dreamer*. New York: Scholastic, Inc., 1994.
[grades K–2; angle measurement; also two- and three-dimensional geometry]

Froman, Robert. *Angles Are as Easy as Pie*. New York: Thomas Y. Crowell, 1975.
[grades K–2]

Grifalconi, Ann. *The Village of Round and Square Houses*. Boston: Little Brown, 1986.
[grades K–3; also two- and three-dimensional geometry][3]

Hamm, Diane Johnston. *How Many Feet in Bed?* New York: Aladdin Paperbacks, 1991.
[grades pre-K–1]

Hightower, Susan. *Twelve Snails to One Lizard: A Tale of Mischief and Measurement*. New York: Simon & Schuster, 1997.
[grades K–2]

Hoban, Tana. *Is It Larger?* New York: Greenwillow Books, 1985.
[grades pre-K–1]

Hutchins, Pat. *Clocks and More Clocks*. New York: Macmillan, 1970.
[grades K–3]

---

[3] For a lesson that relates this book to geometry and measurement see: Catherine L. Kuhns. "Building Mathematical Connections with *Village of Round and Square Houses*," *Teaching Children Mathematics* 10, no. 2 (October 2003): pp. 120–24.

Lasky, Kathryn. *The Librarian Who Measured the Earth.* Boston: Little, Brown, and Co., 1994.
[grades K–2]

Leedy, Loreen. *Measuring Penny.* New York: Henry Holt, 1997.
[grades K–2; standard and non-standard measures]

Lionni, Leo. *Inch by Inch.* New York: Mulberry Books, 1960.
[grades K–2]

Mathis, Sharon Bell. *The Hundred Penny Box.* New York: Viking Press, 1986.
[grades K–2]

Murphy, Stuart *J. Bigger, Better, Best.* New York: Harper Collins Juvenile Books, 2002.
[grades K–3]

———. *Game Time!* New York: Harper Trophy, 2000.
[grades K–2; time]

———. *Racing Around.* New York: Harper Trophy, 2002.
[grades K–2; perimeter]

———. *Room for Ripley.* New York: Harper Trophy, 2000.
[grades K–2; capacity]

———. *Super Sand Castle Saturday.* New York: Harper Trophy, 1999.
[grades K–2]

Myller, Rolf. *How Big Is a Foot?* New York: Atheneum Books for Children, 1972.
[grades K–2]

Nagda, Anne Whitehead, and Cindy Bickel. *Tiger Math: Learning to Graph from a Baby Tiger.* New York: Henry Holt, 2000.
[grades 2–5]

Nesbit, Edith. *Melisande.* Orlando, Fla.: Harcourt, Brace, Jovanovich, 1989.
[grades K–2]

Nolan, Helen, and Tracy Walker. *How Much, How Many, How Far, How Heavy, How Long, How Tall Is 1000?* Toronto: Kids Can Press, Ltd., 1995.
[grades K–2]

Pluckrose, Henry. *Big & Little.* New York: Franklin Watts, 1987.
[grades K–2]

———. *Capacity.* New York: Franklin Watts, 1988.
[grades K–2]

———. *Length.* New York: Franklin Watts, 1988.
[grades K–2]

———. *Weight.* New York: Franklin Watts, 1988.
[grades K–2]

Rex, Michael. *The Fattest, Tallest, Biggest Snowman Ever (Hello Math Reader—Level 3).* New York: Scholastic, Inc., 1997.
[grades K–3]

Schwartz, David. *G is for Googol: A Math Alphabet Book.* Berkeley, Ca.: Tricycle, 1998.
[grades 3–6; also two- and three-dimensional geometry]

Scieszka, Jon, and Lane Smith. *Math Curse.* New York: Viking, 1995.
[grades 1 and up]

Silverstein, Shel. *Where the Sidewalk Ends.* New York: HarperCollins, 1981.
[grades 3–6; also two- and three-dimensional geometry]

Sundby, Scott. *Cut Down to Size at High Noon.* Watertown, Mass.: Charlesbridge Publishing, 2000.
[grades 3–6]

Tomko, Diana. *The Ten-Second Race.* Huntington Beach, Ca.: Creative Teaching Press, 1998.
[grades K–3; time]

Zimelman, Nathan. *Sold! A Mathematics Adventure.* Watertown, Mass.: Charlesbridge Publishing, 2000.
[grades 3–6]

Transformational Geometry

Brown, Jeff. *Stanley, Flat Again!* New York: Harper Collins, 2003.
[grades 2–4; also two- and three-dimensional geometry]

Ernst, Lisa Campbell. *Sam Johnson and the Blue Ribbon Quilt.* New York: Lothrop, Lee and Shepard, 1983.
[grades pre-K–3]

Escher, M. C., and Michael Solomon Sachs. *The Pop-Up Book of M. C. Escher.* Petaluma, Ca.: Pomegranate Artbooks, 1991.
[grades 5 and up; tessellations]

Flournoy, Valerie. *The Patchwork Quilt.* New York: Dial Books, 1985.
[grades K–2]

Hoban, Tana. *Shadows and Reflections.* New York: Greenwillow Books, 1990.
[grades K–3; also two- and three-dimensional geometry]

Hopkinson, Deborah. *Sweet Clara and the Freedom Quilt.* New York: Knopf, 1998.
[grades K–3; also multicultural]

Jonas, Ann. *The Quilt.* New York: Puffin, 1994.
[grades K–3; also multicultural]

———. *Reflections.* New York: Greenwillow, 1987.
[grades K–3]

———. *Round Trip.* New York: Scholastic, Inc., 1983
[grades K–2; transformations]

Murphy, Pat. *By Nature's Design.* San Francisco: Chronicle Books, 1993.
[grades 5 and up; symmetry; also visualization and spatial reasoning]

Murphy, Stuart. *Let's Fly a Kite.* New York: Harper Trophy, 2000.
[grades K–2; symmetry]

Pappas, Theoni. *The Adventure of Penrose the Mathematical Cat.* San Carlos, CA: Wide World Pub Tetra, 1997.
[grades 2–7; transformations; also two- and three-dimensional geometry]

Paul, Ann Whitford. *Eight Hands Round: A Patchwork Alphabet.* New York: HarperCollins Publishers, 1991.
[grades K–2]

Pluckrose, Henry. *Pattern.* New York: Franklin Watts, 1988.
[grades K–2; symmetry; also visualization and spatial reasoning]

Polacco, Patricia. *The Keeping Quilt.* New York: Simon and Shuster, 1988.
[grades K–3; also multicultural]

Sandved, Kjell B. *The Butterfly Alphabet.* New York: Scholastic Inc., 1999.
[grades K–2; symmetry; also two- and three-dimensional geometry]

Sitomer, Mindel, and Harry Sitomer. *What Is Symmetry?* New York: Thomas Y. Crowell, 1970.
[grades pre-K–1; symmetry; also visualization and spatial reasoning]

Smucker, Barbara. *Selina and the Bear Paw Quilt.* New York: Crown Publishing Group, 1996.
[grades 1–3]

Tompert, Ann. *Grandfather Tang's Story: A Tale Told with Tangrams.* New York: Crown Publishers, 1990.
[grades 1–4; two- and three-dimensional geometry; also visualization and spatial reasoning]

Walter, Marion. *Look at Annette.* New York: M. Evans and Co., 1977.
[grades K–3; symmetry and transformations; also visualization and spatial reasoning]

———. *The Mirror Puzzle Book.* Suffolk: Tarquin Publications, 1988.
[grades 3–6; symmetry and reflection; also visualization and spatial reasoning]

Willing, Karen and Julie B. Dock. *Quilting Now and Then.* Ashland, Ore.: Now and Then Pubs, 1994.
[grades K–3]

Two- and Three-Dimensional Geometry

Abbott, Edwin. *Flatland: A Romance of Many Dimensions.* Princeton, N.J.: Princeton University Press, 1991.[4]
[grades 5 and up]

Abel, Simone. *Shapely Sheep.* Brookfield, Conn.: Millbrook, 1999.
[grades pre-K–1; shapes]

Axelrod, Amy. *Pigs on the Ball: Fun with Math and Sports.* New York: Simon & Schuster Books for Young Readers, 1998.
[grades K–3; shapes and angles]

Brown, Jeff. *Flat Stanley.* New York: Harper Trophy, 1996.
[grades 2–4]

———. *Stanley, Flat Again!* New York: Harper Collins, 2003.
[grades 2–4; transformational geometry]

---

[4] Available online at http://downlode.org/etext/flatland/.

Brown, Marcia. *Listen to a Shape*. New York: Franklin Watts, 1979.
[grades 1–4; shapes]

Browne, Anthony. *The Shape Game*. New York: Farrar Straus & Giroux, 2003.
[grades K–4; shapes].

Burns, Marilyn. *The Greedy Triangle*. New York: Scholastic, 1994.
[grades K–3; shapes]

———. *The I Hate Mathematics Book*. Boston: Little, Brown, and Co., 1975.
[grades 4–6; also measurement]

———. *Math for Smarty Pants*. Boston: Little, Brown, and Co., 1982.
[grades 4–6; shapes]

Carle, Eric. *My Very First Book of Shapes*. New York: Thomas Y. Crowell, 1974.
[grades pre-K–2; shapes]

Dodds, Dayle A. *The Shape of Things*. Cambridge, Mass.: Candlewick, 1994.
[grade K; shapes]

Ehlert, Lois. *Color Farm*. New York: J. B. Lippincott, 1990.
[grades pre-K–1; shapes]

———. *Color Zoo*. New York: HarperCollins Publishers, 1989.
[grades pre-K–1; shapes]

Emberley, Ed. *The Wing of a Flea: A Book about Shapes*. Boston: Little, Brown, and Co., 1988.
[grades 1–3; shapes]

Fadiman, Clifton. *Fantasia Mathematics*. New York: Copernicus Books, 1997.
[grades 4 and up; shapes]

Falwell, Cathryn. *Shape Space*. New York: Clarion Books, 1993.
[grades 2 and up; shapes]

Feldman, Judy. *Shapes in Nature*. Chicago: Children's Press, 1991.
[grades K–2; shapes]

Friedman, Aileen. *A Cloak for the Dreamer*. New York: Scholastic, Inc., 1994.
[grades K–2; shapes; also measurement]

Friskey, Margaret. *Three Sides and the Round One*. Chicago, IL: Children's Press, 1973.
[grades 1–3; shapes]

Greene, Rhonda G. *When a Line Bends . . . A Shape Begins*. New York: Scholastic, Inc., 1997.
[grades K–2; shapes]

Grifalconi, Ann. *The Village of Round and Square Houses*. Boston: Little Brown, 1986.
[grades K–3; shapes; also measurement][5]

Grover, Max. *Circles and Squares Everywhere*. New York: Harcourt, 1996.
[grades K–3; shapes]

Hansen-Smith, Bradford. *The Hands-on Marvelous Ball Book*. New York: W. H. Freeman and Co., 1995.
[grades 4–7]

Hoban, Tana. *Circles, Triangles, and Squares*. New York: Macmillan Publishing Co., Inc., 1974.
[grades K–2; shapes]

————. *Round Round Round*. New York: Scholastic, Inc., 1983.
[grades pre-K–1; shapes]

————. *Shadows and Reflections*. New York: Greenwillow Books, 1990.
[grades K–3; also transformational geometry]

————. *Shapes, Shapes, Shapes*. New York: Greenwillow Books, 1986.
[grades K–2; shapes]

————. *So Many Circles, So Many Squares*. New York: Greenwillow, 1998.
[grades pre-K–2; shapes]

Hulme, Joy N. *Sea Squares*. New York: Hyperion Books for Children, 1991.
[grades K–2; shapes]

Hunt, Janie. *Round and Square*. Brookfield, Conn.: Millbrook, 1998.
[grades pre-K–1; shapes]

Juster, Norton. *The Dot and the Line: A Romance in Lower Mathematics*. New York: Random House, 1977.
[grades K–2]

McGrath, Barbara. *The M&M's Brand Counting Book*. Watertown, Ma.: Charlesbridge Publishing, 1994.
[grades K–2; shapes]

---

[5] For a lesson that relates this book to geometry and measurement, see Kuhns, "Building Mathematical Connections," pp. 120–24.

Murphy, Stuart J. *Captain Invincible and the Space Shapes.* New York: Harper Trophy, 2001.
[grades K–4; three-dimensional shapes]

————. *Circus Shapes.* New York: Harper Trophy, 1998.
[grades K–2; shapes]

Neuschwander, Cindy. *Sir Cumference and the Dragon of Pi: A Math Adventure.* Watertown, Mass.: Charlesbridge Publishing, 1999.
[grades 2–7]

————. *Sir Cumference and the First Round Table: A Math Adventure.* Watertown, Mass.: Charlesbridge Publishing, 1997.
[grades 2–7; circles]

————. *Sir Cumference and the Great Knight of Angleland: A Math Adventure.* Watertown, Mass.: Charlesbridge Publishing, 2001.
[grades 4–7; angles]

————. *Sir* Cumference *and the Sword in the Cone: A Math Adventure.* Watertown, MA: Charlesbridge Publishing, 2003.
[grades 4–7; three-dimensional geometry]

Pallotta, Jerry. *Icky Bug Shapes.* New York: Scholastic Books, 2004.
[grades K–3; shapes]

Pappas, Theoni. *The Adventure of Penrose the Mathematical Cat.* San Carlos, CA: Wide World Pub Tetra, 1997.
[grades 2–7; shapes; also transformational geometry]

Pluckrose, Henry. *Sorting.* New York: Franklin Watts, 1988.
[grades K–2]

Podendorf, Illa. *Shapes: Sides, Curves and Corners.* Chicago, Il: Children's Press, 1970.
[grades K–4; shapes]

Reid, Margarette S. *The Button Box.* Glenview, Il.: Scott Foresman, 1990.
[grades pre-K–1]

Rogers, Paul. *The Shapes Game.* New York: Henry Holt, 1989.
[grades K–2; shapes]

Ross, Catherine Sheldrick. *Circles: Fun Ideas for Getting A-Round in Math.* Reading, Mass.: Addison-Wesley Publishing Co., 1992.
[grades 3–6; shapes]

————. *Squares: Shapes in Math, Science and Nature.* Toronto: Kids Can Press, 1996.
[grades 4 and up; shapes]

——. *Triangles: Shapes in Math, Science and Nature.* Toronto: Kids Can Press, 1997.
[grades 4–7; shapes]

Sandved, Kjell B. *The Butterfly Alphabet.* New York: Scholastic Inc., 1999.
[grades K–2; shapes; also transformational geometry]

Schwartz, David. *G is for Googol: A Math Alphabet Book.* Berkeley, Ca.: Tricycle, 1998.
[grades 3–6; also measurement]

Seuss, Dr. *The Shape of Me and Other Stuff.* New York: Random House, 1988.
[grades pre-K–1; shapes]

Silverstein, Shel. *A Light in the Attic.* New York: HarperCollins, 1981.
[grades 3–6; shapes]

——. *The Missing Piece.* New York: Harper and Row, 1976.
[grades K–3; circles]

——. *The Missing Piece Meets the Big O.* New York: HarperCollins, 1981.
[grades 3–6; circles]

——. *Where the Sidewalk Ends.* New York: HarperCollins, 1981.
[grades 3–6; also measurement]

Testa, Fluvio. *If You Look Around You.* New York: Dial Books for Young Readers, 1983.
[grades K–3; shapes]

Tompert, Ann. *Grandfather Tang's Story: A Tale Told with Tangrams.* New York: Crown Publishers, 1990.
[grades 1–4; also transformational geometry; also visualization and spatial reasoning]

Visualization and Spatial Reasoning

Baum, Arline. *Opt. An Illusionary Tale.* New York: Viking, 1987.
[grades 1–4]

Berenstain, Stan, and Jan Berenstain. *The Berenstain Bears: Inside, Outside, Upside Down.* New York: Random House Books for Young Readers, 1997.
[grades pre-K–1]

Hoban, Tana. *Spirals, Curves, Fanshapes, and Lines.* New York: Greenwillow Books, 1992.
[grades K and up]

Murphy, Pat. *By Nature's Design.* San Francisco: Chronicle Books, 1993.
[grades 5 and up; visualization; also transformational geometry]

Murphy, Stuart. *Bug Dance.* New York: Harper Trophy, 2002.
[grades pre-K–1; visualization; also coordinate geometry]

———. *The Greatest Gymnast of All: Opposites.* New York: Harper Trophy, 1998.
[grades pre-K–2]

Pluckrose, Henry. *Pattern.* New York: Franklin Watts, 1988.
[grades K–2; also transformational geometry]

Sitomer, Mindel, and Harry Sitomer. *What Is Symmetry?* New York: Thomas Y. Crowell, 1970.
[grades pre-K–1; also transformational geometry]

Tompert, Ann. *Grandfather Tang's Story: A Tale Told with Tangrams.* New York: Crown Publishers, 1990.
[grades 1–4; also transformational geometry; also two- and three-dimensional geometry]

Van Allsburg, Chris. *Two Bad Ants.* Boston: Houghton Mifflin, 1988.
[grades K–3; visualization]

Walter, Marion. *Look at Annette.* New York: M. Evans and Co., 1977.
[grades K–3; also transformational geometry]

———. *The Mirror Puzzle Book.* Suffolk: Tarquin Publications, 1988.
[grades 3–6; also transformational geometry]

Multicultural

Hopkinson, Deborah. *Sweet Clara and the Freedom Quilt.* New York: Knopf, 1998.
[grades K–3; also transformational geometry]

Jonas, Ann. *The Quilt.* New York: Puffin, 1994.
[grades K–3; also transformational geometry]

Polacco, Patricia. *The Keeping Quilt.* New York: Simon and Shuster, 1988.
[grades K–3; also transformational geometry]

Shannon, George. *More Stories to Solve: Fifteen Folktales from around the World.*
New York: Greenwillow Publishing, 1985.
[grades 3–6]

———. *Stories to Solve: Folktales from around the World.* New York: Greenwillow
Publishing, 1985.
[grades 3–6]

MANIPULATIVES

Instructional materials and manipulatives are critical in the teaching of geometry and measurement. Many students have trouble connecting the new concepts with their everyday lives and what they already know about their environment. Also, some students are tactile learners and even more are visual learners. Providing students with hands-on activities that allow them to feel and see mathematics and to explore and discover concepts and relationships is an essential first step in the learning process.

When students encounter a new concept, they need to start with concrete representations. This is especially true in the early grades. Once students feel comfortable with the concrete representations they can be moved to instruction involving visual representations. Eventually, when students are developmentally ready, they should feel comfortable using abstract representations. What follows is a list of instructional materials that are useful in teaching measurement and geometry. Examples of how some of these manipulatives can be used in the classroom appear in Chapter 4.

Many of these products are available via Web sites, catalogs, and textbook publishers.

See the Web sites section on page 210 for some examples.

algebra tiles
attribute blocks
balance scale
base-10 blocks
Battleship game
blocks
calculator
calendar
cardboard "bricks" for preschool
clay
compass
containers for liquid measure
      (customary/metric)
cubes (centimeter cubes, one-inch cubes)
Cuisenaire® Rods
dominoes
dot paper
flexible straws
fraction circles
fraction squares
geoboards (rectangular and circular)
geo-dot paper
geometric solids
GeoSolids™

graph paper (various sizes)
hinged mirror
JOVO® Click 'N Construct
   manipulatives
kaleidoscope
Klikko™
K'NEX™
links
liquid measure set
maps
mass/weight set
The Master Ruler®
      (customary and metric)
mazes
meter stick
Mira™
mosaics
nets for Platonic solids
number lines
origami paper
paperclips
pattern blocks
patty paper
pentominoes

Platonic solid models
Polydrons™
protractors
puzzles
quilts
rulers (English/metric)
spaghetti
square tiles (one-inch)
string
tangrams
tape measure (customary/metric)
thermometer (Fahrenheit/centigrade)
tissue paper
toothpicks and gum drops
triangle grid paper
trundle wheel
tubes (cardboard paper towel tubes, etc.)
Unifix® cubes
yardstick
yarn
Zome™ Geometry

TECHNOLOGY

Appropriate uses of technology can enhance learning and motivate students. This section includes brief descriptions of software and Web sites that can be used to improve geometry and measurement instruction in grades K–5. This list will continue to be updated on the IMAGES Web site (http://images.rbs.org). Your comments and suggestions are welcome.

For additional information about technology, see pages 13 and 49.

Software

The best software is open-ended and allows students to explore, look for patterns, and make and test conjectures. What appears here is a selection of programs that exemplify this approach. Main criteria for choosing software were whether the program: (1) actively engages students; and (2) facilitates learning new concepts in the context of a problem situation.

Nearly all of the software listed here focuses on geometry and/or measurement and is designed for use by students under the guidance of a teacher. One exception is the *Cognitive Tutor*, which is designed to increase teachers' content knowledge. *Exemplars Math* also provides a wealth of examples of student work and associated rubrics that will help teachers become better at assessing student work.

Cabri Geometry™ II
This dynamic, visual geometry software product allows you to check conjectures using Euclid's five postulates. Along with Geometer's Sketchpad®, Cabri is one of the best known of the dynamic geometry software packages. Texas Instruments. http://www.education.ti.com [grades 3–16]

Cognitive Tutor®: Geometry
This is a secondary mathematics program by the same organization that developed *Cognitive Tutor®: Algebra*, one of the programs designated as exemplary by the U.S. Department of Education's Mathematics and Science Expert Panel. It is included here as a resource for teachers wanting to improve their content knowledge. This program uses a combination of technology and a text to provide the instruction. Carnegie Learning, Inc. http://www.carnegielearning.com [grades 6–12]

Exemplars Math
This series includes two CD-ROMs. *Best of MATH I* contains 180 K–8 assessment and instruction tasks. *Best of MATH II* contains over 100 K–8 assessment and instruction tasks, uses a Web-based platform, and can be networked. All tasks are grouped grades K–2, 3–5, and 6–8. Both CDs include scoring rubrics and benchmark student papers and can be searched by standard or content area. Both allow you to edit tasks to meet specific needs. Exemplars. http://www.exemplars.com [grades K–8]

The Factory Deluxe
As students design, build, and ship products, they learn about shapes, rotations, angle measurement, and formulas. Sunburst. http://www.sunburst.com [grades 4–8]

Geometry Inventor™
This dynamic, visual software is similar to the Geometer's Sketchpad® (see below). You can graph relationships between two measures to show, for example, that the ratio of the circumference of a circle to its diameter is a constant. LOGAL Tangible MATH. http://www.riverdeep.net [grades 3–16]

The Geometer's Sketchpad®
This software is open-ended in the best sense, since it is limited only by the imagination of the teacher. Students can plot points in the plane or in a coordinate system. The software knows what constructions are possible based on what objects have been selected. Students select constructions from a menu and can measure length and perimeter, area, and angles. Students can also test conjectures by altering their construction to determine if a certain property holds for many shapes of the same type. Key Curriculum Press. http://www.keypress.com [grades 3–16]

Microworlds™
This is the Logo program (also called turtle graphics), with many add-ons. In addition to being able to program the turtle to create geometric shapes, students can create a multimedia environment using sound and video. The software can be used for a multidisciplinary unit that integrates math and art or math and music. Logo Computer Systems, Inc. http://www.lcsi.com [grades 3–8]

Pythagoras®
This dynamic, visual software is similar to Geometer's Sketchpad® in its design and use. The software has many built-in shapes to make it easier to create polygons or circles, explore their properties, and easily scale (dilate) figures. Dalin, Inc., Educational Software. http://www.interactivemathworld.com [grades 3–16]

Shape Up!
This program allows students to create and explore two- and three-dimensional shapes and learn names and properties of shapes. Other concepts include similarity, congruence, and transformations. Students can write about their work. Sunburst. http://www.sunburst.com [grades K–8]

SPEX+
Students develop spatial reasoning abilities as they create a room in two dimensions and then view a three-dimensional version of the room. The program requires students to measure and rotate objects. The Knowledge Tree, Inc. http://www.theknowledgetreeinc.com [grades 5–9]

TABS+

Using basic shapes, students can create and manipulate three-dimensional shapes. Models can be wire frames or solids, which can be dilated, rotated, and viewed from the front, side, or top. Shapes can be animated. Nets can be created from three-dimensional models, printed, and used to create the three-dimensional model. The Knowledge Tree, Inc. http://www.theknowledgetreeinc.com [grades 3–12]

The Tenth Planet™ Geometry Bundle

This series consists of six titles: *Spatial Relationships* and *Introduction to Patterns* (grades pre-K–1), *Combining Shapes* and *Creating Patterns from Shapes* (grades 1–2), *Shapes within Shapes* and *Mirror Symmetry* (grades 2–5). Sound, animation, and active engagement motivate students to explore geometric concepts. Sunburst. http://www.sunburst.com

Tessellation Exploration®

Students use transformations to create tessellations. Students are asked to predict and describe the results of transformations. Stamps included with the software allow students to create great-looking tessellations that can be printed or shown to the class using the Slide Show feature. Tom Snyder Productions. http://www.tomsnyder.com [grades 4–8]

Web Sites

Web sites are valuable resources for teachers and students in search of current ideas and activities in mathematics. Since the quality of Web sites varies widely, a teacher should explore a site thoroughly for its mathematical content before suggesting it to students. The selections presented here are only a sample of the high-quality sites that are available.

Some sites are commercial, while others are non-profit organizations offering free educational resources. Some of the following sites are targeted specifically to teachers, offering lesson plans and activities for use in the classroom. Others offer links to other sites that will assist teachers striving to improve measurement and geometry learning in their classroom. Some sites describe educational research in terms that will be most readily usable to teachers trying to incorporate the research in their classes.

Certain sites have activities for students as well as ideas for teachers. A few sites, such as the Research for Better Schools site, are resource sites. They provide software, Web site, video, and/or curriculum reviews, as well as links to professional development opportunities and other useful sites. We have provided brief descriptions to assist you in finding the type of site you are looking for.

All Web sites are current as of February 2004.

Links for Sample State Mathematics Standards:

California: http://www.cde.ca.gov/standards/

Minnesota: http://education.state.mn.us/content/009199.pdf

North Carolina:
http://www.ncpublicschools.org/curriculum/mathematics/standard2003/toc.html

Pennsylvania: http://www.pde.state.pa.us/

Texas: http://www.tea.state.tx.us/rules/tac/chapter111/ch111a.html#111.15

AIMS Education Foundation

http://www.aimsedu.org

AIMS (Activities Integrating Math and Science) offers an online database of hundreds of activities that can also be ordered through the Web site. Some sample activities are available for free, including measurement and geometry activities.

All about Geometry

http://www.aaamath.com/geo.html

These Web pages teach a wide variety of geometry facts and provide interactive practice.

Association for Supervision and Curriculum Development (ASCD)

http://www.ascd.org

ASCD is an international professional education association with more than 160,000 members. This site offers links to the many publications and professional development opportunities affiliated with ASCD, as well as the diverse products available through the online store.

Big Wind Kite Factory

http://www.aloha.net/~bigwind/20kidskites.html

The Big Wind Kite Factory in Moloka'i, Hawaii, shows how to make classroom kites.

Columbia Education Center

http://www.col-ed.org

This site includes over 600 lesson plans and Web activities contributed by classroom teachers, teacher resources with links to education Web sites, and information about educational grant opportunities.

Coolmath 4 Kids

http://www.coolmath4kids.com/geometrystuff.html

The Polyhedra Gallery has colorful pictures and diagrams of the platonic solids and semi-regular polyhedra. Lesson plan topics include tessellations, congruence, and interior angles of regular polygons.

Education World Math Center

http://www.educationworld.com/math

This site includes resources for mathematics educators including lesson plans, mathematics articles, professional development resources, and mathematics Web site reviews and links. Measurement and geometry problems are available in the Math Worksheet Library; there are teacher lessons plans in geometry and measurement.

The Educator's Reference Desk (Formerly Ask ERIC - Educational Resources Information Center)
http://eduref.org/cgi-bin/lessons.cgi/Mathematics/Geometry
The Educator's Reference Desk is a Web site from the U.S. Department of Education which includes lesson plans, links to online education materials, and all the archived questions that were previously available at askeric.org. This page offers geometry lesson plans that can be used at the elementary school level. Measurement lesson plans are available at http://eduref.org/cgi-bin/lessons.cgi/Mathematics/Measurement.
[Note: The ERIC Web site which featured a database with more than one million abstracts of documents and journal articles on education research and practice is being reengineered as of January 2004; during the transition period all materials should still be available at http://www.eric.ed.gov.]

Eisenhower National Clearinghouse (ENC)
http://www.enc.org/
ENC collects teaching materials for K–12 mathematics and science educators and disseminates information about federally funded programs. This site contains links to more than 100 sites related to geometry. See the *Classroom Calendar* (http://www.enc.org/features/calendar/?ls=ho) for weekly entries containing topic overviews, ready-to-go activities, and suggested curriculum materials.

M. C. Escher
http://www.iproject.com/escher/teaching/teaching.html
This site contains lesson plans for connecting the art of Escher to the teaching of geometry (and other topics). It also includes links to related articles in *School Arts* magazine.

ETA/Cuisenaire
http://www.etacuisenaire.com
This company sells more than 150 manipulative-based and supplemental educational materials related to geometry and measurement.

The Geometry Center
http://www.scienceu.com/geometry
This Web page is part of the Science U Web site. Some of the elementary geometry activities include triangle tilings and polyhedra, symmetry and tiling, and tetrahedral puzzles.

The Geometry Junkyard
http://www.ics.uci.edu/~eppstein/junkyard
This resource site for teachers includes various topics in geometry with links to other sites. The origami page of this site (http://www.ics.uci.edu/~eppstein/junkyard/origami.html) has links to other sites with colorful photos of origami foldings.

Geometry Step-by-Step from the Land of the Incas

http://Agutie.homestead.com/files/index.html

This colorful, interactive site includes a mix of sound, science, and Incan history related to the study of geometry. Although the site is more appropriate for high school students, elementary school teachers can learn about concepts that upper elementary students could explore in historical and multicultural contexts.

Goudreau Museum of Mathematics in Art and Science

http://www.mathmuseum.org/

Visit the Web site of this museum (in New Hyde Park, NY) for information about their annual Pi Day Contest.

Helping Your Child Learn Math

http://www.ed.gov/pubs/parents/Math/index.html

The online version of this booklet (published in 1999 by the U.S. Department of Education) provides activities for families with elementary school-aged children. It is designed to help parents to have fun with their children while reinforcing mathematical skills. Many activities are related to measurement and estimation.

Interactive Games

http://www.oswego.org/staff/cchamber/techno/games.htm

This site includes interactive mathematics games and allows the user to create games and quizzes. Two of the pre-made games involve graphing points on the coordinate plane and numerous games involve time.

Investigating Patterns: Symmetry and Tessellations

http://www.camosun.bc.ca/~jbritton/jbsymteslk.htm

Educational consultant and textbook author Jill Britton is the author of this site, listing Web resources for grade 5–8 mathematics. It includes tutorials and fun activities for students and printable activity sheets and lesson plans for teachers. It contains topics such as soap bubbles and honeycombs, Islamic tessellations, M. C. Escher, symmetry by paper folding, and more.

The Joy of Pi

http://www.joyofpi.com/

Find out about the book published by Davis Blatner and discover links to other places on the Web to have fun with pi.

Juvenile Literature Related to Math

http://www.coastal.edu/library/mathlit.htm

The Kimbel Library at Coastal Carolina University has correlated many children's books with mathematics topics, including measurement, shapes, symmetry, and tangrams.

Cynthia Lanius
http://math.rice.edu/~lanius/Lessons/index.html
Cynthia Lanius, Executive Director of the Center for Excellence and Equity in Education (CEEE) at Rice University, authored these lessons in geometry and other areas of mathematics.

The Lesson Plans Page
http://www.lessonplanspage.com/Math.htm
This site includes free lesson plans for grades pre-K–1, 2–3, and 4–5 in the areas of geometry, measurement, and shapes and architecture.

Literature for Science and Mathematics: Kindergarten through Grade Twelve
http://www.cde.ca.gov/ci/scimathlit/
Sponsored by the California Department of Education, this site includes science and math related literature for children. Titles are listed for both geometry and measurement.

Making Tracks Towards Area
http://library.thinkquest.org/TQ0311000/
Students from South Decatur Junior-Senior High School were the winners of the ThinkQuest USA 2003 contest for the state of Indiana. On this site children can learn about finding area of circles, triangles, squares, rectangles, and other polygons.

Math Central
http://MathCentral.uregina.ca/index.html
This site is an Internet service for mathematics teachers and students. Use the search feature in the "Resource Room" section to find geometry and measurement activities and resources.

The Math Forum at Drexel University
http://www.mathforum.org
The Math Forum offers mathematics resources by subject and problems of the week. In particular, see these activities:
- *Chameleon Graphing*
  http://mathforum.org/cgraph
- *Varnelle Moore's Primary Math Activities*
  http://mathforum.org/varnelle
- *Tom Scavo's Tangrams*
  http://www.mathforum.org/trscavo/tangrams.html

Math Fun Facts
http://www.math.hmc.edu/funfacts/
These "Math Fun Facts" from the Harvey Mudd College Mathematics Department can be used to enrich mathematics lessons. Use the search feature at the easy level to find geometry fun facts. One of the activities you will find introduces Pick's Theorem.

Maths Thesaurus
http://thesaurus.maths.org/
This site provides an alphabetized listing of mathematics definitions; each definition also includes links to related and/or similar words.

Mathworld (Wolfram Research)
http://mathworld.wolfram.com/Cube.html
This page of Mathworld includes diagrams of all the possible nets for a cube. Explore this mathematics Web site for other polyhedra nets, mathematical art, and origami. Diagrams and photographs are colorful and some are animated.

NASA "Why?" Files
http://whyfiles.larc.nasa.gov
The "Why" files integrate mathematics, science, and technology with a distance learning format. Each episode includes online investigation, activities/worksheets, free educator's guide, related resources, and implementation strategy.

National Council of Teachers of Mathematics (NCTM)
http://www.nctm.org
This site features professional development opportunities, Web resources, teaching resources, and classroom activities. Click on "Teachers Corner."

NCTM Illuminations
http://www.illuminations.nctm.org
NCTM provides ready-to-use, online interactive multimedia math investigations, mathematics education Web resources reviewed by an NCTM panel, and Internet-based lesson plans. Visit http://illuminations.nctm.org/imath/3-5/GeometricSolids/index.html for an interactive investigation, "Exploring Geometric Solids and Their Properties."

National Library of Virtual Manipulatives for Interactive Mathematics
http://www.matti.usu.edu
Utah State University, working under a grant from the National Science Foundation, has made available online dozens of free pre-K–12 mathematics manipulatives. Every manipulative is correlated to NCTM standards. Geometry and measurement activities are appropriate for grades K–2 or 3–5. New online manipulatives are added each month.

National Metric Week
http://lamar.colostate.edu/~hillger/ideas.htm
This site includes ideas from the U.S. Metric Association for celebrating National Metric Week.

Native American Geometry
http://www.earthmeasure.com
Students can learn geometry through creating Native American designs. This site explores constructions of regular polygons and connects geometry, art, and history. The site is divided into four areas: foundations, anthropology, design, and education.

Origami Mathematics

http://merrimack.edu/~thull/OrigamiMath.html

This page was created by mathematics professor Thomas Hull. It contains a mathematics bibliography, models and tutorials, and links to other origami mathematics pages.

Origami USA

http://www.origami-usa.org/

This very complete site, run by a membership organization devoted to origami, has a model index, lists origami resources on the Internet, and features fun diagrams, quizzes, and puzzles.

Pattern Block Program

http://www.arcytech.org/java/patterns/patterns_i.shtml

On this interactive site students can easily manipulate pattern blocks to create shapes and designs.

PBS Teacher Source

http://www.pbs.org/teachersource/math.htm

This site includes activities for classroom use, including excellent geometry and measurement resources for preschool and grades K–2 and 3–5.

PBS's "News Hour Extra" Teacher Resources

http://www.pbs.org/newshour/extra/teachers/math/

Each "News Hour Extra" story includes a lesson plan for teachers that connects school subjects to important news events around the world. Currently available on this page is a measurement lesson, "A Gigabyte of Music, How Much Is That?"

Pearson Learning Group

http://www.pearsonlearning.com/

The Pearson Learning Group, which includes the imprint Dale Seymour Publications, sells more than 100 programs in geometry, from kits to units. Search by subject and grade level.

Pop-up Art

http://www.robertsabuda.com

Robert Sabuda had created delightful pop-up versions of classic children's books. His Web site includes patterns for pop-ups that can be printed and then made by children. Geometric concepts can be reinforced by making the pop-ups.

Practical Uses of Math and Science

http://pumas.jpl.nasa.gov

This site is an online journal of mathematics and science examples for pre-college students. Measurement and geometry activities for elementary school students are available.

Research for Better Schools

http://www.rbs.org

A special section is devoted to the mathematics and science state resources in the mid-Atlantic region (ENC access centers, informal mathematics and science education, professional development, and technology resources), as well as free publications.

Saskatchewan Education

http://www.sasked.gov.sk.ca/docs/elemath/

Saskatchewan Education created this site, "Mathematics 1–5: A Curriculum Guide for the Elementary Level."

Thinking Fountain Shapes Cluster

http://www.smm.org/sln/tf/nav/shapescluster.html

The Science Museum of Minnesota presents books, activities, and hands-on experiments related to shapes.

Visual Geometry Dictionary for Kids and for Kids' Teachers

http://www.math.okstate.edu/%7Erpsc/dict/Dictionary.html

Pre-service students at Oklahoma State University prepared an online, visual geometry dictionary for children and their teachers.

VIDEOS

Videos have the advantage of showing mathematics content in action, and they can be a valuable resource for instruction. When a teacher has the opportunity to view another teacher's classroom, he or she can benefit from seeing teaching strategies that work and how they look in practice. Similarly, when students see mathematics at work in real-life situations, they can relate better to the mathematics concepts involved.

The videos listed in this section can be used in one of three ways:
- to be shown directly to students
- to deepen teachers' content knowledge
- to model the teaching of mathematics concepts.

Videos and Web links are current as of February 2004.

Annenberg/CPB Videos—*Teaching Math: A Video Library, K–4* (1997)
This series of videos shows how the NCTM standards are used in elementary classrooms across America: small, large, rural, suburban, and inner-city. The entire series contains 52 video programs, but the 11 related to geometry and measurement (described below) can be ordered individually by calling 1-800-LEARNER. Videos range from 15 to 30 minutes in length. For more information visit http://www.learner.org.

Balloon Travel is an integrated mathematics/science lesson, in which second- and third-graders collect data to answer questions such as, "What is the farthest a balloon can travel before falling?" To answer the question, they must understand distance, volume, capacity, and time. NCTM standards addressed: measurement, estimation, connection, problem solving.

Circumference/Diameter includes reviewing the meaning of radius, diameter, center, and circumference with fourth-graders. Students work in teams to measure circular objects throughout the room. They are then challenged to find the relationship between the circumference and the diameter. NCTM standards addressed: geometry and spatial sense, measurement, connections, reasoning.

How Long is a Minute? shows first-graders observing the second hand of a clock and counting by fives as they watch the second hand rotate for one minute. Students do 15-second trials of three activities and estimate how many times the activities can be done in a minute. To determine the time measurements, students use mental math strategies like skip counting. NCTM standards addressed: measurement, estimation, reasoning, connections.

Meter Cords models how third- and fourth-graders use linear measurement in learning about decimals. Students measure different items with a meter divided into 10 parts and then learn to write their measurements using decimal notation. NCTM standards addressed: measurement, fractions and decimals, connections, communications.

Annenberg/CPB Videos (continued)

Pattern Blocks portrays second-graders learning the mathematical terms for pattern-block pieces: hexagon, trapezoid, square, triangle, and rhombus. Ideas about fractions emerge as students spot size relationships between shapes. NCTM standards addressed: geometry and spatial sense, number sense and numeration, reasoning, connections.

Pencil Box Staining challenges fourth-graders with the task of finding out how much stain to buy from the hardware store. Students encounter problems as they work with many mathematical ideas in the context of a real application. Students work in groups with pencil box pieces and a ruler, calculator, and instruction sheet. NCTM standards addressed: measurement, fractions and decimals, problem solving, reasoning.

A Rocket Shape reveals how second- and third-graders subdivide a square to recreate a rocket shape. After completing their rockets, they reconvene as a class to discuss their difficulties and problem-solving strategies. NCTM standards addressed: geometry and spatial sense, measurement, problem solving, reasoning.

Shapes from Squares depicts an activity in which a second/third-grade class develops spatial sense as they subdivide and change squares to create different shapes. The language of geometry—square, trapezoid, hexagon, etc.—grows naturally from their explorations. NCTM standards addressed: geometry and spatial sense, communication, reasoning.

Thanksgiving Quilt shows how first graders, by creating quilt squares from construction paper, develop spatial sense as they discuss and handle different shapes. They connect geometric ideas to number ideas as they cut squares into congruent triangles. NCTM standards addressed: geometry and spatial sense, patterns and relationships, communication, connections.

This Small House presents second- and third-graders using calculators, paper and pencil, and mental math within a realistic task. Students plan the decorating of their milk carton houses using spatial sense to select appropriate furnishings while staying within their allocated budget. NCTM standards addressed: whole number computation, geometry and spatial sense, connections, communication.

Windows, Dinos, and Ants pictures first graders using standard and non-standard units to measure ant farm tunnels, dinosaurs, and the length from the classroom window to the playground. As they work in groups, students communicate and make connections. They use their heights to measure the length of a Tyrannosaurus Rex. NCTM standards addressed: measurement, number sense and numeration, problem solving, reasoning.

Marilyn Burns Tapes

These video programs feature classroom lessons and cover a variety of topics to help teachers and administrators implement the NCTM standards. Teacher's guides are included, which facilitate the use of these resources for staff development and in-service workshops. Available from Dale Seymour Publications (Pearson Learning Center) at 1-800-872-1100.

Mathematics: With Manipulatives is a series of six 20-minute videotapes for K–6 staff development. In each videotape Marilyn Burns shows how to use specific manipulatives. The titles of the tapes are: "Pattern Blocks," "Cuisenaire Rods," "Base Ten Blocks," "Geoboards," "Color Tiles," and "Six Models (Unifix® Cubes, Multilink Cubes, Color Cubes, Tangrams, Attribute Blocks, and Two-Color Counters)."

Mathematics: What Are You Teaching My Child? is an engaging 20-minute

video program that addresses mathematics issues that are vital to teachers, families, and students. Topics include why paper and pencil computational proficiency isn't enough; how to integrate manipulatives into the classroom to help implement the NCTM standards; collaborative learning; the role of problem-solving and reasoning skills; and how to build parental understanding and support for a mathematics curriculum. This is an excellent resource for parent outreach programs as well as in-service and pre-service education for grades K–12.

Mathematics: Assessing Understanding is a series of three videos that look at how the interview can be used to assess student understanding.

Donald Duck in Mathemagic Land

This classic Disney video follows Donald Duck through a journey of discovery of the diversity and value of mathematics. Teachers and students love this animated, humorous video that shows the magic side of mathematics. Available at many libraries.

The Fantastic World of M. C. Escher

This video reveals the intrigue of how M. C. Escher's artwork seems to weave magically and transform from one form into another. This 50-minute video provides a sense of what the man behind the art was all about. Included are first-person accounts from the artist's friends, computer-animated recreations of Escher's work, and views of his sources of inspiration in Italy and Spain. Available from http://www.amazon.com.

How Do You Spell Parallel? Visiting Middle School Math (1997)

In this 19-minute video, two seventh-grade teachers and one sixth-grade teacher discuss and model changes teachers are making in instruction. Students are actively involved and motivated by real-life examples. The teachers explain a geometry project, use hands-on activities, communicate concepts, and connect geometry to other mathematical topics.

Available from the Mathematics and Science Education Center, Northwest Regional Educational Laboratory (101 SW Main St., Suite 500, Portland, OR 97204) at 503-275-9500.

Math Monsters Videotape Series:
2. Standard and Non-standard Measurement **and** *5. Geometry*
These two videos in the series can be useful to introduce or reinforce topics and allow students to be actively involved. Available at http://www.mathmonsters.com.

PBS Mathline: *Elementary School Math Project*
The Elementary School Math Project (ESMP), for teachers K–5, features video lessons modeling the teaching of mathematical concepts. It shows how these concepts can be developed over time in the classroom and provides a forum for discussing issues relating to teaching at the elementary level. Available under the TeacherLine section at http://www.pbs.org/teachersource/math.htm.

Geometry and Spatial Relations: **ESMP Tape Four** (#VC1574) includes three different activities:
1. "Tessellations WOW!" (grade 1)—Identifying and using shapes such as sponge designs, crackers, and other applications to create tessellations (22 minutes).
2. "Sidewalk Capers" (grade 3)—Exploring spatial relationships of various shapes that tessellate and have the same area (28 minutes).
3. "Mirror, Mirror" (grade 5)—Using spatial reasoning and angle measure to determine which regular polygons will tessellate (29 minutes).

Geometry and Spatial Relations: **ESMP Tape Five** (# VC1575) is divided into three parts:
1. "It's a Perfect Fit," part 1—Identifying, describing, and classifying two-dimensional shapes (27 minutes).
2. "It's a Perfect Fit," part 2—Identifying and describing numerical relationships among pattern block shapes (16 minutes).
3. "It's a Perfect Fit," Part 3—Combining geoblocks to make three-dimensional shapes (17 minutes).

Measurement: **ESMP Tape Six** (# VC1576) features three sections:
1. "Sand Babies" (grade 1)—Measuring the weight of students when they were born, their present height, and the area of their feet (24 minutes).
2. "Bubble Mania" (grade 3)—Measuring the diameter, circumference, and the area of circles made by a bubble print (23 minutes).
3. "It Takes Ten" (grade 5)—Estimating and measuring through a variety of lab experiences (26 minutes).

TIMSS CD: Teaching Mathematics in Seven Countries (1999)

This is a four-CD set that includes videos from eighth grade mathematics lessons in seven countries: Australia, the Czech Republic, Hong Kong SAR, Japan, Netherlands, Switzerland, and the United States. As a component of the TIMSS 1999 video study, the CDs are intended for use by professional developers and district administrators in order to conduct professional development with teachers. The software, designed by LessonLab, Inc., offers numerous features to enhance the study of these lessons. The features include subtitles of each video, user-friendly maneuvering within each video, transcripts of the lessons, commentary by observers, and an index of key points in the lessons. The CDs are compatible with Macintosh and Windows. The CDs are for sale at http://www.rbs.org/catalog/pubs/pd57.shtml.

TIMSS Videotape: Classroom Study (1995)

This video survey of eighth-grade mathematics lessons in Germany, Japan, and the United States is the first attempt to collect videotaped records of classroom instruction from nationally representative samples of students, aimed at improving student learning in school. For more information visit http://isc.bc.edu/. Available free of charge from the National Center for Education Statistics (U.S. Dept. of Education, 1990 K Street, NW, Washington, DE 20006).

Video 5: Geometry (2001)

This teacher-to-teacher video presents concepts of lines and angles, midpoints and bisectors, classification of angles, diagonals and angles of polygons, congruency, lines and planes in space, prisms, and pyramids. The teacher explains terms clearly and models the solving of related problems. The latter part of the video shows the use of the SAS and SSS congruence theorems. The video provides an excellent, quick review of basic geometric concepts. Available through Prentice Hall Publishers.

Appendix A

Correlations to State Standards

Effective implementation of state standards for geometry and measurement is a critical goal of IMAGES. This section presents aspects of the various state academic standards for mathematics that pertain to the five IMAGES content strands for students in grades K–3 and 4–5:[1] visualization and spatial reasoning; two- and three-dimensional geometry; coordinate geometry; transformational geometry; measurement. This appendix includes only elements of the state standards that apply to geometry and measurement.

The IMAGES content for students may be broader than that presented in various state standards and goes beyond what each state's programs assess. Just as teachers must know content beyond that which they are teaching, students need to learn more than what will appear on any given test.

Appendix A1: California State Standards

Appendix A2: Minnesota State Standards

Appendix A3: North Carolina State Standards

Appendix A4: Pennsylvania State Standards

Appendix A5: Texas State Standards

---

[1] Standards in this appendix are organized by the lettering and numbering consistent with the original state documents. Please refer to the original state documents, whose Web links are on page 210, for comprehensive state standards.

APPENDIX A1: California State Standards[2]

A1.a: Visualization and Spatial Reasoning

> Grades K–3 (*Mathematics Content Standards for California Public Schools*, Measurement and Geometry, 2.0, grade 3)
>
> Students describe and compare the attributes of plane and solid geometric figures and use their understanding to show relationships and solve problems:
> 2.1 Identify, describe, and classify polygons (including pentagons, hexagons, and octagons).
> 2.2 Identify attributes of triangles (e.g., two equal sides for the isosceles triangle, three equal sides for the equilateral triangle, right angle for the right triangle).
> 2.3 Identify attributes of quadrilaterals (e.g., parallel sides for the parallelogram, right angles for the rectangle, equal sides and right angles for the square).
> 2.4 Identify right angles in geometric figures or in appropriate objects and determine whether other angles are greater or less than a right angle.
> 2.5 Identify, describe, and classify common three-dimensional geometric objects (e.g., cube, rectangular solid, sphere, prism, pyramid, cone, cylinder).
> 2.6 Identify common solid objects that are the components needed to make a more complex solid object.

> Grades 4–5 (*Mathematics Content Standards for California Public Schools*, Measurement and Geometry, 2.0, grade 5)
>
> Students identify, describe, and classify the properties of, and the relationships between, plane and solid geometric figures:
> 2.1 Measure, identify, and draw angles, perpendicular and parallel lines, rectangles, and triangles by using appropriate tools (e.g., straightedge, ruler, compass, protractor, drawing software).
> 2.3 Visualize and draw two-dimensional views of three-dimensional objects made from rectangular solids.

---

[2] Available online at http://www.cde.ca.gov/standards/

A1.b: Two- and Three-Dimensional Geometry

Grades K–3 (*Mathematics Content Standards for California Public Schools*, Measurement and Geometry, 2.0, grade 3)

Students describe and compare the attributes of plane and solid geometric figures and use their understanding to show relationships and solve problems:
2.1 Identify, describe, and classify polygons (including pentagons, hexagons, and octagons).
2.2 Identify attributes of triangles (e.g., two equal sides for the isosceles triangle, three equal sides for the equilateral triangle, right angle for the right triangle).
2.3 Identify attributes of quadrilaterals (e.g., parallel sides for the parallelogram, right angles for the rectangle, equal sides and right angles for the square).
2.4 Identify right angles in geometric figures or in appropriate objects and determine whether other angles are greater or less than a right angle.
2.5 Identify, describe, and classify common three-dimensional geometric objects (e.g., cube, rectangular solid, sphere, prism, pyramid, cone, cylinder).
2.6 Identify common solid objects that are the components needed to make a more complex solid object.

Grades 4–5

Grade 4 (*Mathematics Content Standards for California Public Schools*, Measurement and Geometry, 3.0, grade 4)

Students demonstrate an understanding of plane and solid geometric objects and use this knowledge to show relationships and solve problems:
3.2 Identify the radius and diameter of a circle.
3.3 Identify congruent figures.
3.7 Know the definitions of different triangles (e.g., equilateral, isosceles, scalene) and identify their attributes.
3.8 Know the definition of different quadrilaterals (e.g., rhombus, square, rectangle, parallelogram, trapezoid).

Grade 5 (*Mathematics Content Standards for California Public Schools*, Measurement and Geometry, 2.0, grade 5)

Students identify, describe, and classify the properties of, and the relationships between, plane and solid geometric figures:
2.1 Measure, identify, and draw angles, perpendicular and parallel lines, rectangles, and triangles by using appropriate tools (e.g., straightedge, ruler, compass, protractor, drawing software).
2.2 Know that the sum of the angles of any triangle is 180° and the sum of the angles of any quadrilateral is 360° and use this information to solve problems.
2.3 Visualize and draw two-dimensional views of three-dimensional objects made from rectangular solids.

A1.c: Coordinate Geometry

Grades K–3 (*Mathematics Content Standards for California Public Schools*, Measurement and Geometry, 2.0, grade 1)

Students identify common geometric figures, classify them by common attributes, and describe their relative position or their location in space:
2.3 Give and follow directions about location.
2.4 Arrange and describe objects in space by proximity, position, and direction (e.g., near, far, below, above, up, down, behind, in front of, next to, left or right of).

Grades 4–5

Grade 4 (*Mathematics Content Standards for California Public Schools*, Measurement and Geometry, 2.0, grade 4)

Students use two-dimensional coordinate grids to represent points and graph lines and simple figures:
2.1 Draw the points corresponding to linear relationships on graph paper (e.g., draw 10 points on the graph of the equation $y=3x$ and connect them by using a straight line).
2.2 Understand that the length of a horizontal line segment equals the difference of the x-coordinates.
2.3 Understand that the length of a vertical line segment equals the difference of the y-coordinates.

Grade 5 (*Mathematics Content Standards for California Public Schools*, Algebra and Functions, 1.0, grade 5)

Students use variables in simple expressions, compute the value of the expression for specific values of the variable, and plot and interpret the results:
1.4 Identify and graph ordered pairs in the four quadrants of the coordinate plane.

A1.d: Transformational Geometry

Grades K–3 (*Mathematics Content Standards for California Public Schools*, Measurement and Geometry, 2.0, grade 3)

Students describe and compare the attributes of plane and solid geometric figures and use their understanding to show relationships and solve problems:
2.1 Identify, describe, and classify polygons (including pentagons, hexagons, and octagons).
2.5 Identify, describe, and classify common three-dimensional geometric objects (e.g., cube, rectangular solid, sphere, prism, pyramid, cone, cylinder).

Grades 4–5 (*Mathematics Content Standards for California Public Schools*, Measurement and Geometry, 3.0, grade 4)

Students demonstrate an understanding of plane and solid geometric objects and use this knowledge to show relationships and solve problems:
3.4 Identify figures that have bilateral and rotational symmetry.

A1.e: Measurement

Grades K–3 (*Mathematics Content Standards for California Public Schools*, Measurement and Geometry, 1.0, grade 3)

Students choose and use appropriate units and measurement tools to quantify the properties of objects:
1.1 Choose the appropriate tools and units (metric and U.S.) and estimate and measure the length, liquid volume, and weight/mass of given objects.
1.2 Estimate or determine the area and volume of solid figures by covering them with squares or by counting the number of cubes that would fill them.
1.3 Find the perimeter of a polygon with integer sides.
1.4 Carry out simple unit conversions within a system of measurement (e.g., centimeters and meters, hour and minutes).

Grades 4–5 (*Mathematics Content Standards for California Public Schools*, Measurement and Geometry, 1.0, grade 5)

Students understand and compute the volumes and areas of simple objects:
1.1 Derive and use the formula for the area of a triangle and of a parallelogram by comparing it with the formula for the area of a rectangle (i.e., two of the same triangles make a parallelogram with twice the area; a parallelogram is compared with a rectangle of the same area by cutting and pasting a right triangle on the parallelogram).
1.2 Construct a cube and rectangular box from two-dimensional patterns and use these patterns to compute the surface area for these objects.
1.3 Understand the concept of volume and use the appropriate units in common measuring systems (i.e., cubic centimeter, cubic meter, cubic inch, cubic yard to compute the volume of rectangular solids).
1.4 Differentiate between, and use appropriate units of measures for, two- and three-dimensional objects (i.e., find the perimeter, area, volume).

Appendix A2: Minnesota State Standards[3]

A2.a: Visualization and Spatial Reasoning

Grades K–3

Grade K (*Minnesota Academic Standards, Mathematics K–12*, Spatial Sense, Geometry, and Measurement, grade K)

Understand meaning of terms used to describe location and placement of objects.
The student will:
1. Locate and describe placement of objects with terms such as: on, inside, outside, above, below, over, under, beside, between, in front of, behind, next to, top, bottom.

Grade 3 (*Minnesota Academic Standards, Mathematics K–12*, Spatial Sense, Geometry, and Measurement, grades K and 3)

Classify shapes by specified attributes. Identify simple shapes within complex shapes.
The student will:
1. Identify, describe and classify two-dimensional shapes according to number and length of sides and kinds of angles.
2. Identify common two- and three-dimensional shapes that are components of more complex shapes.

Grades 4–5

Grade 4 (*Minnesota Academic Standards, Mathematics K–12*, Spatial Sense, Geometry, and Measurement, grade 4)

Understand spatial relationships and describe them using language such as congruent, similar, parallel and perpendicular. The student will:
1. Identify congruent and similar figures.
2. Identify parallel and perpendicular lines.

Grade 5 (*Minnesota Academic Standards, Mathematics K–12*, Spatial Sense, Geometry, and Measurement, grade 5)

Sort, classify, compare and describe two- and three-dimensional objects.
The student will:
1. Sort three-dimensional objects according to number and shape of faces, number of edges and vertices.
2. Classify polygons as regular or irregular.

---

[3] Available online at http://education.state.mn.us/content/009199.pdf.

A2.b: Two- and Three-Dimensional Geometry

Grades K–3 (*Minnesota Academic Standards, Mathematics K–12*, Spatial Sense, Geometry, and Measurement, grade 3)

Classify shapes by specified attributes. Identify simple shapes within complex shapes. The student will:
1. Identify, describe and classify two-dimensional shapes according to number and length of sides and kinds of angles.
2. Identify common two- and three-dimensional shapes that are components of more complex shapes.

Grades 4–5 (*Minnesota Academic Standards, Mathematics K–12*, Spatial Sense, Geometry, and Measurement, grade 5)

Sort, classify, compare and describe two- and three-dimensional objects. The student will:
1. Sort three-dimensional objects according to number and shape of faces, number of edges and vertices.
2. Classify, compare and identify acute, right and obtuse angles.
3. Classify polygons as regular or irregular.
4. Know the sum of the angles in triangles and quadrilaterals.

A2.c: Coordinate Geometry

Grades K–3 (*Minnesota Academic Standards, Mathematics K–12*)

none

Grades 4–5 (*Minnesota Academic Standards, Mathematics K–12*, Spatial Sense, Geometry, and Measurement, grade 6)

Demonstrate understanding of the rectangular coordinate system. The student will:
1. Demonstrate understanding of the four quadrants in a rectangular coordinate system by writing and plotting ordered pairs.

A2.d: Transformational Geometry

Grades K–3 (*Minnesota Academic Standards, Mathematics K–12*, Spatial Sense, Geometry, and Measurement, grade 3)

Understand the concept of reflection symmetry as applied to geometric shapes. Understand how representations of shapes are affected by various motions. The student will:
1. Identify lines of symmetry in geometric shapes.
2. Recognize and predict the position and orientation of a shape after a single flip, slide, or turn.

Grades 4–5 (*Minnesota Academic Standards, Mathematics K–12*, Spatial Sense, Geometry, and Measurement, grade 5)

Understand the concepts of reflection and rotation symmetry as applied to two-dimensional shapes. The student will:
1. Identify reflection and rotation symmetries in two-dimensional shapes and designs.

A2.e: Measurement

Grades K–3 (*Minnesota Academic Standards, Mathematics K–12*, Spatial Sense, Geometry, and Measurement, grade 3)

Measure and calculate length, time, weight, temperature and money using appropriate tools and units to solve real-world and mathematical problems.
The student will:
1. Select an appropriate tool and identify the appropriate unit to measure time, length, weight and temperature.
2. Find the perimeter of a polygon with whole number sides.
3. Know relationships between units of length in a system of measurement, such as 12 inches equals 1 foot or 100 centimeters equals 1 meter.
4. Tell time to the minute using digital and analog time.
5. Determine elapsed time to the minute.

Grades 4–5 (*Minnesota Academic Standards, Mathematics K–12*, Spatial Sense, Geometry, and Measurement, grade 5)

Measure and calculate length, area and capacity using appropriate tools and units to solve real-world and mathematical problems. The student will:
1. Find the area and perimeter of a triangle by measuring or using a grid, and label the answer with appropriate units.
2. Use a two-dimensional pattern of a cube or rectangular box to compute the surface area.
3. Select and apply the appropriate units and tools to measure perimeter, area, and capacity.

Appendix A3: North Carolina State Standards[4]

A3.a: Visualization and Spatial Reasoning

Grades K–3

Grade 2 (*Mathematics Standard Course Study and Grade Level Competencies*, grade 2)

3.02 Describe the change in attributes as two- and three-dimensional figures are cut and rearranged.
3.03 Identify and make:
    a. Symmetric figures.
    b. Congruent figures.

Grade 3 (*Mathematics Standard Course Study and Grade Level Competencies*, grade 3)

5.01 Describe and extend numeric and geometric patterns.

Grades 4–5

Grade 4 (*Mathematics Standard Course Study and Grade Level Competencies*, grade 4)

Competency goal 3: The learner will recognize and use geometric properties and relationships.

Grade 5 (*Mathematics Standard Course Study and Grade Level Competencies*, grade 5)

3.03 Classify plane figures according to types of symmetry (line, rotational).

A3.b: Two- and Three-Dimensional Geometry

Grades K–3

Grade 2 (*Mathematics Standard Course Study and Grade Level Competencies*, grade 2)

3.01 Combine simple figures to create a given shape.

Grade 3 (*Mathematics Standard Course Study and Grade Level Competencies*, grade 3)

Competency goal 3: The learner will recognize and use basic geometric properties of two- and three-dimensional figures.
3.01 Use appropriate vocabulary to compare, describe, and classify two- and three-dimensional figures.

---

[4] Available online at http://www.ncpublicschools.org/curriculum/mathematics/standard2003/toc.html

Grades 4–5

Grade 4 (*Mathematics Standard Course Study and Grade Level Competencies*, grade 4)

3.02 Describe the relative position of lines using concepts of parallelism and perpendicularity.

Grade 5 (*Mathematics Standard Course Study and Grade Level Competencies*, grade 5)

Competency goal 3: The learner will understand and use properties and relationships of plane figures. Objectives:
3.01 Identify, define, describe, and accurately represent triangles, quadrilaterals, and other polygons.
3.02 Make and test conjectures about polygons involving:
    c. Sum of the measures of interior angles.
    d. Lengths of sides and diagonals.
    e. Parallelism and perpendicularity of sides and diagonals.
3.04 Solve problems involving the properties of triangles, quadrilaterals, and other polygons.
    a. Sum of the measures of interior angles.
    b. Lengths of sides and diagonals.
    c. Parallelism and perpendicularity of sides and diagonals.

A3.c: Coordinate Geometry

Grades K–3 (*Mathematics Standard Course Study and Grade Level Competencies*, grade 3)

3.02 Use a rectangular coordinate system to solve problems.
    a. Graph and identify points with whole number and/or letter coordinates.
    b. Describe the path between given points

Grades 4–5 (*Mathematics Standard Course Study and Grade Level Competencies*, grade 4)

3.01 Use the coordinate system to describe the location and relative position of points and draw figures in the first quadrant.
3.02 Describe the relative position of lines using concepts of parallelism and perpendicularity.

A3.d: Transformational Geometry

> Grades K–3 (*Mathematics Standard Course Study and Grade Level Competencies, grade 2*)
>
> Competency goal 3: The learner will perform simple transformations.

> Grades 4–5 (*Mathematics Standard Course Study and Grade Level Competencies, grade 4*)
>
> 3.03 Identify, predict, and describe the results of transformations of plane figures.
> f. Reflections.
> g. Translations.
> h. Rotations.

A3.e: Measurement

> Grades K–3 (*Mathematics Standard Course Study and Grade Level Competencies, grade 3*)
>
> Competency goal 2: The learner will recognize and use standard units of metric and customary measurement. Objectives:
> 2.01 Solve problems using measurement concepts and procedures involving:
> i. Elapsed time.
> j. Equivalent measures within the same measurement system.
> 2.02 Estimate and measure using appropriate units.
> d. Capacity (cups, pints, quarts, gallons, liters).
> e. Length (miles, kilometers).
> f. Mass (ounces, pounds, grams, kilograms).
> g. Temperature (Fahrenheit, Celsius).

Grades 4–5

Grade 4 (*Mathematics Standard Course Study and Grade Level Competencies*, grade 4)

Competency goal 2: The learner will understand and use perimeter and area. Objectives:
2.01 Develop strategies to determine the area of rectangles and the perimeter of plane figures.
2.02 Solve problems involving perimeter of plane figures and areas of rectangles.

Grade 5 (*Mathematics Standard Course Study and Grade Level Competencies*, grade 5)

Competency goal 2: The learner will recognize and use standard units of metric and customary measurement. Objectives:
2.01 Estimate the measure of an object in one system given the measure of that object in another system.
2.02 Identify, estimate, and measure the angles of plane figures using appropriate tools.

Appendix A4: Pennsylvania State Standards [5]

A4.a: Visualization and Spatial Reasoning

Grades K–3 (*Pennsylvania Academic Standards for Mathematics*, 2.9.3, Geometry)

A. Name and label geometric shapes in two and three dimensions (e.g., circle/sphere, square/cube, triangle/pyramid, rectangle/prism).
B. Build geometric shapes using concrete objects (e.g., manipulatives).
C. Draw two- and three-dimensional geometric shapes and construct rectangles, squares and triangles on the geoboard and on graph paper satisfying specific criteria.
D. Find and describe geometric figures in real life.
I. Predict how shapes can be changed by combining or dividing them.

Grades 4–5 (*Pennsylvania Academic Standards for Mathematics*, 2.9.5, Geometry)

D. Describe in words how geometric shapes are constructed.
E. Construct two- and three-dimensional shapes and figures using manipulatives, geoboards and computer software.
F. Find familiar solids in the environment and describe them.
H. Describe the relationship between the perimeter and area of triangles, quadrilaterals and circles.
I. Represent and use the concepts of line, point and plane.
J. Define the basic properties of squares, pyramids, parallelograms, quadrilaterals, trapezoids, polygons, rectangles, rhombi, circles, triangles, cubes, prisms, spheres and cylinders.
L. Identify properties of geometric figures (e.g., parallel, perpendicular, similar, congruent, symmetrical).

A4.b: Two- and Three-Dimensional Geometry

Grades K–3 (*Pennsylvania Academic Standards for Mathematics*, 2.9.3, Geometry)

A. Name and label geometric shapes in two and three dimensions (e.g., circle/sphere, square/cube, triangle/pyramid, rectangle/prism).
B. Build geometric shapes using concrete objects (e.g., manipulatives).
C. Draw two- and three-dimensional geometric shapes and construct rectangles, squares and triangles on the geoboard and on graph paper satisfying specific criteria.
D. Find and describe geometric figures in real life.
I. Predict how shapes can be changed by combining or dividing them.

---

[5] The complete standards are available from the Pennsylvania Department of Education, "Academic Standards for Mathematics," *Pennsylvania Bulletin* 29, no. 3 (Jan. 1999): pp. 427–41. Available online at http://www.pde.state.pa.us/.

Grades 4–5 (*Pennsylvania Academic Standards for Mathematics*, 2.9.5, Geometry)

A. Give formal definitions of geometric figures.
B. Classify and compare triangles and quadrilaterals according to sides or angles.
C. Identify and measure circles, their diameters and their radii.
D. Describe in words how geometric shapes are constructed.
E. Construct two- and three-dimensional shapes and figures using manipulatives, geoboards and computer software.
F. Find familiar solids in the environment and describe them.
I. Represent and use the concepts of line, point and plane.
J. Define the basic properties of squares, pyramids, parallelograms, quadrilaterals, trapezoids, polygons, rectangles, rhombi, circles, triangles, cubes, prisms, spheres and cylinders.
L. Identify properties of geometric figures (e.g., parallel, perpendicular, similar, congruent, symmetrical).

A4.c: Coordinate Geometry

Grades 4–5 (*Pennsylvania Academic Standards for Mathematics*, 2.8.5, Algebra and Functions)

H. Locate and identify points on a coordinate system.

A4.d: Transformational Geometry

Grades K–3 (*Pennsylvania Academic Standards for Mathematics*, 2.9.3, Geometry)

A. Name and label geometric shapes in two and three dimensions (e.g., circle/sphere, square/cube, triangle/pyramid, rectangle/prism).
B. Build geometric shapes using concrete objects (e.g., manipulatives).
D. Find and describe geometric figures in real life.
E. Identify and draw lines of symmetry in geometric figures.
F. Identify symmetry in nature.
G. Fold paper to demonstrate the reflections about a line.
H. Show relationships between and among figures using reflections.

Grades 4–5 (*Pennsylvania Academic Standards for Mathematics*, 2.9.5, Geometry)

E. Construct two- and three-dimensional shapes and figures using manipulatives, geoboards and computer software.
G. Create an original tessellation.
K. Analyze simple transformations of geometric figures and rotations of line segments.
L. Identify properties of geometric figures (e.g., parallel, perpendicular, similar, congruent, symmetrical).

A4.e: Measurement

Grades K–3 (*Pennsylvania Academic Standards for Mathematics*, 2.3.3, Measurement and Estimation)

A. Compare measurable characteristics of different objects on the same dimensions (e.g., time, temperature, area, length, weight, capacity, perimeter).
B. Determine the measurement of objects with non-standard and standard units (e.g., U.S. customary and metric).
C. Determine and compare elapsed times.
D. Tell time (analog and digital) to the minute.
E. Determine the appropriate unit of measure.
F. Use concrete objects to determine area and perimeter.
G. Estimate and verify measurements.
H. Demonstrate that a single object has different attributes that can be measured in different ways (e.g., length, mass, weight, time, area, temperature, capacity, perimeter).

Grades 4–5 (*Pennsylvania Academic Standards for Mathematics*, 2.3.5, Measurement and Estimation)

A. Select and use appropriate instruments and units for measuring quantities (e.g., perimeter, volume, area, weight, time, temperature).
B. Select and use standard tools to measure the size of figures with specified accuracy, including length, width, perimeter and area.
C. Estimate, refine and verify specified measurement of objects.
D. Convert linear measurements within the same system.
E. Add and subtract measurements.

IMAGES
Improving Measurement and Geometry in Elementary Schools

Appendix A5: Texas State Standards[6]

A5a: Visualization and Spatial Reasoning

Grades K–3

Grade 2 (*Texas Essential Knowledge and Skills for Mathematics*, grade 2)

7. Geometry and spatial reasoning. The student uses attributes to identify, compare, and contrast shapes and solids. The student is expected to:
   A. identify attributes of any shape or solid;
   B. use attributes to describe how two shapes or two solids are alike or different;
   C. cut geometric shapes apart and identify the new shapes made.

Grade 3 (*Texas Essential Knowledge and Skills for Mathematics*, grade 3)

6. Patterns, relationships, and algebraic thinking. The student uses patterns to solve problems. The student is expected to:
   A. identify and extend whole-number and geometric patterns to make predictions and solve problems
9. Geometry and spatial reasoning. The student recognizes congruence and symmetry. The student is expected to:
   A. identify congruent shapes;
   B. create shapes with lines of symmetry using concrete models and technology;
   C. identify lines of symmetry in shapes.

Grades 4–5 (*Texas Essential Knowledge and Skills for Mathematics*, grade 4)

9. Geometry and spatial reasoning. The student connects transformations to congruence and symmetry. The student is expected to:
   A. demonstrate translations, reflections, and rotations using concrete models;
   B. use translations, reflections, and rotations to verify that two shapes are congruent;
   C. use reflections to verify that a shape has symmetry.

---

[6] Available online at http://www.tea.state.tx.us/rules/tac/chapter111/ch111a.html#111.15

A5.b: Two- and Three-Dimensional Geometry

Grades K–3

Grade 2 (*Texas Essential Knowledge and Skills for Mathematics*, grade 2)

7. Geometry and spatial reasoning. The student uses attributes to identify, compare, and contrast shapes and solids. The student is expected to:
   A. identify attributes of any shape or solid;
   B. use attributes to describe how two shapes or two solids are alike or different;
   C. cut geometric shapes apart and identify the new shapes made.

Grade 3 (*Texas Essential Knowledge and Skills for Mathematics*, grade 3)

8. Geometry and spatial reasoning. The student uses formal geometric vocabulary. The student is expected to name, describe, and compare shapes and solids using formal geometric vocabulary.
9. Geometry and spatial reasoning. The student recognizes congruence and symmetry. The student is expected to:
   A. identify congruent shapes;
   B. create shapes with lines of symmetry using concrete models and technology;
   C. identify lines of symmetry in shapes.

Grades 4–5

Grade 4 (*Texas Essential Knowledge and Skills for Mathematics*, grade 4)

8. Geometry and spatial reasoning. The student identifies and describes lines, shapes, and solids using formal geometric language. The student is expected to:
   A. identify right, acute, and obtuse angles;
   B. identify models of parallel and perpendicular lines; and
   C. describe shapes and solids in terms of vertices, edges, and faces.

Grade 5 (*Texas Essential Knowledge and Skills for Mathematics*, grade 5)

7. Geometry and spatial reasoning. The student generates geometric definitions using critical attributes. The student is expected to:
   A. identify critical attributes including parallel, perpendicular, and congruent parts of geometric shapes and solids; and
   B. use critical attributes to define geometric shapes or solids.

A5.c: Coordinate Geometry

Grades K–3 (*Texas Essential Knowledge and Skills for Mathematics,* grade 3)

10. Geometry and spatial reasoning. The student recognizes that numbers can be represented by points on a line. The student is expected to locate and name points on a line using whole numbers and fractions such as halves.

Grades 4–5

Grade 4 (*Texas Essential Knowledge and Skills for Mathematics,* grade 4)

10. Geometry and spatial reasoning. The student recognizes the connection between numbers and points on a number line. The student is expected to locate and name points on a number line using whole numbers, fractions such as halves and fourths, and decimals such as tenths.

Grade 5 (*Texas Essential Knowledge and Skills for Mathematics,* grade 5)

9. Geometry and spatial reasoning. The student recognizes the connection between ordered pairs of numbers and locations of points on a plane. The student is expected to locate and name points on a coordinate grid using ordered pairs of whole numbers.

A5.d: Transformational Geometry

Grades K–3 (*Texas Essential Knowledge and Skills for Mathematics*)

none

Grades 4–5

Grade 4 (*Texas Essential Knowledge and Skills for Mathematics,* grade 4)

9. Geometry and spatial reasoning. The student connects transformations to congruence and symmetry. The student is expected to:
   A. demonstrate translations, reflections, and rotations using concrete models;
   B. use translations, reflections, and rotations to verify that two shapes are congruent;
   C. use reflections to verify that a shape has symmetry.

Grade 5 (*Texas Essential Knowledge and Skills for Mathematics,* grade 5)

8. Geometry and spatial reasoning. The student models transformations. The student is expected to:
   A. sketch the results of translations, rotations, and reflections; and
   B. describe the transformation that generates one figure from the other when given two congruent figures.

A5.e: Measurement

Grades K–3

Grade 2 (*Texas Essential Knowledge and Skills for Mathematics*, grade 2)

9. Measurement. The student recognizes and uses models that approximate standard units (metric and customary) of length, weight, capacity, and time. The student is expected to:
A. identify concrete models that approximate standard units of length, capacity, and weight;
B. measure length, capacity, and weight using concrete models that approximate standard units;
C. describe activities that take approximately one second, one minute, and one hour.
10. Measurement. The student uses standard tools to measure time and temperature. The student is expected to:
A. read a thermometer to gather data; and
B. describe time on a clock using hours and minutes.

Grade 3 (*Texas Essential Knowledge and Skills for Mathematics*, grade 3)

11. Measurement. The student selects and uses appropriate units and procedures to measure length and area. The student is expected to:
A. estimate and measure lengths using standard units such as inch, foot, yard, centimeter, decimeter, and meter;
B. use linear measure to find the perimeter of a shape; and
C. use concrete models of square units to determine the area of shapes.
12. Measurement. The student measures time and temperature. The student is expected to:
A. tell and write time shown on traditional and digital clocks; and
B. use a thermometer to measure temperature.
13. Measurement. The student applies measurement concepts. The student is expected to measure to solve problems involving length, area, temperature, and time.

Grades 4–5

Grade 4 (*Texas Essential Knowledge and Skills for Mathematics*, grade 4)

11. Measurement. The student selects and uses appropriate units and procedures to measure weight and capacity. The student is expected to:
    A. estimate and measure weight using standard units including ounces, pounds, grams, and kilograms; and
    B. estimate and measure capacity using standard units including milliliters, liters, cups, pints, quarts, and gallons.
12. Measurement. The student applies measurement concepts. The student is expected to measure to solve problems involving length, including perimeter, time, temperature, and area.

Grade 5 (*Texas Essential Knowledge and Skills for Mathematics*, grade 5)

10. Measurement. The student selects and uses appropriate units and procedures to measure volume. The student is expected to:
    A. measure volume using concrete models of cubic units; and
    B. estimate volume in cubic units.
11. Measurement. The student applies measurement concepts. The student is expected to:
    A. measure to solve problems involving length (including perimeter), weight, capacity, time, temperature, and area; and
    B. describe numerical relationships between units of measure within the same measurement system such as an inch is one-twelfth of a foot.

Appendix B

Acronyms

AAUW: American Association of University Women

AIMS: Activities Integrating Mathematics and Science; the AIMS Education Foundation

ASCD: Association for Supervision and Curriculum Development

CESTA: Commonwealth Excellence in Science Teaching Alliance

CPB: Corporation for Public Broadcasting

ENC: Eisenhower National Clearinghouse

EPR: Every Pupil Response

ERIC: Educational Resources Information Center

ESMP: Elementary School Mathematics Project

MAA: Mathematical Association of America

NAEP: National Assessment of Educational Progress

NASA: National Aeronautics and Space Administration

McREL: Mid-continent Research for Education and Learning

NCTM: National Council of Teachers of Mathematics

NSF: National Science Foundation

NSTA: National Science Teachers Association

PBS: Public Broadcasting Service

PDE: Pennsylvania Department of Education

PSSA: Pennsylvania System of School Assessment

RBS: Research for Better Schools

TIMSS: Third International Mathematics and Science Study (1995)

TIMSS: Trends in International Mathematics and Science Study (2003 and beyond)

TIMSS-R: Third International Mathematics and Science Study—Repeat (1999)

Appendix C

Glossary of Assessment Terms

Anecdotal notes: Short notes written during a lesson, as children work in groups or individually, or after a lesson.

Anecdotal notebook: A notebook where a teacher records observations of students.

Anecdotal note cards: An alternative system to an anecdotal notebook, in which the teacher records observations using one note card per child. One way to facilitate this process is to select five children per day for observation. The cards can be kept together on a ring.

Assessment: The gathering of evidence about a student's knowledge of, ability to use, and disposition towards a subject, and the making of inferences from this evidence. These inferences can also be a valuable tool for making instructional decisions. Assessment should always support and enhance students' learning.

Assessment standards: Criteria for judging the quality of assessment practices that embody a vision of assessment consistent with the curriculum and teaching standards derived from shared philosophies of mathematics, cognition, and learning.[7]

Criterion-referenced assessment: A test that measures student achievement against well-defined criteria; assigns levels of proficiency of performance; and/or assesses mastery of a specific domain or area of knowledge.

Formative assessment: Forms of assessment that help the teacher understand what the students know, do not know, and might need in terms of instruction. Ideally, these assessments are going on all the time, as the teacher uses the feedback to enable students to learn better.

Interviews: An interaction in which a teacher presents a child with a planned sequence of questions. These exchanges can be a rich source of information about how the child is constructing concepts or using procedures, and they also give the teacher direction for modifying instruction.

Journal writing: A series of writings in which a student reflects on his or her learning. As journals can include diagrams, graphs, labels, and symbols, journal writing can be a more inclusive form of communication than an oral response. In many cases it also deepens the cognitive process.

Labels/adhesive notes: These small papers free the teacher from carrying a notebook around the room. After an observation is complete, the labels and adhesive notes should be inserted into the teacher's filing system.

---

[7] National Council of Teachers of Mathematics. *Assessment Standards for School Mathematics* (Reston, Va.: National Council of Teachers of Mathematics, 1995), p. 87.

Norm-referenced assessment: A test that measures a student's quantitative scores (such as how many items the student answered correctly) against a normal distribution of scores by other students of the same age or grade. This kind of testing is often used to rank students, measure their relative standing, and assess their general knowledge across broad areas.[8]

Observation: A systematic plan for gathering useful pieces of information about students. This can include what a student does or does not know and/or can or cannot do. This information in turn makes it possible to plan ways to encourage students' strengths and work on weaknesses.

Observation tools: Instruments and techniques that help teachers to record useful data about students' learning in a systematic way.

Peer assessment: A group activity in which students listen to, discuss, and analyze each others' strategies for solving problems. The teacher can learn about the students by observing these discussions.

Performance task: A physical activity or production of some significance, which when carried out or brought to completion, displays a student's knowledge and judgement while engaged in the task.[9]

Portfolio: A collection of a student's work over a period of time (a term, a year) that can be used for assessment by the teacher and by the student. It can include special problem-solving tasks, writings, investigations, projects, and reports—not only on paper but also on audio- or videotapes and/or computer disks. By dating each of the entries in the portfolio, the student (and the teacher) can use it to see the growth of his or her work. Portfolios can be "learner-managed" (organized by the student), teacher-managed, or both.[10]

Probing questions: A teaching/assessment strategy that provides insight into the mental processes a student is using by engaging him or her in conversation about the subject or the understanding of the subject.

Prompting questions: A process by which a teacher supports a student by giving hints that point the student toward appropriate strategies to use to solve problems.

Questioning: A way of teaching that actively invites students to convey what they are thinking. Good questions, prepared before a lesson, will also help a teacher determine whether students use varied approaches to a problem and how well students can explain their own thinking. This process complements observation.

---

[8] National Council of Teachers of Mathematics, *Assessment Standards*, p. 89.

[9] National Council of Teachers of Mathematics, *Assessment Standards*, p. 90.

[10] Alan Trussell-Cullen, *Assessment in the Learner-Centered Classroom* (Carlsbad, Ca.: Dominie Press, Inc., 1998), p. 100.

Rubric: A hierarchy of performance standards and expectations used to evaluate student performance on a task. Either task-specific or general, the rubric makes it possible to determine a student's score based on overall performance, as opposed to simply the number of correct or incorrect items. A sample rubric could consist of a scale of three to six points that are used to rate performance. If they are shared with the students, rubrics can engage and empower students in the learning process.

Self-assessment: The process by which students evaluate their own work, given criteria established by the teacher.

Summative assessments: Graded work that measures the quality of students' performance or summarizes student learning at some point in a class.

Teacher-designed written tests: These are tests that are constructed by a classroom teacher or group of teachers. These not only help determine a student's grades, but also can inform and guide a teacher's instruction and be an efficient way to gather information. They do not provide a complete assessment of students' knowledge, but only one piece of the puzzle. Teacher-made tests should be thoughtful and well constructed, and should include a variety of different items, such as skills problems, selected-response problems, and constructed-response (or "open-ended") problems, which can be either brief or extended.

Think-alouds: A teaching/assessment strategy in which one verbalizes his or her thought process. A teacher should incorporate this into the daily practice of teaching, modeling it first, and then encouraging students to try it as well. Think-alouds can be especially helpful in revealing how a student arrived at a particular answer.

Work samples: These can include projects, written assignments, and other student products that the teacher collects and evaluates. Scoring, which involves judgement and analyzing the work, makes it possible to learn about the students.[11]

Writing prompts: Statements that provide students with a clear, well-defined purpose for a particular writing assignment.[12] A teacher needs to communicate clearly to students exactly what he or she expects in a response, such as whether it should include certain components or be a particular length.

---

[11] Robert Reys et al., *Helping Children Learn Mathematics*, 6th ed. (New York: John Wiley & Sons, 2001), p. 78.

[12] John A. Van de Walle, *Elementary and Middle School Mathematics: Teaching Developmentally*, 4th ed. (New York: Addison Wesley Longman, 2001), p. 74.

Appendix D

Glossary of Geometric and Mathematical Terms

These definitions are available online at the IMAGES Web site (http://images.rbs.org).
For additional definitions of geometry and measurement terms, visit the Web sites
of the Visual Geometry Dictionary for Kids and for Kids' Teachers
(http://www.math.okstate.edu/%7Erpsc/dict/Dictionary.html) and the Maths Thesaurus
(http://thesaurus.maths.org). Also see Christine G. Renne's article, "Is a Rectangle a
Square? Developing Mathematical Vocabulary and Conceptual Understanding,"
Teaching Children Mathematics 10, no. 5 (2004): pp. 258–63.

Acute angle: An angle that measures between 0 and 90 degrees

Acute triangle: A triangle with three acute angles

Adjacent angles: Two angles on a plane that share a common vertex and a common side

∠ A is adjacent to ∠ B

Adjacent sides: In a polygon, two sides that share a common endpoint

Adjacent sides

Algorithm: A step-by-step procedure used for solving a problem

Alternate exterior angles: When two parallel lines are cut by a transversal, the two pairs
of angles on opposite sides of the transversal and outside the parallel lines, and
the angles in each pair are congruent

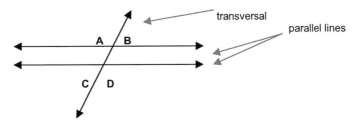

∠ A and ∠ D are alternate exterior angles
∠B and ∠ C are alternate exterior angles

Alternate interior angles: When two parallel lines are cut by a transversal, the two pairs of angles on opposite sides of the transversal and inside the parallel lines, and the angles in each pair are congruent

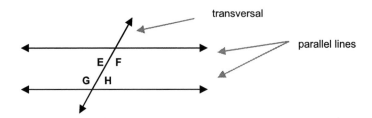

∠ E and ∠ H are alternate interior angles
∠ F and ∠ G are alternate interior angles

Altitude: Height; the perpendicular distance from a vertex of a polygon to its opposite side

Analytic geometry: Geometry that deals with the relation between algebra and geometry, using graphs and equations of lines, curves, and surfaces to develop and prove relationships

Angle: The union of two rays with the same endpoint (its vertex); the amount of rotation of a ray about a fixed ray

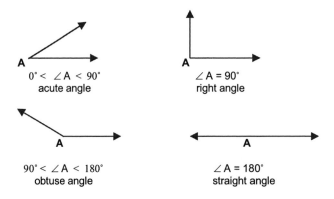

Apex: The point off the base of a pyramid where the triangular sides meet

Arc: A part of a circle; the set of points on the circle between two points on the circle, plus those two endpoints

Area: The number of square units in a closed two-dimensional or plane shape

Axiom: A basic assumption that is accepted without proof

Axis: One of the number lines that form a coordinate system

Axis of symmetry: A line that divides a shape into two congruent halves

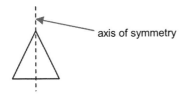

Base: The side of a shape used as the foundation for the shape; the face of a solid used as the foundation for the solid

Bisect: To cut something (such as a line segment or an angle) into two equal parts

Bisector: A straight line that divides an object into two equal parts

Capacity: The amount a container will hold such as fluid ounces or liters

Cartesian coordinate system: See **Coordinate plane**

Center of a circle: A fixed point equidistant from all points on the circle

Center of rotation: The only point in the plane that remains unchanged under a rotation of the plane

Chord: A line segment joining two points on a circle

Circle: A set of all points in a plane that are the same distance (**radius**) from a fixed point (**center**)

Circular cone: A three-dimensional shape with one circular base and a vertex that is not in the same plane as the base

Circumference: The perimeter of a circle

Clockwise rotation: Rotation about a point in a clockwise direction

Collinear points: Three or more points on the same line in a plane or in space

Collinear rays: Two rays that are subsets of the same line in a plane or in space

Compass: A tool used to draw circles of different radii or mark off equal lengths

Complementary angles: Two angles for which the sum of their measures is 90 degrees

Concave (non-convex): A shape with the property that the line segment connecting any two interior points is not totally contained in the shape; Not convex

Congruence: The relationship between two geometric shapes having the same size and shape (**congruent shapes**)

Contraction: See **dilation**

Convex shape: A shape with the property that the line segment connecting any two interior points is contained in the shape

Coordinate: On a number line, the number paired with a point. In the coordinate plane, the numbers which are paired with a point. Point (2,4) has x-coordinate 2 and y-coordinate 4.

Coordinate plane: The number plane formed by two perpendicular number lines that intersect at their zero points (also called the **Cartesian coordinate system**)

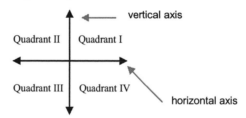

Corollary: A statement that is readily proved deductively by applying a theorem

Corresponding angles: When two parallel lines are cut by a transversal, the pairs of angles that are on the same side of the transversal (one inside the parallel lines and one outside the parallel lines) and are congruent

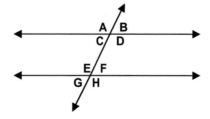

These pairs of angles are corresponding angles:

∠A and ∠E
∠C and ∠G
∠B and ∠F
∠D and ∠H.

Corresponding parts (angles and sides): Angles and sides in the same position on two shapes. In congruent shapes, the corresponding angles and sides are congruent.

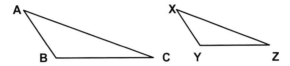

Corresponding sides are: $\overline{AB}$ and $\overline{XY}$; $\overline{AC}$ and $\overline{XZ}$; and $\overline{BC}$ and $\overline{YZ}$

Corresponding angles are: $\angle A$ and $\angle X$; $\angle B$ and $\angle Y$; and $\angle C$ and $\angle Z$

Counterclockwise rotation: Rotation about a point opposite the rotation of a clock hand

Cube: A rectangular polyhedron composed of six congruent squares

Cylinder: A solid shape whose bases are formed by congruent circles in parallel planes and whose lateral surface is curved. The segment whose endpoints are the centers of the circular bases is called the **axis of the cylinder**. The altitude is a segment perpendicular to the base planes with an endpoint in each plane.

Decagon: A polygon of ten sides

Definition: A statement that gives the meaning of a word or symbol in terms that have been previously defined or are accepted as undefined

Degree: The standard unit for angle measure; one revolution is 360 degrees; a unit for measuring temperature

Diagonal: A segment connecting two non-adjacent vertices of a polygon

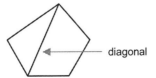

diagonal

Diameter: A chord containing the center of a circle or sphere; the segment whose endpoints are points on a circle (or sphere) that contains the center of the circle (or sphere) as its midpoint

Dilation: A transformation in which each point P in the plane is mapped to a point P' on the ray OP where O is a fixed point in the plane. The position if P' is determined by the scale factor k by choosing P' so $OP' = k\, OP$. If k is less than one the transformation is called a **contraction**. Informally, a dilation transforms a polygon to a similar shape in which the sides are proportional.

Dimensions: Length, width, and/or height of a plane or solid shape

Edge: The line of a three-dimensional shape where two plane faces meet

Equiangular: A term used to indicate that all angles of a polygon have the same measure

Equilateral: A term used to indicate that all the sides of a polygon are equal in length

equilateral polygons

Euclidean geometry: The geometry (plane or solid) based on Euclid's postulates

Euler's formula: The relationship between the number of vertices, the number of faces, and the number of edges of any polygon (V + F = E + 2)

Face: One of the plane surfaces of a polyhedron bounded by edges

Function in two variables: A set of ordered pairs (x, y) in which each value of x is paired with exactly one value of y

Geometry: The study of space and properties of shapes in space

Glide reflection: A transformation that consists of a translation parallel to a fixed line followed by a reflection about the line

Hexagon: A polygon of six sides

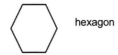

hexagon

Hypotenuse: The side in a right triangle that is opposite the right angle

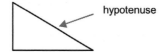

hypotenuse

Image: The shape formed by a transformation of a shape (the **pre-image**)

Interior angles: Angles on the inside of a shape

$\angle$ A, $\angle$ B, $\angle$ C, $\angle$ D, and $\angle$ E are interior angles

Intersecting lines: Two different lines that contain exactly one point in common

Isometric drawing: A drawing where length, width, and height are represented by lines 120 degrees apart, with all measurements in the same scale

Isosceles trapezoid: A quadrilateral with one pair of sides that are parallel and another pair of sides that are not parallel but have equal lengths; the base angles are equal in measurement.

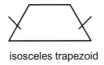

isosceles trapezoid

Isosceles triangle: A triangle with two congruent sides

isosceles triangle

Kite: Quadrilateral with two distinct pairs of adjacent sides that are congruent

Lattice point: A point in a coordinate plane with integer coordinates

Leg: In a right triangle, a side that is not the hypotenuse

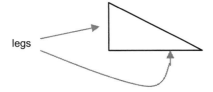

legs

Lemma: A theorem proven only for use in the proof of more important theorems

Length of a segment: The distance between the endpoints of a segment

Line: An undefined term for an infinite, one-dimensional object

Line of reflection: A line used to create a reflection of a shape

Line segment: Part of a line consisting of two endpoints and all the points on the line between them

Line of symmetry: A line that divides a shape into two congruent halves

Midpoint: A point that divides a line segment into two congruent segments

Net of a polyhedron: A pattern that can be cut out, folded, and glued together to make a three-dimensional model of a solid

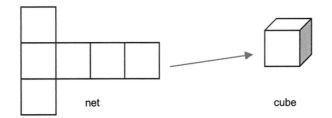

net   cube

Network: A set of vertices and edges

Non-collinear points: Points that do not lie on the same line

Non-Euclidean geometry: Any geometry that changes at least one of Euclid's postulates

Number line: A line with an origin (0) and a unit length that allows for each integer to be assigned a point in the line

Obtuse angle: An angle with measure of between 90 and 180 degrees

Obtuse triangle: A triangle with one interior angle that is obtuse

Octagon: A polygon of eight sides

One-dimensional: Having length but no width, e.g., lines, rays, and segments

Ordered pair: A pair of numbers in which the order is specified, used to locate a point in a coordinate plane

Origin: On the coordinate plane the point where the two perpendicular lines (axes) intersect or the point (0,0)

Parallel lines: Lines in the same plane that do not intersect

parallel lines

Parallel planes: Two planes in three-dimensional space that never meet

Parallelogram: A quadrilateral with opposite sides that are parallel

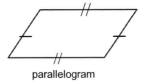

parallelogram

Pentagon: A polygon with five sides

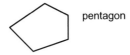

pentagon

Pentomino: Five equal-sized squares that can be attached edge-to-edge to form a three-dimensional shape

Examples of pentominoes   Non-examples of pentominoes

Perimeter of a polygon: The sum of the lengths of all sides of a polygon; the distance around a closed plane shape

Perpendicular: Forming a right angle

right angle

Pi: The ratio of the circumference of a circle to its diameter

Pick's theorem: Given a polygon where each vertex is on a pin of a geoboard, the area can be found by the formula $A = B/2 + I - 1$, where B is the number of boundary points and I is the number of interior points.

Plane: An undefined term for a flat, infinite two-dimensional shape

Plane geometry: The geometry that deals with shapes in a two-dimensional plane

Platonic solids: See **regular polyhedron**

Point: A location on a line, in a coordinate plane, or in space; an undefined term for a zero-dimensional object (having no length, width, or height)

Polygon: A simple closed shape composed of a finite number of line segments, each of which intersects exactly two of the other segments, one at each endpoint

Polyhedron: A simple closed three-dimensional shape formed by plane polygons

Postulate: A basic assumption that is accepted without proof

Prism: A polyhedron that has two congruent parallel faces and a set of parallel edges that connect corresponding vertices of the two faces

Protractor: A tool used to measure angles

Pyramid: A polyhedron that has one base and a set of edges that meet at a single point (**apex**) that is not in the base; all faces except the base are triangles

Pythagorean theorem: A theorem that states that in any right triangle, the square of the hypotenuse is equal to the sum of the squares of the sides.

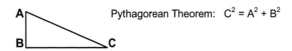

Pythagorean Theorem: $C^2 = A^2 + B^2$

Quadrant: Any one of the four regions into which a plane is divided by a pair of coordinate axes

Quadrilateral: A polygon with four sides

quadrilateral

Radius: A line segment connecting the center of a circle (or sphere) to any point on the circle (or sphere); the length of that line segment

Ray: A part of a line with a single endpoint and that extends infinitely in one direction

Rectangle: A quadrilateral with all interior right angles

rectangle

Reflection (flip): A transformation that maps each point in a plane to a new point that is the same distance from a fixed line (called the **line of reflection**) but on the opposite side of the line; informally, a geometric shape that can be flipped over a line so that the new shape is a mirror image of the original

Regular polygon: A polygon that is equilateral and equiangular

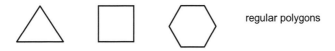

regular polygons

Regular polyhedron: A polyhedron whose faces are congruent regular polygons and where each vertex figure (how the polygons meet at a vertex) is identical; also called a **Platonic solid**

Rhombus: A parallelogram with four congruent sides

rhombus

Right angle: An angle with a measure of 90 degrees

Right triangle: A triangle that has a right angle

right triangle

Rotation (turn): A transformation that maps every point in a plane shape to its image by rotating the plane through an angle (called the **turn angle**) around a fixed point (called the **turn center** or **center of rotation**)

Rotational symmetry: A term that describes a shape that remains unchanged when it is turned less than 360 degrees about a fixed point

Scalene triangle: A triangle with no two sides of the same length

scalene triangle

Segment: A set of points containing two endpoints and all points along the straight line between the two endpoints; a part of a circle between an arc and its chord

Semicircle: Half of a circle

Set: A group of objects or numbers, which are called **elements of the set**

Similar shapes: Two shapes that have the same shape—corresponding angles that are congruent and corresponding sides that are proportional

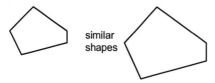

similar shapes

Simple closed curve: A set of points in a plane that can be drawn such that the initial and final points are the same and the curve never intersects itself; it divides the plane into three regions: the region inside the curve, the curve, and the region outside the curve.

Simple closed surface: A surface without holes that encloses a hollow region; it divides space into three regions: the region interior to the surface, the surface, and the region exterior to the surface.

Slide: See **translation**

Solid geometry: Geometry that deals with shapes and their properties in three-dimensional space

Sphere: A shape in space whose points are the same distance from a fixed point (the center)

Spherical geometry: Geometry that deals with shapes on the surface of the sphere

Square: An equilateral and equiangular quadrilateral

square

Straight angle: An angle with measure of 180 degrees

Supplementary angles: Two angles for which the sum of their measures is 180 degrees

Surface area: The total area of the outside of a three-dimensional shape

Symmetry: Correspondence in size, shape, and relative position of parts on opposite sides of a dividing line or median plane or about a center or axis

Synthetic geometry: Geometry that explores properties of geometric objects without algebra

Tangram: A Chinese puzzle made up of a square cut into seven pieces that can be rearranged to make various shapes

Tessellation: A repetitive pattern of polygons that covers (or tiles) a plane with no gaps and no overlaps

Tetrahedron: A polyhedron with four faces

Theorem: A statement that can be proven using logical (deductive) reasoning

Three-dimensional: Having length, width, and thickness

Transformation of the plane: A one-to-one correspondence that maps each point *P* (called the **preimage**) in the plane to a point *P'* (called the **image**) in the plane

Translation (slide): A transformation of a plane where every point *P* is moved in the same direction and the same distance to a new point *P'*; moving a shape along a straight line without it flipping, rotating, or reflecting

Transversal: A straight line that crosses two or more given lines

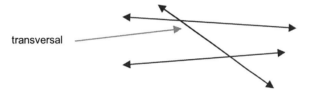

Trapezoid: A quadrilateral with exactly one pair of parallel sides

Triangle: A polygon with three sides

Two-dimensional: Having both length and width, but no thickness

Undefined term: A term—such as *point, line, plane,* and *space*—that is accepted without definition

Vertex: The point where two rays forming an angle meet, the point where two sides of a polygon meet, or the point where three or more faces of a polygon meet

Vertical angles: A pair of non-adjacent angles formed by intersecting lines; also called **vertically opposite angles**

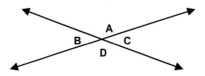

∠ **A** and ∠ **D** are vertical angles; and ∠ **B** and ∠ **C** are vertical angles

Volume: Amount of space enclosed by a simple closed surface, measured in cubic units

X-axis: The horizontal number line in a plane

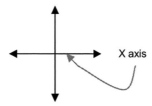

Y-axis: The vertical number line in a coordinate plane

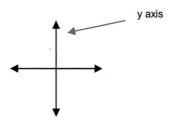

INDEX